C000005229

SAILING

into

SOLITUDE

2011 EDITION

VALENTINE HOWELLS

1st Edition
Published in the U.K. by Temple Press
Published in the U.S.A by Dodd Mead & Company
(Library of Congress Catalogue Card Number 66-24273)

2011 Edition
Published by: Landsker Publications Ltd
Paperback ISBN: 978-0-9542732-2-4
Hardback ISBN: 978-0-9542732-9-3

Ebook Editions

Published by: Landsker Publications Ltd.
PDF Version ISBN: 978-0-9542732-1-7
E-Pub Version ISBN: 978-0-9542732-7-9

Copyright © Valentine Howells 2011

Valentine Howells has asserted his right under the Copyright, Designs and Patents Act, 1988 to be identified as the author of this work.

All rights reserved. No part of this publication may be reproduced, stored in a retrieval system, or transmitted in any form or by any means without the written permission of the publisher, nor be otherwise circulated in any form or binding or cover other than that in which it is published and without similar condition being imposed on the subsequent purchaser.

INTRODUCTION

This book, the 2011 edition of *Sailing into Solitude* offers a transparently honest account of what happened when the author was fortunate enough to be able to take part in the first single-handed transatlantic small boat race, across the North Atlantic, from Plymouth to New York. An event now known by the international yachting community as OSTAR 1960.

From this start point, and to whittle it down to the barest of bare essentials, all you really need to know is that David Lewis came along in a boat called *Cardinal Vertue*, Francis Chichester had the benefit of *Gipsy Moth*, Blondie Hasler sailed *Jester*, and Jean Lacombe had the temerity to embark on an ocean passage to New York, from Plymouth, England, in a vessel (*Cap Horn*) that was little bigger than a dinghy.

So far – so apparently simple enough.

Yet how can it be, that an experienced seaman, in a boat called *Eira*, was careless enough to allow himself to be manoeuvred into a position, while alone, in a small boat, in the middle of the Western Ocean, only to find he was being pissed on by a horse.

That, surely, will take a bit of explaining.

But all will be crystal clear, when you get to the end of that particular tunnel.

Dodd Mead & Company: New York

From the days of Joshua Slocum there have been many interesting accounts by 'single-handed' sailors of their adventures on the high seas. This one differs markedly from most of them, in its intensely personal exploration of how it feels to be alone in the unremitting partnership of sea and boat during a long ocean voyage. The emphasis is far more on the inner man, than on the usual outward events.

Such a book takes a lot of doing, and it is Howells' frank, searching introspection that gives it its unusual content, and his sheer ability to write entertainingly, penetratingly, and originally that pulls it off.

Val Howells is over six feet tall, with a large black beard. His boat was a Folkboat, twenty-five feet overall, little more than nineteen feet on the waterline, with the cabin space offering no more than four feet ten inches of headroom. By any standards, a small boat to embark on an ocean passage; yet he and four others, in widely assorted craft, set out from England to race across the Atlantic to New York.

The circumstances that befall them are peculiar enough, but what will enthral the reader most are the things that go on in this man's imaginative mind and very human body.

Temple Press: London

Sailing into Solitude is much more than just another yachting yarn. The passage of an ocean is described as the exciting experience it certainly was; but this book is more than that, for it tells the story of another journey, to the *'land that is walled with mirrors'*. That revealing place where every posture, every façade, stands naked to the truthful eye. Perhaps many of us trudge this road, not all of us are honest enough to tell of our adventures.

Here it is; the laughter and the pain, the effort and the failure, the boldness and the fear, which will lead us to a better understanding of ourselves.

Val Howells has not only succeeded in crossing the Atlantic, but has managed to convey the haunting fear of his own insignificance, measured beside the immense forces of the elements. To be completely alone, and yet to have to share the unremitting partnership of sea and boat would try the least imaginative.

The author emerges from this gigantic undertaking, a chastened and most human companion, as he gives us a memorable picture of one man's battle with the sea, and himself.

Russian Edition

' ... readers interested in transatlantic racing probably won't find many relevant details here. The author himself makes the point that there are many books dedicated to that type of voyaging, and it's not his intention to add to the list; rather, he invites the reader to actually sail 'with' him. And he keeps his promise; you do get crammed aboard a small vessel (a Scandinavian Folkboat) and are then offered the opportunity of sharing his experiences, which do not in any way include a 'challenge' to the ocean.

It should be noted that *Sailing into Solitude* is not a diary, transposed into book form, shortly after the event, but a serious attempt to describe his emotions which vary from *'I'm lonely, I'm scared, I'll be glad when this is over'* to the degree of self-analysis which is honest enough to admit that, on more than one occasion, he recognised that he was verging on being *'unstable'*, even mentally *'unbalanced'*.

Yet when reading this book, you should always bear in mind the irony employed by the author. High-pitched phrases are studiously avoided; indeed, his speech is rough, sometimes even rude, as he regularly makes fun of himself. Nevertheless, with it all, this volume offers artistic value - you read it, from the first page to the last, on what seems a single breath.

Times Literary Supplement

Val Howells is an unusual man, and he has produced a remarkable book.

He occasionally verges on something like a parody of Dylan Thomas, but by and large, his is an honest and vivid description of what it means for an extrovert Welshman to imprison himself voluntarily for two months in a small boat. Pain and discomfort, fear and loneliness, depressions and hallucinations are candidly and imaginatively described.

Self-pity however is always overwhelmed by a gusty humour, and his account of a week's sojourn in Bermuda, when he found himself unable to come to terms once more with ordinary life, is particularly memorable.

All sorts of people are sailing vast distances alone these days, but it's a safe bet that none of them will write a book quite like this.

Previous Work

SAILING INTO SOLITUDE

1st Edition
Published in the U.K. by Temple Press
Published in the U.S.A by Dodd Mead & Company
(Library of Congress Catalogue Card Number 66-24273)

UP THAT PARTICLAR CREEK

Pavilion Publications
1st and 2nd Editions
ISBN 0 9542732 0 6

BBC Wales TV

ALONE IN A BOAT
(Producer: John Ormond)

MINERS IN THE PINK
(Producer: Selwyn Roderick)

AN OBSESSION IN THE FAMILY
(Producer: Derek Trimby)

I, A STRANGER
(Producer: Selwyn Roderick)

VALENTINE'S NIGHT
(five part series)
(Producer: Derek Trimby)

BBC 2

THE JOLLY RODGERED SEA
(Producer: Selwyn Roderick)

Chapter Headings

1 - (1) - 8

can I come lend a hand, on the trip down to Plymouth ?
certainly Jack, if you fancy being cook.

11 - (2) - 15

the men and boats are gathering
but we only have time for a hesitant glance

29 - (3) - 35

what sailor departed without a small noggin ?
who lived to regret it, the day of the race ?

47 - (4) - 54

some things
are not as easy as they look

55 - (5) - 69

settle now to the rhythm of the ocean
we face a fair long haul

71 - (6) - 85

a narrow squeak
a message home
an altering view of the sea

87 - (7) - 99

take your time
you may miss it when it's gone

101 - (8) - 125

sail on
past temptation
and the saddening thought
so many rocks to be avoided

127 - (9) - 160

alone
all, all alone
but are you sure ?

161 - (10) - 184

and so
you think you know yourself

185 - (11) - 211

a change of view

213 - (12) - 230

are there fairies at the bottom of your garden ?
or
are the sands of time always this abrasive ?

233 - (13) - 243

so near
and not so far

245 - (14) - 247

why must you do it ?

1

can I come lend a hand, on the trip down to Plymouth ?
certainly, Jack, if you fancy being cook

what about me ?
have you room for a small one ?

go get your kit
and we'll see how you stow

It's just a short hop from Saundersfoot, to Plymouth (England), a hundred miles or so, no more than a routine trip, but one made interesting by the presence of a crew. I was glad to have them on board, enjoying their company, so much better than sailing alone that I felt obliged to treat them with at least some degree of consideration.

'… Eight Bells, lads, time to change watches, come on down to a nice warm bunk.'

'If you don't mind, Val, we'll stay on deck for a while, it's a lovely day and it seems a pity to spend it below.'

'… O.K. Bert, it's up to you, but I'll take over the tiller.'

It's lunchtime, and Jack the cook proceeds to open the meal; slabs of corned dog, plastered with French mustard, followed by buttered bread rolls, a handful of pickled onions, helped down by several cans of ale are ravished by some. Others, complaining of an over-hearty breakfast, make do with a few plain biscuits and a cup of milk and sugarless tea.

Having enjoyed the grub, my four-hour stint on deck soon passes, and I'm watch below once more, climbing into a cold sleeping bag. I can hardly complain about that, as the other watch have kept me company throughout my trick at the tiller. Yet the thought does occur - that they might be a trifle shy of bedding down in a recently vacated berth? This prim little doubt prompting the recollection of another friend, who devoted a large part of his tremendous energy getting into bed with anybody's wife - while complaining bitterly if someone else's sweaty hands touched the steering wheel of his pride and joy of a car. However, my present companions are not cursed with this type of fastidiousness. They are not the sort of people who would be fussy about climbing into a friend's perhaps smelly sleeping bag, without a riposte of their own.

'Good grief, Howells, when did you last change your socks?'

Having slept my watch below, I'm wakened by Jack, cursing, because he can't get the stove alight; and then find it's way past the time I should have climbed out of my cart.

'... I'll be up on deck directly, lads. Why didn't you call me before?'

'It's all right Val, we didn't want to bother you, it's such a marvellous evening we're quite happy carrying on.'

When I do eventually stick my head out of the hatch, I can see the day is indeed drawing to a masterly conclusion. The sun has turned its duty to the west and is about to warm another continent, while we're having difficulty lighting the primus. The swell, though not any higher, has noticeably increased in length, with the boat climbing to the top of each advancing undulation, to hang on the crest, then move quietly down the watery lip, to lie cradled in the welcoming arms of the trough. Dark in the lengthening shadows, while the backs of the eastbound swells glisten in the lowering rays of the sun. Too fine a moment to spend below, so we sit in the cockpit, speaking very little.

As the light fades, it's noticeably colder, prompting a warming tot of rum.

'... you lads ought to go below, after all, it's my watch, and you'll be on again at midnight.'

They persist in their objection to any horizontal work, and when they decline a steaming brew, as well as the tot, I'm beginning to appreciate what might be troubling them.

'... are you feeling alright?'

'Good Lord, yes. I'm O.K. But I'll stay up here for a while, and not tempt providence by going below.'

They have now been in the cockpit for over twelve hours, and I must say that I've always found my bunk as tempting as any providence; however, their business, is their business, so I happily retire below.

Midnight comes, and I feel guilty letting my shipmates face another four, long yawned hours of the graveyard watch.

Viewed from a warm sleeping bag, the open hatch reveals a swinging arc of stars, twinkling coldly out of a lamp-black sky, accentuating the homely feel of the cabin - making it a difficult place to leave - yet I feel, I should at least show willing.

' ... are you devils still up there?'

'Yes, we're still here.'

' ... if you wish, you can change watches with me, and take a spell out of the cockpit.'

'No, we're both managing quite well, and I don't want to go below.'
'Neither do I.'
' ... O.K., be it on your own heads. Any shipping about?'
'Nothing to bother us.'
' ... give me a shout if you have any doubt, and definitely at four
AM.'
'Right-ho, will do, good night.'
' ... good night.'

The feeling of guilt departs with embarrassing ease when presented with the continuing pleasure of a warm bunk. My conscience, such as it is, prompts me to the opinion that, if they don't feel well, perhaps they *should* keep out of the cabin.

I've suffered from seasickness on two occasions in the past; once while taking my turn as cook on a schooner, and again when leaving Spain the previous year.

When you're alone in a small boat the malady is overcome by stark necessity - you pull your finger out, and get on with the job. Aboard the schooner, years ago, as a very young man, I had the undoubted benefit of the rude boot of a bellowing bosun threatening my tight as a drum little bum - a slight exaggeration, but it turns out to be excellent therapy.

So I know what it's like to be seasick.

The first, almost unnoticed dampness of the palms. Then the excess of saliva, which wells constantly, regardless of how often you spit. A slight headache prompts you to touch an ice-cold forehead with the back of a trembling hand. Your stomach tightens, gathering for the humiliating spout of disgusting bile, which no matter how you 'will' it to stay put, gushes out, and forces your astonished eye to acknowledge the apprehensive horror of your thoroughly beastly self.

Small boats on large oceans are hardy animals to live with, and having spent time enough afloat, I have some idea of what those on deck are thinking. Stay in the fresh air. Keep on doing something. Concentrate on an essential task. To go below is bound to lead to a loss of control. Avoid bending. Far better to maintain an upright posture (if I remain on deck I'll be all right) able to offer perhaps a passable imitation of a seamanlike response.

'Eight Bells, and all's well, with a fine clear night.'

When I stick my head out of the hatch, I can see they are far removed from the time-honoured status of 'all's well'. At the very least, they're in need of a little encouragement.

'... good morning lads. How are you feeling? You don't look too good.'

'I feel awful. I've just been sick.'

'... I'm sorry to hear that, come below.'

' No, I must stay on deck. I'm going to be sick again.'

What can you do to help him at this stage in the game? Not a damned thing, apart from expressing a pious hope.

'... you ought to get your head down.'

'No, absolutely not. I'm staying here.'

And that's that for a while.

Comes the dawn, with the breeze freshening, we must reduce sail, replacing the genoa with the working jib, pulling down two reefs in the mainsail.

With the wind, the sea is rising, moderately at first, then rough enough to make the deck a dismal place, as we hold our course for the Longships, then pass inside the Wolf, exposed to the weight of a boisterous sou'easterly breeze.

All this time, they remain on deck.

Viewed from the comfort of the companionway, their faces loom palely from a dark surround of oilskin coat and hat. At unmercifully frequent intervals they're being deluged by a spatter of ice-cold spray. Taken one with another, they look, and occasionally sound, awful.

'... come on, you devils. You *must* come below.'

My friend Bert lifts his head from leeward, turning a sorrowful face, its only patch of colour being the watery pupils of grey and listless eyes, but I'm glad to hear him murmur.

'Yes, I think I will come below.'

'... good man. I'll wrap you up in a nice warm bunk. If you feel you're going to be sick, just spew into the bucket. I don't give a damn. I've spewed into it myself on more than one occasion.'

Down he comes; his watch keeping mate remains on deck.

'... what about you?'

'I'll stay up here. I haven't been sick yet, and I'm determined to avoid it.'

'... O.K. Are you cold?'

'Absolutely perished.'

'... wet?'

'It's just starting to run down the back of my neck.'

I pass him a dry towel, which he winds around his throat, as a hopefully effective barrier against the encroaching misery.

It takes several hours to weather Land's End and then the Runnelstone Buoy. This is a formidable corner at any time, and having to beat against an adverse tide is making our task a long, drawn-out, and bruising affair.

During the forenoon we make it, and can ease sheets a trifle. Then the weather takes a change for the better. The breeze moderates, veers a point, and to crown it all, the sun comes out as we broad reach our way up The Channel.

Time to shame some life into the crew.

'... where's the cook? Come on Jack, shake a leg. Only biscuits for breakfast? There had better be stew for lunch, or the chances are you're going to get tossed in the 'oggin.'

Our Chef de cuisine is deep in the horrors of seasickness.

'... come on, you restless bum. Get up off your backside, we're hungry (a gentle version of the previously rude bosun's boot). All to no avail: right now, Jack wishes looks could kill, as he opens one eye, and views me as a butcher might appraise a beast - marking the spot for the knife.

'Do you mean to tell me, you want food?'

'... that's correct, Jack, lots of it, and soon.'

'Dear God, it's inhuman.'

Nevertheless, he gets up, and while I empty buckets and clean around the deck, he makes an effort to light the stove. After ten minutes, there's a pale wisp, of what could be smoke emerging from the companionway hatch.

Then sounds emanate from below.

A saucepan clatters to the deck.

The sound of a body, or part of a body, striking the coachroof with a resounding thump, followed by a groan and a string of mumbled obscenities. A cloud of what certainly *is* smoke billows from the companionway hatch, framing Jack's pale face, smudged with soot, one eyebrow mostly gone.

'... what the hell's going on, Jack?'

'I'm afraid the ship's on fire' (this with a deadpan look) a mumble of barely connected words which only a man wracked by a night of seasickness could possibly aspire to. It's also obvious, not only that he doesn't give a damn that the vessel's on fire, his last remaining hope is, she's going to be reduced to a smouldering hulk.

The stove, flooded with blazing paraffin, is flaring to the deckhead. The flames have already caught a towel and the sleeve of somebody's sweater; soon smothered by a squirt from a small fire extinguisher, which

5

has waited patiently for this significant moment of triumph, while the stove, brought under control, is once again roaring noisily away.

'... there you are, Jack, she's going a treat. Do you feel well enough to cook a meal?'

This prompts a malevolent stare, as he growls. 'Stand back, I'm going to cook something on this blasted stove, even if it kills me. What do you want? A stew?'

This is more like my old friend Jack, it seems there's hope for him yet. So while we're waiting for the broth, the improving weather enables us to sit in the cockpit, enjoying the afternoon sun.

The fact that we're reaching, with the breeze just abaft the beam, brings the crew back to near-normality. Almost to the point where those who have been on deck for upwards of thirty hours, without food and little to drink, are beginning to realize that a bunk is a useful item of equipment aboard any sort of a boat. Nevertheless, although they want to turn in, they also want something hot in their bellies.

'... any sign of the stew, cook?'

Silence: while the boat moves gracefully, even if slowly, to the lift of the following swell, yet fast enough to rattle an empty stomach.

'... you down there, Jack? Pass out a few biscuits, there's a good lad, we'd like to make some sort of start on the grub.'

A hand appears, offering a tin of ship's biscuits, a jar of Marmite, and a knife (we snatch them, and eat). The hardtack is dry, and the Marmite is hot enough to burn the tip of your tongue; as a culinary delight, it's not far removed from bone-dry sawdust and mustard.

'... come on, Jack. Where's the ruddy stew?'

At length, after a belly rumbling age, he appears, head rising slowly, above the coaming of the companionway hatch.

Our cook's sparse hair is shiny with sweat, and sticks greasily to his scalp. His face is pale, his eyes sunken, only dark eyebrows show signs of life. Despite the fact that one of these eyebrows has been badly singed, they draw together as if for protection from leering lips, whose paleness is accentuated by an unshaven jowl - but with it all, he is actually trying to smile as he murmurs.

'   'Stew's up, chaps.'

'... and about time, Jack. We're faint from lack of nourishment, lad.'

He extends two hands, offering mugs of something or other; in each there tinkles a spoon.

I wonder why?

His hands are shaking, as he presents a believable image of the person tasked with offering Cleopatra the asp. We take what's given, and holding the precious bowls close to our chests, view what's supposed to be the stew.

In my mug, which is less than half-full, there swills a dark brown liquid. Dark it may be, but it's also thin - the dipping spoon displays a liquid with the consistency of un-milked tea.

Stew, my foot. His broth is nothing more than a scrape of Marmite, over which he's poured a little water.

'... Jack, what in God's name do you call this?'

The face he turns in our direction conveys the burden of a Shakespearean tragedy, as he sighs.

'I'm afraid.' (while leaning outboard, heaving his heart up).

'I'm afraid, it was the best.' (followed by another stomach-knotting retch).

'The best that I could do.' (so saying, and with a ghastly grin, he disappears below).

I, for one, can't drink the stuff.

It's not the taste, or the fact that the 'stew' is barely warm.

It's not merely its anaemic appearance.

It's just, well (words fail me) but you probably know what I mean.

The weather keeps fining away as we run up the Channel, and with the eased motion of the boat the spirits of the crew are likewise soaring. Having survived the agonies of Hell they are now beginning to feel somewhat larger than life, and are moving about the boat with the assurance of old seadogs, casting critical eyes over sheets and halyards that previously could have gone to the devil.

'I think that genoa sheet could do with a tweak, Val.' (so I lever it in, the half-an-inch suggested).

A short time later, the watch changes, with a new man at the helm.

'Look at this genoa, it's as hard as a blasted board, not a bit of flow in it.' (so I apologise, and, at his direction, ease the damned sheet out).

Then they are hungry.

'Your turn to brew-up, isn't it, Val?' (so I make them tea and toast).

But believe or not, I'm glad they're feeling better.

As we near Plymouth, the tension mounts, prompted by the realisation that we have been *at sea*, and are about to make - *a landfall*.

They all become navigators, attacking pristine charts with needle-sharp pencils, while their sticky mugs of cocoa leave disgusting rings on previously unblemished paper.

'Don't you think we should haul a little to the nor'ard, Val? We seem to be making a lot of leeway.' (there's no need to reply, when he's next at the tiller, he will be holding her up no matter what I say).

We have now run our distance, and everyone's keeping a sharp lookout. There's a haze, bringing the visibility down to not much more than a mile, so I'm once more in charge, conscious of eyes that are darting questioning glances.

'Isn't it time we saw something?' (it certainly is; but I display a nonchalant air, as if quite unworried).

'By my reckoning,' he says, 'we should be right by the entrance to Plymouth Sound.' (by my reckoning, we're ashore, but there's no need to tell him that).

Then Hawk-Eye sees something fine on the starboard bow.

'Land-Ho!' he bawls, (if he was Christopher Columbus, he couldn't be better pleased).

Then a thought strikes him.

'What point is that?'

Ever since we've seen the loom of the land, I've been racking my brains in an effort to identify the silhouette. However, it's such an indistinct shape, I'm not quite sure what it is, so I pretend I didn't hear him - but it doesn't gain me a thing.

'What point is that?'

He knows very well I heard him the first time, so he's now certain I'm not sure of our position, which prompts a hard-eyed look that conveys nothing of his previous indisposition. I could have nursed the sod through cholera, but it wouldn't make the slightest difference - nevertheless, I have to say something.

'… it looks like Rame Head.'

He's delighted.

I've admitted it ('it *looks like*', Rame Head).

Now we're all on the same level. Everyone discusses our possible whereabouts. What action we should take. How the tide is likely to be setting. What the breeze will do. Our likely time of arrival at the harbour.

It turns out that it *is* Rame Head, so we sail close-to, then when we've made the necessary mile to wind'ard, ease sheets, soon bringing the breakwater into view. Plymouth stands behind it, grey stone buildings march in orderly rows across the face and brow of the hill, as is required by a barrack town

neat, but a little austere.

Photo: **Eileen Ramsay/PPL**

left to right & clockwise

**Francis Chichester, Sheila Chichester, Blondie Hasler
David Lewis, Valentine Howells**

there is a significant omission

Jean Lacombe

had not yet arrived in Plymouth
and thereafter, as far as some of the press were concerned
it sometimes seemed that he had been airbrushed out of the event

2

the men and boats are gathering
but we only have time for a hesitant glance

David [1] and I were the first to arrive at Plymouth, but after a few days Blondie [2] and then Francis [3] sailed in to join the fleet, and our boats lay conveniently grouped together at the eastern end of the basin.

Comparing *Gipsy Moth* with the other three, I was immediately struck by her size and power, and began to wonder why the race was being organised on a first boat home basis, without any system of handicapping; because alongside a forty-foot ocean racer, which is what *Gipsy Moth* is, and a good one at that, a Folkboat [4] looks like a sailing canoe and a Vertue a tubby weekender. So when I had the opportunity, I tackled Blondie about the discrepancy in size.

'Well, Val,' he said, with a quiet smile and a bright twinkle in his eye, 'we thought, that is, the Committee in its wisdom thought, that whatever system of handicapping was adopted, it wouldn't be perfect, and this being the case, it would be bound to weigh unfairly on someone, with the possibility of reducing the entry.'

'… that's fair enough Blondie, but it's a sight too ingenious for me. By refusing a handicap the whole thing is biased in favour of the faster boat; look at her,' (pointing to *Gipsy Moth*) 'all Francis has to do is keep sailing, and he's bound to win.'

'That may well be so,' replied Blondie, 'but a bigger boat in some ways imposes her own limitations when sailed single-handed. He may find her too much for him.'

I could see, as Blondie made the remark, that he didn't truly believe it. The debate revolved around the size of boat that could be sailed efficiently by one man. A fifty-ton schooner would probably be too much for anybody, then, as you come down the scale, the argument sheds much of its force, until by the time you compare a twelve-tonner with a five-tonner it may be swayed by other considerations. To be sailed at say eighty per cent of maximum efficiency, the work on deck might be heavier aboard the bigger boat, but the deck on which you work would be a much more congenial place, while more powerful winches and tackles obviate the lack of beef. Waterline length is the thing that counts, and that depends on the depth of your pocket, more than on the size of your biceps. Taking one thing with

(1) these numbers indicate that the relevant information will be provided at the end of this chapter.

another, I believed the smaller boats were at a near hopeless disadvantage, and told Blondie this.

'Don't say too much,' he replied, 'the entry is small enough as it is.'

Excitement mounted as the starting date drew near, we all seemed to have masses of work that needed doing aboard our respective boats, and the arrival of the long-promised radio sets, held up 'til now in Customs, gave us even more to do. These sets were on loan from the Radio Corporation of America. That we had been provided with them, was due entirely to the efforts of Bruce Robinson of the *Slocum Society*. [5]

Although it was kind of the people concerned, this kit, arriving at the eleventh hour created several problems. In the first instance they were radio-telephones, working on a frequency which limited their range to not much more than thirty miles. To get over this difficulty, Bruce had worked out an ingenious, but complicated, schedule with Pan-American Airlines whose planes, while on the North-Atlantic hop were supposed to relay our messages. This seemed a pretty long shot, but perhaps not sufficient in itself to justify refusal of the equipment. The bigger drawback was the necessity of installing a large accumulator to meet the power requirement, as I didn't have charging equipment or indeed a motor of any sort aboard the Folkboat *Eira*.

The installation of the radios had been entrusted to the Royal Navy, who did their best under what must have seemed to them to be somewhat chaotic circumstances. Their expert came aboard my boat, opened the for'ard hatch, stood on the flap, and promptly broke the hinges. After this contretemps we circled each other warily for a while, before coming to grips with the problem of where to put the radio, the antenna, and the gigantic, lorry-sized lead-acid battery.

When the technical type broke the hatch, it was on the tip of my tongue to tell him where to put the stuff, but I managed to take a leaf out of their well-mannered book and played the silent service myself.

The transmitter we screwed to the deckhead. The antenna was taped to the rigging and led to the top of the mast. However, the massive accumulator just wouldn't fit anywhere.

To the casual observer, a boat that is twenty-five feet long might be expected to offer room enough for this relatively small bit of equipment. In practice, the amount of available space is strictly limited. This being the case because we were trying to include items that were in addition to those long

(5) *information concerning the Slocum Society will be found later in the text.*

planned for. And furthermore, you can't just plant an object weighing in excess one hundred pounds just anywhere in a small boat. It's got to be somewhere fairly low, easily accessible and, in this instance, preferably a well ventilated position.

Fair enough; and there was one place that exactly met those requirements, however, that pièce de résistance, the toilet, was already there.

Admittedly, it was only a bucket, but I had spent much time and thought on its precise location. The headroom was just right, immediately under the for'ard hatch, which ensured a reviving draft of fresher air. The straining bars were strategically positioned, and through-bolted. What might appear to the untutored eye as nothing more than a simple plastic bucket, was really an engine of magnificence and purpose, designed and constructed to provide long and useful service. Even so, 'you'll have to move this bucket.' said the man from the Senior Service.

I sighed, at the utter vandalism of it all. When *will* people learn, what to keep, and what to throw away?

Regardless of this difference of opinion, the battery at length held pride of place, lashed down with many turns of codline through the handles at each end. With the outraged member of the crew partly sustained throughout these tribulations by the thought that, if it all worked, I would at least be able keep my promise to my wife - because, like many a journeying husband, I had rashly given my word that I would do my very best to get a message through every other day.

Each preparing boat had an air about it all its own.

With Francis, aboard the flagship of the fleet, his wife Sheila ensured that order reigned supreme. The vessel's stores came at their appointed time, and they were duly stowed. The press were dealt with, wooed, or fended off, as precedence dictated, and court was held with pomp and circumstance, if the occasional, perhaps unwitting gaffe is ignored.

'It's a pity your wife can't be here to see you off, Valentine.'

'… she's just had a baby.'

'What a shame.'

On *Jester*, Blondie worked quietly, while friends and visitors dropped in for a chat and a drink, and regardless of the accumulation of supplies it was easy to discern a plan.

Lists were being pencilled-in, consulted, lengthened, carefully amended. Throughout it all shone an experienced seaman's neatness and the habits of a lifetime spent in boats. On this favoured vessel, in the midst of a tumultuous gale, at dead of night, the skipper would be able to reach for the box of matches required to light the galley stove, and they would be there, in their place, secure and dry.

'Oh, before you go, Val, sign the visitor's book, there's a good chap.'

He also thanked me, for what I regarded as privilege.

On board *Cardinal Vertue* David occasionally appeared from around, behind, or out of colossal piles of jam, rope, sails, beer, fenders, boxes of apples, bottles of gin, a pair of climbing boots, an ice axe, a case of whisky, tins of shark repellent, packets of matches, half-a-dozen water jugs, a whole clutch of Calor Gas bottles, pairs of silk stockings, the occasional brassiere and, as seductive a pair of black lace panties as you would ever wish to see, nicely filled, of course.

At first sight, some of these endearing items seemed a little out of place aboard a boat that was entered for a single-handed transatlantic race, until I was told, they (the beguiling bits) belonged to his girlfriend who, as he put it, 'had offered her services' and was helping prepare the hooker for sea.

On board *Eira*, apart from the excited Celtic shouts of my friends, who were bravely preparing a boat they were sure was going to bear me to a watery grave, there was some semblance of order, but under those tidy rows of tinned baked beans were several pairs of sweaty socks. And when we eventually got to sea, I found I'd forgotten an important book of Navigational Tables.

Blondie Hasler was the man who captured my attention.

Francis, David, and myself had merely purchased boats of a size and suitability that the extent of our financial resources would allow. They were essentially small cruisers or (in one case) an ocean-racer, which had been adapted for single-handed sailing, principally by adding a self-steering device.

Lt Colonel H.G.Hasler's boat, on the other hand, displayed a radical approach to the problems of ocean voyaging, and for me was nothing less than a notice board which announced - *attention, mind at work.*

Blondie was, of course, quite unassuming about the rig, saying that the Chinese had done it all before, a mere five thousand years ago. Nobody should swallow that, because *Jester* was, and is, the result of the application of an original mind, backed by a wealth of experience, to the age-old problem of how to cross an ocean and stay dry.

I admired the man and his boat, which reflects and illuminates the character of the owner/designer more than any other vessel I'm familiar with.

'... what are those side flaps for, Blondie?'

'Well, when you're under way and well-heeled, you can use the weather hatch to get out on deck, if you want to. And the lee one is handy for being sick out of.'

'... one of the limitations of the rig, it seems to me, Blondie, is the fact that it's impossible to set any specifically light-weather canvas - you're stuck with two hundred and fifty-two square feet - while on a conventional boat, you can play around with genoas and light-weather kites and in that way double the sail area.'

'But you have to get out on deck to do it.' (I know, Blondie; I know).

'... I'm also worried about the un-stayed mast, which must wave around in an alarming manner, much in the style of a fly-fishing rod.'

'There was a time when the wings of a biplane required yards of wire to keep them in place.'

touché, Blondie, touché.

photo: **Eileen Ramsay/PPL**

the four boats that started, and finished
the first single-handed transatlantic race
1960

in the foreground

Gipsy Moth 3

left to right

the Folkboat *Eira*, the modified Folkboat *Jester* and *Cardinal Vertue*

photo: **Eileen Ramsay/PPL**

David Lewis [1] & *Cardinal Vertue*

the bird depicted on the self-steering wind vane is a kiwi, which David
was proud to display as representative of his adoptive country,
and perhaps an acknowledgement that he also harboured an imp which
is at least partly illustrated in the Eileen Ramsay portrait (opposite)

photo: **Eileen Ramsay/PPL**

David Lewis [1]

aboard

Cardinal Vertue

with the self-steering gear supposedly in charge of the vessel

photo: **Patrick Ward**   courtesy: **The Observer**

the modified Folkboat

Jester

the application of a seafaring mind to the age-old problem of how to cross
an ocean, in a small boat and
stay dry

photo: **Patrick Ward**   courtesy: **The Observer**

Lt Colonel H.G.Hasler [2]

known affectionately by international yachting community as

Blondie

photo: **Eileen Ramsay/PPL**

Gipsy Moth 3

designed by Robert Clark to the owner's specification 1957
built by John Tyrell at Arklow, Eire, completed September 1959
self-steering gear (known as 'Miranda') designed by the owner
length overall 39ft 7ins; waterline length 28 ft
maximum beam 10ft 2ins
Draught 6ft 5 ins
tonnage: Thames 13 tons; net registered 9 tons. Iron keel, 4 tons
planking, mahogany; deck beams, spruce; deck, half-inch ply
mast, boom, and spinnaker booms, hollow spruce spars

photo: **Eileen Ramsay/PPL**

Francis Chichester [3]

in some ways, a reticent character, as people can afford to be, who have so
many record-breaking accomplishments to their credit (he was a pioneer
aviator) they have no need to embellish their image

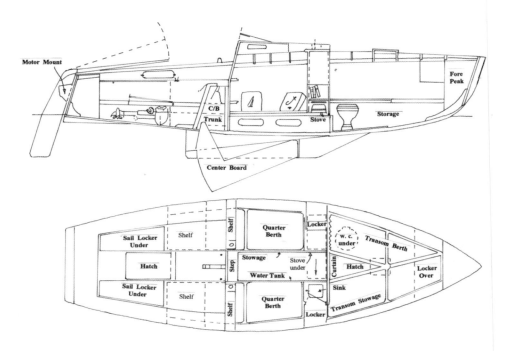

Cap Horn

length overall 21ft 4 ins; waterline length 19 ft 8 ins; beam 7 ft 1 inch
draft, centreboard up 2 ft 2 ins; draft, centreboard down 4 ft zero ins
displacement 2350 lbs; ballast (cast iron) 800 lbs
average headroom, main cabin 4 feet zero inches

By ocean-going standards, this is a small vessel, but not necessarily an
unseaworthy craft, particularly when sailed by an experienced seaman who
had built his own boat, and then sailed that yacht (*Hippocampe*: 18 feet
overall) from France, to New York, via the Caribbean. A varied seafaring
experience which put Jean Lacombe comfortably ahead of most of his fellow
competitors in the first single-handed transatlantic race. Nevertheless, *Cap
Horn* didn't have the ghost of a competitive hope when up against *Gipsy
Moth 3*, and it says a great deal for Jean's sanguine demeanour that he
accepted that fact, with a smile, coupled with a good-natured shrug to his
shoulders. The outboard motor illustrated above was not aboard the vessel
when undertaking ocean passages (what use would it be?). The limited
stowage space, coupled with the weight restriction, rendered that awkward
little item (smelly, and a fire risk) as nothing more than a joke.

photo: **Eileen Ramsay/PPL**

Jean Lacombe,[4] having just completed a single-handed transatlantic passage, from New York to Plymouth, in a vessel that was little bigger than a dinghy, arrived just in time to attend The Observer-sponsored party which was held at the harbour-side restaurant known as Pedro's (see accompanying text).

However; Jean, as an experienced seaman, knew that he needed a few days rest before embarking on yet another transatlantic passage, but this time, from Plymouth *to* New York.

These are major undertakings, and Eileen Ramsay has effectively captured the physical cost that comes with such a challenge.

part of the art of seamanship?
knowing when to stop

photo: **Squibbs Studio**, Tenby   the Folkboat *Eira*

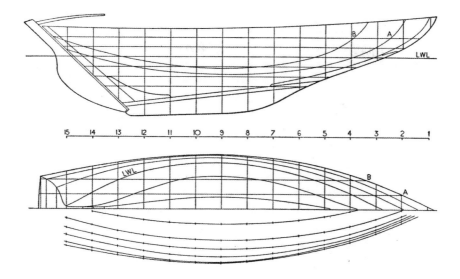

The yacht *Eira* was based on a standard Scandinavia Folkboat. The lines of the vessel were unchanged (19 feet and six inches of waterline length) and the freeboard, scantlings, and traditional clinker method of construction were representative of the original concept.

However, Folkboats were intended as weekenders, with large cockpits and lightly rigged masts, not attributes that lend themselves to North Atlantic passages. So the decision was taken, by the owner, to convert the cockpit into a very small self-draining area, separated from the accommodation by a 'bridgedeck' which gave assurance that when she shipped a big one (only a matter of time) the resultant deluge didn't flood the saloon and subsequently sink the vessel.

The mast supports were strengthened to include a double-spreader rig, with inner & outer forestays, runners, and twin standing backstays. The end-result being, that while the craft might be small, she could (should) survive a knock-down, recover, and sail confidently on.

The coachroof was extended just forward of the mast in order to not only provide a little more headroom, but also improve the ventilation (the 'bucket and chuck it') was located directly under the hatch.

photo: **Squibbs Studio, Tenby**

the proud owner of the Folkboat

Eira
(named for his wife)

after having been reluctantly persuaded
to join with some of the partying members of the

Saundersfoot Sailing Club

what sailor departed without a small noggin ?
who lived to regret it the day of the race ?

The time spent in Mill Bay Basin went all too quickly and the day came that had been set aside for *The Observer's* dinner to commemorate the first ever, East/West Single-handed transatlantic Race. This was held at *Pedro's,* [6] and as is usually the case with events of this nature, the establishment had been chosen not only because of its excellent reputation, but because the venue was well within staggering distance of the dock.

The competitors attended with some of their supporters.

The organising committee of the Royal Western Yacht Club of England [7] were also represented.

And the men who wore the puzzled expressions were from The *Observer,* [8] no doubt wondering how, through a smudge of printers ink, they ever came to be involved with this raggle-taggled mob.

Somebody, no doubt it was Chris Brasher, had obviously taken care to see the evening a success, which was just as well, because when I turned up at the restaurant, the event seemed to have the doom of the Last Supper lurking in the foyer. This impression may have been engendered by the fact that I had kept off the booze all day, determined to at least start on the right foot, because I have sometimes been embarrassed by arriving at the rip-roaring, back slapping stage, while other people are sipping sherry, prior to spooning up the soup. More often than not, I don't realize this until the next day, when it's too late for anything other than a shudder.

However, we all marched gaily along on this particular evening. The wine flowed as wine should when provided by a sponsor and the party was turning out a great success. Towards the end of the proceedings I noticed a thickset man, sitting by himself at a table in a corner of the room, and having benefited from enough of the smooth stuff to at least partially overcome my natural shyness (?) I went over and introduced myself.

'... Howells,' I said, holding out my hand, 'I'm sailing the Folkboat *Eira.'*

'I'm the Frenchman, Jean Lacombe,' he replied, while getting to his feet, 'I'm sailing the yacht *Cap Horn,* and I come from the port of Le Havre.'

This is a gambit I really must try out on some unsuspecting empire builder.

'How do you do, I'm the Welshman Dai John Edwards, sailing a boat called *Snow* and I come from Gwaencaegurwen.'

The French can get away with it. I'm not sure about the Celts, yet it's surely worth a try?

Jean had just arrived in Plymouth after a hard passage. The rumour was, he'd recently sailed from New York, either way, he was tired and said he would rest-up for a day or two, even if it meant a late start. He made this remark after a careful look at his roistering companions, and I'm still not sure how to take it.

Having got the bit between our teeth at *Pedro's*, I and half-a-dozen other tiddly lads from Pembrokeshire were foolish enough to have more drinks at our hotel, and it was very late indeed when we tottered up to bed. Even then, I couldn't sleep. I was fully wound and my mind revolved around the race, the boats, and the other competitors. I lay in bed thinking about my wife Eira, at home in Saundersfoot. At the same time trying to console myself by reflecting that the circumstances were perhaps better than some others who were entered for the race, and had so far failed to show.

Piver (rhymes with diver) had built his trimaran in California, trailed it four thousand miles across the 'States, and at this moment was bound for Plymouth, certain to arrive too late to be accepted as an entry.

We had heard great reports of the multihulls, how fast they were, how seaworthy, and I was disappointed that Piver was not going to give us a demonstration of these radical newcomers to the ocean racing fleet.

The German who had entered was a bit of a mystery. He had been reported sailed from Hamburg, so far hadn't turned up, another probable non-starter.

A gent by the name of Elison had entered a boat called *Blue Haze*, a West Solent One Design. He was reported sailed from Abersoch but, due to gear failure, had put into Fishguard Harbour for shelter (another non-runner). And I would have hated to have that happen to me, the months of preparation, all the sweat and toil, then the terrible letdown when things go horribly wrong.

With these disasters in the forefront of my mind, I had little difficulty convincing myself that I was a very lucky fellow to be starting in the race the next day. Before I fell asleep, I 'phoned the night porter, fixed a call for 0500 hrs., and while I was at it, ordered two boiled eggs and four aspirins for breakfast - oh, the desperate evils of drink.

The morning came, and I felt awful. It required an effort of will to tackle breakfast, but I knew it was important to start on the right foot, while readily admitting that it was a pity I hadn't stumbled across this priceless gem before getting involved in the previous evening's booze-up.

The day was dull and grey, which matched the state of my head.

When I looked up at the sky (ouch!) I could see that we had been blessed with a sou'westerly breeze, about Beaufort five to six, overcast, with probable rain showers, not a pleasant prospect.

When I got down to the tub, I noticed Blondie at work on *Jester;* then David, and finally Francis appeared and began working on their boats.

I fussed about *Eira,* but there was nothing of a major nature to do, so I just mucked about, feeling grumpy and irritable. The two boiled eggs sat on my stomach as so much lead shot, and I regretted having eaten them.

By eight-thirty I had done all that needed doing and was reduced to killing time. My friends were there, and I tried my best to be civil; it was an uphill task, and we were probably all glad when the naval launch came alongside to give *Eira* a tow to the torpedo camber.

Jester and *Gipsy Moth* had already gone, Blondie under tow, with Francis using his auxiliary. This move had been arranged some days previously, the object being to provide everyone with the opportunity of scrubbing the topsides of his boat, in order to get rid of the stinking oil smears that had accumulated on the hulls while we lay at the leeward end of the commercial dock.

When the naval coxswain of the harbour launch went ahead, the tow rope snatched at the bows of *Eira,* causing the vessel's stern to strike the hull of the tank landing craft which we had lain alongside. I shouted at the coxswain, laying my tongue to a stream of oaths that cast doubt on his parentage, his sex, his ability, and that of the Senior Service as a whole. Taking one thing with another, it was a real giveaway of the nervous tension I was suffering from. And worse than that, the sort of bad manners which I regretted as soon as I had formed the sentences, which leapt out of my mouth as cats released from a bag - when we arrived at the camber, I went over to him and apologised.

My friends, John and Lloyd, were soon engaged on the job of removing the scum of oil, helped by detergents supplied by the Navy. While they were at this task, which I was grateful they were doing for me, I walked along the dock to find out if the other competitors were displaying the jangling nerves that I myself was feeling.

Blondie seemed cool, calm, and purposeful, checking items of rigging, he greeted me with a smile.

Francis was busy, but his activities seemed designed to conceal his irritability, all I got out of him was a grunt.

David was circulating with the rapidity of a fly in a bottle, moving fast but getting nowhere. But he did help me, when I asked him if it might be a good idea to postpone the start - the timid type, hoping for better weather - he said, 'absolutely not, let's get to hell out of here right now.'

My support team had hired a launch from which to view the proceedings, and this turned up at nine-fifteen to tow *Eira* out to somewhere near the start line.

The torpedo camber was located in a sheltered spot, and it was difficult to estimate the wind speed that would obtain clear out in the bay. The low grey clouds seemed to be moving fast overhead so, while still in the lee, I tied down two reefs and hanked on the small jib. Then it was time to leave, and *Eira* was towed out, expertly this time, by the launch hired from Mashford's Yard.

The breeze was not as fresh out in Plymouth Sound as I had expected, and this meant that the boat was under-canvassed. It seemed a good fault, as there was always the possibility of the weather deteriorating. In any case, for the next twenty minutes or so, we would only be jilling about.

Francis was manoeuvring *Gipsy Moth* under full mainsail, and she, and he, looked great. David was rushing about the bay with the keenness of a young bull trying to join a herd of passing heifers, some of whom were in season.

And Blondie?

Had the situation well in hand, tacking *Jester* quietly to and fro, at the weather-end of the line (of course).

The ten-minute gun crashed out, and I noted it on my wristwatch.

By the time the five-minute gun was due, I had started to shiver with the build-up of nervous tension. Unable to sit in the cockpit, I hopped up and down, up and down, up and down, totally out of control.

As the final minutes ticked away, I managed to regain some semblance of normality by standing back from myself and deliberately slowing my rate of breathing, taking a succession of deep breaths that did much to steady my nerves. My stomach felt incredibly tight - those two hard boiled eggs lay like ballast in a bilge.

At last, the starting gun boomed out, and we were off.

Blondie made the best start, smack on the line at the gun, and up at the weather-end (where else?).

David was well there, as was Francis, who was a little astern of *Eira*.

I watched him get out of the cockpit, move for'ard, and start winching up a good-sized genoa.

Gipsy Moth was reaching under a mainsail and when the genny was hoisted, surged forward, even before the sail was sheeted home. She was coming up astern of *Eira* and travelling twice as fast, as I was still jogging along under a double-reefed main. If I hadn't altered course to leeward there would have been a collision. When Francis passed, a mere boat's length to windward, he was still on the foredeck and Miranda, as he calls his self-steering gear, was in charge of the vessel. The irony of the situation amused me, and helped steady my nerves. *Overtaking boat keeps clear,* says the international yacht racing rule. Hoist a protest flag, and put the cat amongst the pigeons?

Having indulged in a near-enough hysterical giggle, I decided that, perhaps, it just wouldn't do. It was unthinkable; even if he had rammed me fair and square, I wouldn't have protested. As he passed, I waved, thinking, as I did so, that's the last I'll see of him.

Eira was now tail-end-Charlie, and I felt I had better do something about it. When I was about the job of shaking the reef out of the mainsail, a spectator launch came close alongside, and I could see Chris Brasher waving, so I thought I'd better put on a display of cheerfulness.

'... it's a good job it's a long race, Chris', delivered with as much of an air of nonchalance as I could muster. The truth was, I felt awful, nervous and fearful, just hoped it didn't show.

Under the full mainsail, *Eira* picked up speed, and by the time we had cleared the breakwater we were on level terms with David and Blondie, although *Jester* was the windward boat of the group.

The two Folkboats and the Vertue were evenly matched. *Jester* was carrying full sail, and moving well, seemingly slightly closer-winded than the other two. *Eira* was also tramping along and I just cracked the main and jib sheets to keep her footing with her rivals. In a short time, even though we had only made a few seaward miles, *Gipsy Moth* was well ahead, little more than a white sail, which occasionally showed from the top of a wave.

We were now clear of the land and the sea was building, with the fresh westerly breeze blowing over the ebb tide kicking up a sizeable lump.

I set the self-steering gear and went below for something to drink.

The movement was violent, and together with my indigestion (or was it fear?) my stomach felt queasy and myself generally rotten. My mouth was dry, so I settled on a glass of lime juice and water.

Back on deck, the spray was starting to fly, and the boat, close-hauled on starboard, was well heeled with her lee rail occasionally pushed right under. Just the sort of conditions I had hoped we would avoid at the start of the race, brought about by a depression moving towards the British

Isles, with fresh to strong sou'westerly winds expected in the Channel and Western Approaches.

Tackling a single-handed passage, of whatever duration, is a job to cause the best to stop and think awhile. The start of a single-handed passage across the Western Ocean is a major undertaking which, when he's about it, must cause the boldest man to ponder the risks involved, recognising that at the very least they give rise to apprehension.

The start of the first-ever East to West single-handed transatlantic race had got me in the gut. I cursed the adverse weather, and longed for moderate conditions. The breeze held steady, and we beat out of the Channel, lee-bowing the tide. By one o'clock in the afternoon we had the Eddystone Light about a mile and a half abeam to starboard, and the English coast was out of sight.

I had been keeping an eye on David and Blondie, noting that *Cardinal Vertue* was closing up astern, tramping along under a large genoa. She was going like a train, smashing her way over the crests, then plunging into the troughs, evidently David didn't fancy being last.

Thirty minutes after the Eddystone was abeam, I looked aft again. *Jester* was on the starboard quarter, a mile astern, well up to wind'ard. David was directly astern, but the boat seemed to have changed shape, there was something wrong with the silhouette.

I reached below for the binoculars, had difficulty keeping *Cardinal Vertue* in the field of vision.

As we surged up and over the oncoming swell, still close-hauled and well heeled, with the occasional spatter of spray making the use of the binoculars a chancy affair, it took what seemed an age to confirm what I had suspected at the first glance - *Cardinal Vertue* was partly dismasted.

I just couldn't contain myself, shouting into the wind 'Great Scott, he's lost his topmast.'

For a fleeting second, an unlovely thought broke surface in my mind, then I swept it away as too mean to harbour.

'Poor old David; what bad luck.'

Through the binoculars I could see that the Vertue's mast had snapped just above the hounds, the broken half swaying drunkenly about, still attached by the shrouds and the enveloping genoa. For a minute I debated whether I should go about and offer assistance, on balance concluded there was little I could do - seeing David moving about on deck, apparently unharmed, relieved my principal anxiety.

As I watched the wallowing wreck, which was dropping rapidly astern, I saw *Jester* alter course, reduce sail, and then heave-to within hailing distance of *Cardinal Vertue* (good old Blondie). I didn't think there was much he could do; it gave me a good feeling to see the man running so well and true to form.

Within a few more minutes we had dropped them out of sight, but certainly not out of mind.

The turn of events had shaken me out of what had been in danger of becoming a sad-sack, sorry for myself attitude, which just won't do when you're alone in a small boat.

The enormity of David's bad luck hadn't altered my immediate circumstances. I was still feeling apprehensive of the task that lay ahead. It had certainly knocked the props from under the slightly unreal, withdrawn, crouching attitude that some emotional people adopt when faced with a particularly nasty set of problems.

That might have happened to me.

Life is real, life is earnest.

What caused the accident?

Probably carrying too much sail, and when the boat failed to negotiate the awkward top of a crest, she had fallen off it, and the resultant shock proved too much for the mast.

Are we playing the same fool trick?

How are the bottlescrews and the mast fittings?

I was now wide awake, and aware of my responsibilities to the boat; our partnership, to be successful, had to be honest and long.

That I was in need of a lesson, the events of the past few minutes had made glaringly obvious, with it came the recognition that David had probably been lucky to suffer the reverse when he did.

It would have been much more serious if it had happened in the middle of the Western Ocean.

In all the excitement I had forgotten to stream the log, and I now did this little chore, cribbing the dial setting so that it would have read zero when we were abeam of the Eddystone Light. One of the minor advantages of single-handed sailing is that you can do this sort of thing, and nobody will ever know. Then I went below and wrote up the logbook.

1300 hrs., Eddystone abeam, bearing due North (true), a mile and a half to starboard.

we had made our ocean-going departure

Photo: **Eileen Ramsay/PPL**

the start of the first single-handed transatlantic race

Cardinal Vertue

to windward

the Folkboat

Eira

under-canvassed

THE

PARTY

@

PEDRO'S

the near-waterfront bistro that Chris Brasher [1] chose
as the best venue
for this one-off event

look carefully at the menu,
something has been included which,
to say the very least, is somewhat out of the ordinary

the wines on offer demonstrate
that no expense
was spared

(Chateau d'Yquem, for a group of rollicking sailors ?)

---

(1) *An appreciation of Chris is to be found at the end of the chapter.*

EVE - OF - THE - RACE DINNER
AT PEDRO'S, PLYMOUTH.

10. 6. 60.

M E N U
(Note: Alternatives are not compulsory —
order both or all, if you like.)

SCAMPI RIRA

MELON AUX VERTUS CARDINALES
⸺⸺⸺⸺⸺⸺⸺

CONSOMME DE TORTUE DEUX FOIS TOURNEE
⸺⸺⸺⸺⸺⸺

ESCALOPE TZIGANE A SAUCE PAPILLON DE NUIT
(GARNI A LACOMBE)

LAMB CUTLETS JESTER
(LEGEREMENT BLONDI)

FILETS MIGNONS OCCIDENTALES ROYALES
⸺⸺⸺⸺⸺⸺

FRAISES A CREME OBSERVATEUR
⸺⸺⸺⸺⸺⸺

CAFE NATURE ARROSE DE LIQUEUR SLOCUM
⸺⸺⸺⸺⸺⸺

CIGARES, CIGARETTES, PIQURES DE MESCALIN, ETC.

⸺⸺⸺⸺⸺⸺⸺⸺⸺⸺⸺⸺⸺

EVE-OF-RACE DINNER

OSTAR 1960 @ PEDRO'S

compiled
by
Chris Brasher

SCAMPI EIRA

Melon aux Vertue Cardinales

CONSOMME DE TORTUE DEUX FOIS TOURNEE

ESCALOPE TZIGANE A SAUCE PAPILLON DE NUIT

Garni a Lacombe

LAMB CUTLETS JESTER

Legerement Blondi

FILETS MIGNONS OCCIDENTALES ROYALES

FRAISES A CRÈME OBSERVATEUR

CAFÉ NATURE ARROSE DE LIQUEUR SLOCUM

CIGARES, CIGARETTES, PIQURES DE MESCALIN, ETC

BORDEAUX. Red

	Bot.	½Bot
1. Medoc	10/-	5/6
2. St.Emilion	11/-	6/-
3. St.Julien	11/-	6/6
4. Chateau Pichon Longueville-Lalande	16/-	
5. Chateau Lascombes	11/6	9/-
6. Chateau Pontet Canet		
7. Chateau La Mission Haut Brion Pessac	22/-	
8. Chateau Calon Segur		
9. Chateau Lafite		

BORDEAUX. White

Chateau bottled	37/6	

BURGUNDY. Red vin

	Bot.	½Bot
10. Graves Superieur	11/-	6/-
11. Sol Enclos	12/6	7/-
12. Lauriers Blanc	14/6	8/-
13. Marquis de la Rose	14/6	8/-
14. La Mora Blanc	16/-	9/-
15. Marsac	45/6	8/6
16. Chateau d'Yquem		
Chateau bottled	45/-	
20. Beaujolais	14/6	8/-
21. Pommard 1952	18/6	10/-
22. Nuits St.Georges 1953	20/-	11/-
23. Gevrey-Chambertin 1952	21/-	11/6
24. Beaune 1953	18/6	10/-
25. Fleurie N.V.	15/6	8/6
26. Vosne-Romanee 1950	21/-	11/6

BURGUNDY. White

		Bot.	½Bot
30. Bourgogne Blanc	1953	12/6	7/6
31. Pouilly Fuisse	1953	15/6	8/6
32. Chablis Village	1953	16/6	9/-
33. Meursalt	1953	18/6	10/-

RHONE WINES.

	Vin	Bot.	½Bot
40. Chateau Neuf-du-Pape	1953	15/-	8/6
41. Tavel Rose	1953	15/-	8/6

HOCK.

	Vin	Bot.	½Bot
45. Liebfraumilch Rosengold	1953	21/-	11/-
46. Liebfraumilch Dienhard & Co. Haar Christof Wein	1953	23/-	12/6
47. Liebfraumilch Alberich Saccone & Speed	1953	19/6	10/-
48. Morsteiner Domtal	1955	16/6	10/-

ITALIAN WINES.

	flask	
Chianti Ruffino Red or White	21/6	11/6
Chianti Stravecchio Red or White	12/-	bot
Chianti Orvieto White Sweet or Dry	9/-	
Asti Spumanti, Sparkling Muscatel	25/-	16/-

Spanish Wines.

Rioja Ebreo Red,	10/-	5/6
Santa Lucia White Medium Sweet	10/-	5/6

PORTUGUESE WINES.

Tinto	10/-	5/6
Sec	10/-	5/5

CHAMPAGNE.

Bollinger, Special Cuvee	37/6	20/-
Veuve Clicquot ½ bot	49/6	26/6
N.V. N.V.	37/6	12/-
Heidsieck, Dry Monopole ½ bot	22/6	22/6
Moet & Chandon ¾ bot	37/6	11/6

BORDEAUX Red

Medoc	10/-	5/6
St. Emilion	11/-	6/-
St. Julien	12/-	6/6
Chateau Pichon Longueville L/L	16/-	
Chateau Pontet Canet	17/6	9/-
Chateau La Mission Haut Brion Pessac	22/-	
Chateau Calon Segur	22/-	
Chateau Lafite (Chateau Bottled)	37/6	

BORDEAUX White

Graves Superieur	11/-	6/-
Bel Enclos	12/6	7/-
Lauriers Blanc	14/6	8/-
Marquis de la Rose	14/6	8/-
La Flora Blanc	16/-	9/-
Barsac	15/6	8/6
Chateau d'Yquem (Chateau Bottled)	40/-	

BURGUNDY Red

Beaujolais	14/6	8/-
Pommard '52	18/6	10/-
Nuits St. Georges '53	20/-	11/-
Gevrey-Chambertin '52	21/-	11/6
Beaune '53	18/6	10/-
Fleurie N.V.	15/6	8/6
Vosne-Romanee '50	21/-	11/6

BURGUNDY White

Bourgogne Blanc	12/6	7/-
Poully Fuisse '53	15/6	8/6
Chablis Village '53	16/6	9/-
Mersalt '53	18/6	10/-
Chateau N-du-P '53	15/-	8/6
Tavel Rose '53		

HOCK

Liebfraumilch '53 Rebengold Dienhard & Co	21/-	11/-
Liebfraumilch '53 Hane Christof Wein	23/-	12/6
Liebfraumilch '53 Alberich, Saccone & Speed	19/6	10/-
Miersteiner Domtal '55	18/6	10/-

ITALIAN WINES

Chianti Ruffino (Red or White, by the flask)	21/6	11/6
Chianti Stravecchio (bottle)	12/-	
Chianti Orvieto (White: sweet or dry)	19/-	
Asti Spumanti (Sparkling Muscatel)	29/-	16/-

SPANISH WINES

Rioja Ederara (Red)	10/-	5/6
Santa Lucia. White (medium sweet)	10/-	5/6

PORTUGESE WINES

Tinto	10/-	5/6
Seco	10/-	5/6

CHAMPAGNE

Bolinger (Special Cuvee)	37/6	20/-
Veuve Clicquot	49/6	26/6
Veuve Clicquot (N. V. quarter bottle)		12/-
Heidseick Dry Monopole (N.V.)	37/6	22/6
Moet & Chandon (N.V.)	37/6	22/6
Moet & Chandon (N.V. quarter bottle)		11/6

ROYAL WESTERN YACHT CLUB OF ENGLAND

The club was founded in 1827 as The Plymouth Royal Clarence Regatta Club, renamed The Royal Western Yacht Club in 1833.

At the time there was an Irish yacht club called The Western Yacht Club of Ireland and, for reasons not entirely apparent, the two clubs became affiliated, with early records quoting the Irish and English Divisions of the Royal Western Yacht Club.

However, by 1844, the decision was taken to revert to the original title, with one significant change, so that The Royal Western Yacht Club had 'of England' added to its title.

In 1942, the clubhouse, which at the time was located adjacent to The Grand Hotel, was destroyed by enemy aircraft (the Luftwaffe were bombing Britain at the time) so the Club premises were moved to The Esplanade.

In 1961 The Royal Western and The Royal South Western Yacht Clubs amalgamated and the refurbished West Hoe premises, previously those of the Royal South Western, were officially opened by HRH Philip, Duke of Edinburgh in 1965.

In 1989 the Club moved to the present location, with this significant development being funded through the sale of the West Hoe leasehold.

HRH the Princess Royal opened the present-day clubhouse in May 1989.

The Club first enjoyed the privilege of an Admiralty Warrant that authorized the use of the Blue Ensign as far back as 1842. The current warrant was issued in 1894, with copies of these original documents being reprinted in the Club handbook.

THE
OBSERVER

This British newspaper is published on Sundays.

It is placed, in political terms, in the middle of the broad spectrum of liberal opinion, and can be relied on to take a social democratic line on most issues.

It is the world's oldest Sunday newspaper, with the first issue gracing the news-stands on the 4th December, 1791.

Like most publications of its sort, the business suffered varying fortunes, came close to bankruptcy on more than one occasion. In the modern era, it was purchased by the newspaper magnate Lord Northcliffe in 1908, but disagreements with his editor persuaded the noble lord that he would be better off getting rid of his troublesome pamphlet, and he sold out to William Waldorf Astor in 1911.

Ownership passed to Waldorf's sons in 1948, with David taking over as editor, a position he retained for 27 years, during which time he turned it into a trust-owned business employing, amongst others, George Orwell, Paul Jennings, and C.A.Lejeune.

In 1977, the Astor's sold the by-then ailing newspaper to the US oil giant Atlantic Richfield, now known as ARCO, who sold it on to Lonrho plc in 1981.

Since June 1993, it has been part of the Guardian Media Group.

photo: **Ed Lacey**

courtesy: **George Herringshaw's Sporting Heroes**

Chris Brasher

winning an Olympic Gold medal
Summer Olympics
Melbourne

1956

CHRISTOPHER BRASHER CBE

At the time of the first single-handed transatlantic race Chris was working for The Observer, as their sports correspondent, although he later became Sports Editor, a position he was eminently qualified to occupy.

He was an enthusiastic supporter of the race, in marked contrast to representatives of the Establishment who, on more than one occasion, expressed the opinion that 'this hare-brained scheme could well bring the sport of yachting into disrepute.'

All that got out of Chris and Blondie Hasler was a smile, and a barely disguised look, with a lift of the eyebrows that conveyed the opinion that those old buffers were not only past their sell-by-date, but the sooner they were put out to grass the better for all concerned.

This man from the Press was immensely helpful, nothing was too much trouble. He always seemed to be available, and without him the assemblage of boats and the disparity of their owners may not have coalesced into the happy band that seemed, at one time, almost too good to be true.

4

some things
are not as easy as they look

The first night of the first-ever East/West single-handed transatlantic race drew a darkening veil over the events of the day, and perhaps it was just as well. Not a good start, unfavourable weather, and one of the four competitors out, at least temporarily, nevertheless we *had* crossed the line at the gun.

I kept *Eira* close-hauled on starboard tack, with the self-steering working well, while I retired below, with just a head popping exercise out of the hatch every ten minutes or so to make sure we were clear of whatever shipping might be about. I got out of my oilskins, wrapped a dry towel around my neck to keep a soaking shirt collar away from my skin, and wriggled into my sleeping bag all-standing.

There is not the slightest chance of any sleep during the dark hours ahead. We are beating down channel and will cross and re-cross busy steamer lanes, where only a fool would fail to keep a lookout. I'm cold, and the silk cocoon of the sleeping bag offers warmth to my limbs. However, I soon found, quite apart from the watch keeping requirement, that sleep was impossible. Even though I only had the benefit of three hours shut-eye the previous night, and had started the day with a good imitation of a hangover, I couldn't have slept, even if you had promised me a pension.

The first night at sea, alone, in a small boat.

I've done it dozens of times, and if I have to do it a hundred more, I never expect to be able to relax so soon after the beginning of a passage. I'm too much on edge. There are scores of things picking at my over-sharp senses. It's too early for the body to come to terms with the wild movements of the vessel. Man and boat are mere acquaintances, thrown together in rough circumstances. It takes time to establish a working relationship and a spell of moderate weather before an intimate understanding leads to relative peace of mind.

The noises during the first sleepless night at sea.

The slap and rattle of wind-driven spray.

The threatening *hiss*, of an about-to-break crest.

The thump and groan of a clinker-built wooden vessel, working her way to wind'ard. The whole crazily leaning basket of tricks held together with nothing more substantial than row upon row of small copper nails.

There's no need, in a vessel as small as a Folkboat, to get out of your sleeping bag to see if the course is clear. You just kneel on your bunk, grip the companionway coaming, and wait - if she's just shouldered a big one, and having let the deluge of spray rattle down to leeward, then, cautiously stick your head out of the hatch.

The practised eye can sweep the horizon at night - having been below, in a dark cabin, your night vision is immediately as good as it's going to be - so you are able to absorb the groups of masthead and sidelights that are visible, and from that click of an image form an unhesitating picture of the tracks of the vessels involved.

A group of trawlers to leeward.

A large vessel, up to the nor'ard, showing a green sidelight - looks like a liner, eastbound, possibly heading for Southampton.

A steamer fine on the port bow, masthead lights just open and showing a red sidelight. And there's another feller, astern, showing two near-vertical whites, as well as a red and a green - an overtaking ship, on a threatening course, must keep an eye on him. He could be a supertanker, creaming along at something in excess of eighteen knots, capable of running you down, while barely scratching the paint on his bow, let alone being aware that he's done it.

Another quick look around, to make sure you haven't missed anything, perhaps by being in the trough of a wave, and you can get your head down again, hopefully before collecting another faceful of spray.

Back in your berth, you can think about home. The wife. The children. The weather. The distance to sail. All the pleasures of home sweet home, until fifteen minutes have passed and it's time to do it all over again.

Hurrah for the joys of single-handed sailing.

At one o'clock in the morning, the log having reeled up twenty-seven miles, I judge it time to go about and make a board to the nor'ard. This entails wriggling out of a warm sleeping bag, struggling into clammy oilskins, jamming a hat on my head, checking that everything in the cabin is prepared for the change in attitude, from one well-heeled tack to the other. And having waited for a favourable lurch, climb out of the hatch and settle myself in the cockpit, with the question that's slithering into my mind as a suitable companion to the breeze that's whistling up the arms of my oilskin coat - what in the name of all that's sensibly nautical am I doing in this particular spot?

But there isn't time to bother with questions of this navel gazing sort.

It's time to tack the vessel (back to stark reality).

I'm standing in the cockpit, disconnecting the self-steering vane, clearing the jib sheets, putting the helm up a little, to make sure she's footing well enough before altering course. And having got the feel of the hooker, put the helm down, while offering the traditional shout of *Lee Ho!*

Let go the jib sheet, allow the mainsail and jib to rattle through the eye of the wind, over comes the self-tacking boom, hold her up on the new heading while hardening-in the new jib sheet, and there we have it, on the other tack and working to windward again.

As we changed one board for another, a crash from the cabin told me that I'd missed stowing something prior to going about (let's hope it's nothing important). Never mind, she's tramping along now; time to reset the wind vane, and having adjusted that useful bit of equipment, the self-steering gear's in charge of the Folkboat again.

All done with kindness.

No shouting and roaring, apart from the hail of *Lee-oh*.

This is an idiosyncrasy I've drifted into over the years. An echo of the seamanlike cry heard aboard all vessels under sail as one tack is changed for another, but as there's no one aboard but ourselves, I dispense with the warning shout of *'ready-about'*, in case someone may judge I've gone a little soft in the head.

To carry on the good habit, before going below, I always stand in the hatchway for a few minutes, checking everything on deck. And while about this task, put in a few strokes of the pump to make sure she's dry.

That job done, another sweep of the horizon, to register what shipping's in view. A glance at the compass to check the course made good; and then, satisfied that all's as well as I can make it, slip below and slide the hatch close-to.

It's Sunday morning, and a 'Day of Rest' on shore, but far from restful for those of us working our way to windward.

By half-past four in the afternoon, the wind's freshening and it's time to pull down a reef.

She's a different animal now - over-canvassed and tearing along, being swept by heavy spray and the occasional dollop, with the lee rail forced well under.

The sort of conditions where I always use a safety harness, and work without shoes.

You're troubled by cold feet?

Too bad.

It's blowing hard, and raining, the sail flaps noisily as I let go the halyard, ease the boom into the gallows and harden-in the main sheet (because having something to lean on makes the work a great deal safer).

Pull down the first reef.

Snap-shackle the tack, heave away on the clew pennant, make fast, tie the reef points.

Same again for the second reef.

Ease the main sheet, top up the boom, set up the halyard, ease the topping lift, harden-in the main sheet. Fifteen minutes of the sort of work that separates the sheep from the goats.

Hurrah for the joys of single-handed racing.

But when I go below, after completing the chores on deck - a task which should have provided at least a passable imitation of a self-righteous glow - the truth is, I feel lousy, cold, wet, and dispirited.

Trying to analyse the condition, it comes as something of a shock to realize that I've eaten nothing, and drunk very little since 0500 hours yesterday - no wonder I'm feeling a bit quaint. So I drink a pint of lime juice as a thirsty man might slurp a pint of beer, and as soon as I've done it realize I've made a tactical error.

The cold liquid swills around in my empty belly, where it certainly doesn't belong. I barely have time to grab a bucket before being violently sick.

Spewing your guts into a yellow plastic bucket could be the trigger that prompts the seaman to start walking up the beach, with an anchor hoist on his introspective shoulder.

'What's that?' says the yokel.

And you know you've arrived.

I curse myself for being such a fool. And to ease my pride, try to console myself with the thought that if I had carried out the same exercise ashore (sloshing down that quantity of lime juice) I might have been faced with the same result. It hammered home the lessons learned on my previous single-handed trips. Look after the ship, the mind, and then the body.

Faced with a long passage, I've been tending the vessel, wrestling with the mental challenge, but neglecting the all too common man.

The action of an idiot.

No matter how strong and active a person you are, in a small boat, perhaps more than anywhere else, you just cannot afford to neglect your physical condition, and I have done just that.

I'm a fool.

Regular meals, even if you don't feel like it, eat something.

Hot drinks, an absolute must when making an ocean passage in a small boat, apart from, perhaps, in the high tropics.

I have thrown overboard so much of the hard-earned knowledge, randomly gathered over the years.

I have also underestimated the emotional strain of leaving my wife with a newborn baby and two other children. Embarked on this ocean-going undertaking, my body may have been in a sleeping bag, but my mind has been at the end of a string. As a paper kite, kept aloft by the draft of apprehension which is apt to strike me when starting out on a passage alone.

The fear of failure.

It's time to come down to earth, so I spit in the bucket, wipe my mouth on a towel, in an attempt to rid myself of the revolting spewed-up taste, then settle down to get the primus going. While I'm waiting for the kettle to boil, I take a dose of liquid paraffin that would move a horse, then butter a piece of Danish crispbread, and feel pleased to find that I can keep it in my belly.

It's come to me, that I'm not the only pebble on the beach, there are others just as involved, and I'm certain they are all facing up to it far better than poor little me. I can't conceive of Blondie Hasler snivelling away, full of self-pity, or Francis, and certainly not David.

And then Jean Lacombe, having the balls to set out on a Western Ocean passage in what amounts to little more than a dinghy.

Having weathered my minor crisis, I feel better, which is just as well, because during the forenoon the weather deteriorates, and by eleven o'clock it's blowing Beaufort 6 to 7, with a moderate gale in the offing, but I can at least set about the necessary tasks in a much more confident manner.

Hand the mainsail, and lie under a small jib for a while, virtually hove-to. A few hours of this, then the wind veers a point and moderates, allowing me to reset the double-reefed main. So we're bowling along once more, closed-hauled on starboard tack making good a sou'westerly course.

For lunch, I have a tin of self-heating oxtail soup, thickened by slices of crispbread plastered with beef extract, which proves an unqualified blessing. Probably the easiest way to get a nourishing broth that's ever been devised. This feast, the first decent meal in two days, sets me up as a new man. And while the afternoon is offering little more than a moderate breeze, I turn in, intending to get some much needed sleep.

After the excitement and nervous tension of the start, together with the awkward first night at sea, I'm beginning to unwind, with one natural result being the acceptance that my body needs a rest. Yet I sleep little more then twenty minutes before waking with the feeling there's something amiss.

It's difficult to explain a hunch, or the sixth sense which some individuals develop, I *wake* with the knowledge there's something wrong, and this feeling doesn't come to me as I lie daydreaming in my sleeping bag.

I wake, from sleep, *knowing* there's a problem concerning the boat.

Get up and look out of the hatch, to at least assure myself that we're not about to be run down. Then have a good look about the deck. The mast and fittings. The self-steering gear, all apparently in good order. That being so, whatever it is, must be below, so I sit on the companionway steps and survey the cabin, which is tidy enough with everything in its usual place.

Yet there is still some little thing that my sixth sense, or my guardian angel, call it what you will, is warning me against.

Or is it my nose?

That's it, as I catch another whiff; a strange smell, something very odd indeed.

Working from aft, I check all the lockers - soaking woollen clothing, left to its own devices, runs wild and ferments in an airtight locker - but there's nothing of that nature, and in any case, it's too soon in the passage to have that condition develop.

I sniff about the galley - that seems clear enough.

Then I catch another whiff, faint, yet strangely compelling, suggesting that whatever it is, it's definitely up for'ard. So I squeeze past the mast, kneel on the cabin sole, and cast an eye over the sail bags, spare rope, and the rest of the bits and pieces stowed in the bow of the boat.

We're still close-hauled, and there's an appreciable swell running from the west'ard. As we drive on, she's taking the odd crest over the foredeck, and some of it is making its way down the hatch. This has never been perfect, but since it was strained, during the encounter with the battery-stowing technician in the camber, it's far from watertight.

The next time the boat takes a dollop aboard, I notice a stream of seawater, running from a corner of the hatch, on to the locker where the battery is stored.

That's it, the battery.

I lift the lid from the box: hell's bells, the end and half the side of the battery casing has been pulled off, and the acid has run out. Some of the water dripping down the hatch is finding its way to the exposed lead cells, prompting my mind to leap back twenty years, to a long-forgotten chemistry lesson.

Was it associated with some sort of gas?

Chlorine gas?

I throw the lid of the locker aside, get an oilskin coat and place it over the battery, in order to protect it from further salt water splashes, then retire to the after end of the vessel to think the thing out.

The cause of the accident is plain enough.

The codline securing the battery had been put in place while the boat was at Plymouth, when everything, particularly the line, was bone dry. But when she started taking water on deck, some of it found its way to the lashings, they had contracted and pulled the side out of the battery.

The whole of the radio installation had been a rush job. The battery, in a standard ebonite case, was not really designed for marine use. I should have obtained, or made, a protective wooden box which would have provided a more seamanlike solution.

There was a lesson to be learned, but the immediate problem is what to do right now, both with the battery and the free acid that must be floating around in the bilge. I decide to jettison what remains of the battery, but before setting about the job, dress in seaboots, oilskin trousers, and a waterproof coat, luckily find a pair of gloves, then go for'ard to deal with the task. Difficult enough at the best of times, because of the weight involved; in a confined space, with only crouching headroom and the boat bouncing about, it takes some time to lift what remains of the massive battery out of the locker. Work it slowly aft, dragging it over the cabin sole. Lift it up, and over the top of the companionway steps. Juggle with it there, balanced on the narrow bridgedeck, while I climb out of the cabin and settle myself in the cockpit; and then, waiting until the vessel offers a convenient lurch, throw the damned thing over the side.

Having disposed of the accumulator, I sluice myself down in seawater, to get rid of the stuff that had slopped out of the battery while I had the thing hugged to my chest. Then go below to complete the task, because there's obviously some sulphuric acid in the bilge, and I wonder what effect it might be having on the copper fastenings that hold the boat together.

Fearing the worst, and no doubt going a long way over the top, I flush the boat with dozens of buckets of seawater. And when there's a sloshing amount in the bilge, pump it dry. Then flood the bilge again, pump her dry again. Swilling and pumping away until I'm sure the hull and the locker are acid free.

A tough enough task, and I'm glad to call the job done, and can rest, sitting on the edge of my bunk.

The whole operation has taken three-quarters of an hour's hard slog, and I'm tired, hot, and sweaty.

I think I've earned myself a drink, and pour a stiff Scotch & water, but feel I can't take the first snort of the passage without making some sort of a toast. So I solemnly raise my glass to the Radio Corporation of America, whose fine transmitter is still firmly attached to the deckhead.

And coupled with them, the Toledo Battery Company of Ohio, without whose product

the intricate bag of radio tricks is absolutely useless.

settle now to the rhythm of the ocean
we face a fair long haul

During the struggle with the battery, the weather has moderated, and as I sip my drink, I realize it's time to get rid of the two reefs and reset the full mainsail; but despite the need to attend to the boat, I remain seated on the lee berth, my recent alarm having a salutary effect.

The cabin looks different - not quite so small as previously - but this is a crazy notion.

It *must* be the same size.

Yet it does look bigger.

The gimballed paraffin stove swings to the movement of the hull, squeakily complaining its endlessly supporting role as it maintains the kettle on an even keel.

In the locker under my backside a tin, and then a jar, clunks and clinks in rhythmic accord to the heave of the westerly swell.

A drip of water runs down the after side of the mast, hesitantly at first, then gathering speed as it's swollen by another fugitive from the spray-swept deck. Down the mast it rolls, over the cabin sole and on, into the bilge, to join a million others of its kind - nourishing swill for an imaginative creature.

A few gallons of water sloshing about in the bilge?

Nothing unusual about that, every nail-held plank must work a bit and every wooden boat makes water. No need to be embarrassed on that score (don't the skippers do the same?), but the slap of water in the bilge does much to focus my mind, bring sharp awareness of my peculiar situation.

Sunday evening, a bare yet not uneventful thirty-six hours after the start of the race, and I have just escaped being gassed.

Or is this taking much too alarmist a view?

There has certainly been some danger. The roughish conditions make the closure of the hatches necessary, with the result that the cabin is not well-ventilated. Not knowing the concentration of chlorine gas that has accumulated below, or how much a sleeping man can tolerate, it's pointless to dwell on the accident, but along with other near escapes, its memory recurs from time to time throughout the length of the voyage.

Still I sit, and idle away more time, when I should be on deck, improving the performance of the boat - more sail is obviously needed.

What, I wonder, are the lessons to be learned by the excitement of the last few days?

Prosaically, be reasonable, both drinking and eating, the night before you embark on a single-handed small boat voyage in the teeth of even a moderate sou'westerly breeze - yet any fool knows that.

Then the preparation of the boat, with the salient point being attention to detail. Acceptance of the inescapable fact that it will just not do to rush the preparations. And further on the same tack, I think the outstanding lesson of the exercise so far has been to expect the unexpected, that a small item, the contracting of a lashing, can cause, to say the least, a vicious little drama.

This is what I ponder, as I sip my drink, and find myself being absorbed by my surroundings.

The cabin *is* bigger - there seems more space in it for a diminishing me.

Waiting for a convenient roll, I heave myself off the bunk, and by mounting the lower step of the companionway ladder, slide back the flap, to climb head and shoulders out of the hatch.

A good third of the Scotch and water remains in my tightly-held glass. I look moodily into the swirling amber liquid. Not much help there, rather the reverse; with a disdainful sniff I throw the booze over the side and then, without leaving the companionway, stow the glass in its rack, little boats and long-armed men go well together.

The west-gone light of evening has left the eastern seascape dark and threatening, while the failing light jostles for space between the sea and the ragged edge of the sky.

As the nor'westerly breeze is dealing lightly with the under-canvassed boat, I go on deck, shake out the reefs in the mainsail, set up the luff, and I'm pleased to feel the boat respond so well to such a little effort.

How well worthwhile.

Back in the cockpit, I sit some time, only my feet are cold.

West sou'west she's making, so I can let her tramp along, thinking there will be plenty of time to make a tactical board when the breeze backs, as it's bound to. It can't stay in the northerly quadrant for ever.

When it's dark, I stand in the cockpit and search for steamer's lights, and there they are a'plenty.

Outward bound shipping, plodding westward, no doubt with the intention of clearing Ushant and hauling south for La Coruña, across the Bay of Biscay.

Homeward bounders, even whose hardest nuts would be experiencing the thrill of the 'Channels'. The delightful seafaring complaint, whose symptoms are related to the terminal port of a protracted voyage, with girlfriends, wives and lovers drawing nearer to bed.

And so, satisfied that all is clear ahead, I go below to light the stove, brew up, and have a bite to eat; relaxed, happy enough (poor mug) that things are going well, quite unaware that I'm making yet another error.

Another night of jack-in-the-box productions, performances scheduled at twenty-minute intervals, with occasional rain squalls hampering the cast. A succession of twenty-minute catnaps, some successful, the sleepless others, spent listening to the restless sound of the boat, bring me, by four o'clock on Monday morning, to a pitch of irritation which could only be soothed by the attentions of a good woman, or a first class cook. Preferably both, though I doubt if I could do either of 'em justice.

Four o'clock of a seagoing morning is as good a time as any to give up thinking of staying in bed and decide to cook yourself a hearty breakfast. Nothing elaborate; half a grapefruit, a pair of kippered herrings, bacon, eggs, and sausage, flapjacks with lashings of syrup, hotly buttered toast spread with English marmalade, all strung together with cups of scalding coffee.

And the reality?

One devil of a job to get the primus going (an irritatingly blocked jet) but eventually, a cup of tepid cocoa.

Not to be compared with the imagined repast, but enough to bolster the seaman sufficiently to face the fast approaching dawn.

During the night, the sea has shrunk to a pool that barely floats the boat. A pond, that offers form, but little depth or distance.

Can those twinkling lights really represent the varied environment of a thousand men and women? The bulwark of your own boat confines the imagination, happily limits its necessary strict control. It doesn't do, to mentally roam an ocean, wondering what it has in store, too many possibilities spell disaster.

Daylight provides the opportunity of an hour's undisturbed sleep, and I wake with a feeling of excitement, which has been conspicuously lacking during the previous two days. Though still short of shuteye, and not yet the possessor of my normal appetite, I feel the beginning of companionship with the boat; begin to pick up the customary routine that has been slovenly allowed to slip.

I wash the dirty crockery which has accumulated in the cockpit, not a major task, but satisfying.

I tidy the cabin, pump the bilge, see all well on deck, and then settle down to write the log, that so far only contains the barest of jottings. Being struck by how revealing it is, to look back on a situation, and judge your performance on the amount and style of the recording of events, which could, and should, have been mastered.

So far, navigation has been sketchy.

The bare essentials, wind speeds and direction have been recorded, as have sea conditions, together with course and distances made good, but most significantly, no 'day's work' has been recorded, and the position of the vessel has not been accurately fixed.

The breeze still holds nor'westerly, with the same substantial swell and over-topping crests, so as soon as the sun is high enough to provide an accurate sight, I get the sextant out and make an attempt at an altitude.

Twenty minutes and three spray soakings later, I have a group of sights with which I'm reasonably satisfied. The difficulties encountered are those normal to small craft navigation, and I'm used to overcoming them, indeed, take pride in being able to do so. Worked up, the sights come in near enough to the dead-reckoned position, and I wait impatiently for a meridian altitude, but at noon, a heavily overcast sky combined with a freshening breeze denies me this further satisfaction.

By the time the sun has reached its zenith, the wild motion of the boat, combined with the hindering overcast makes the observation impossible, and it's tempting to curse the weather, as I do feel in need of the sight. There's also the comforting thought of the three thousand miles of open ocean between me and the ultimate landfall, so after wiping my sextant and returning it carefully to its box, I work out the estimated position, bring the log up to date, and then fix lunch, over which I debate my most promising course of action.

The long board on starboard tack, heeled to the nor'westerly breeze, has provided as much westing as it's been possible to make, in the limited distance run. However, we are well to the south'ard of the intended course (the north-about, great circle track), the route that offers the shortest distance between the old world and the new.

And I'm certain that both David and Francis are bound that way.

But why not take the intermediate route?

Barton [9] made a successful passage using it in 1956. It does, after all, avoid the ice and fog inevitably encountered off the Newfoundland Banks.

As I savour a cup of lunchtime tea, it seems to offer a better chance of survival, which is surely the essential element in any small boat passage.

Still sipping tea, I weigh it up.

There are over two thousand miles of ocean between my small vessel and the hoped-for landfall on the eastern seaboard of the 'States. So far, we have achieved little more than a hundred miles in the right direction. And during the time it has taken to make that modest advance, one of the four vessels entered in the race has been partially dismasted, and I've been fortunate to avoid what could have turned out to be a major complication.

After another sip of rapidly cooling tea, the north-about, guaranteed to freeze your balls off route doesn't seem quite so attractive - slow but sure has won some races - why not let another unfortunate competitor bump into a berg, with this being the decision arrived at, certainly a mistake, but maybe understandable in the circumstances.

So we carry on, close-hauled to the nor'westerly breeze, gusting Beaufort 6, which is far too much for a Folkboat under a full mainsail and a working jib.

There's plenty of spray, the rail a'wash more often than not, with the lee berth the only place that offers even a modicum of comfort, so that's where I lie, hoping for a favourable turn in the weather.

During the night, the breeze moderates, the barometer begins to climb, and the sea falls away, leaving only a substantial westerly swell to play about with the boat. A morning sight, crossed later with a meridian altitude puts her at 47 ° 30' North, 6° 53' West, with the log reading 140 miles made good, and this is Tuesday, the fourteenth of June.

Throughout the afternoon the breeze drops again, to barely an air. By 5 o'clock not a puff remains, and without a lee to lean on, the Folkboat's mast describes the wild motions of its creakily supporting hull.

The violent rolling of a small boat in a flat calm may come as a surprise to a landlubber, who might imagine that a lack of wind must lead ultimately to 'a painted ship upon a painted ocean'.

Discard another illusion.

It may be true in well-sheltered places, but it's a most unlikely circumstance in the Western Ocean where, even in the flattest of flat calms, there stirs a swell. Sometimes long and heavy, the possible forerunner of an approaching gale; on others, a barely perceptible heave, but always enough movement to send a ballasted boat rolling heavily about her metacentre.

As the boat rolls, her limply hanging sails thrash against the rigging, being subject to more wear in half-an-hour than they would during a long-

(9) Humphrey Barton: a significant figure in the world of 'crewed' small-boat cruising.

sailed day, had they the satisfaction of a bellyful of wind. So having only one mainsail, I judge it prudent to look after it, and as there seems no prospect of a breeze, hand it (the mainsail) and bring the headsail down on deck.

It's a fine evening, and here we are, ninety nautical miles west of Ushant, just clear of the steamer lanes, and three days out from Plymouth.

Although the main radio is out of action, I still have a small D.F. set which is blessed with its own dry batteries, and a programme from the B.B.C. is doing much to lighten my depression.

My depression?

I'm struck by my own solemnity.

The gay tinkle of the radio seems out of place on an apparently empty ocean. Then I realize I haven't smiled since Friday gone, and I'm the bold buckaroo who would enjoy the voyage 'come what ruddy well may'.

How sorry for yourself can you get?

I come to the conclusion that I'm duty-bound to raise a smile, that it's time to tend to my morale.

Going below, I light the stove, get out a two-gallon jar of fresh water, carefully pour three pints into a saucepan, set it on the flame, then stopper the jar, double checking before re-stowing it in the bilge.

We have thirty gallons of fresh water on board the boat, in fifteen polythene jars. The estimated time of passage being forty days, with a worst-case scenario adding another twenty, gives an aggregate of sixty days afloat. So we have available, as a reasonable guess-estimate, half a gallon of sweet water a day, for drinking, cooking, washing and spilling. Not a great deal, but enough, provided crew discipline is strictly maintained.

As cook/purser, that's my problem.

My water intake has been below this figure since the passage began.

Can I risk a wash?

I need it.

Working a small boat to windward, in anything above a moderate breeze, means that sooner or later you get wet. Not all at once, but neck after head, elbow after wrist, knee after ankle, then your bum is wet, and it's time to change to something drier.

But I have a plan, which entails wearing 'unwashed' woollen underwear next to the skin, over which goes an old-fashioned Welsh flannel shirt, followed by a cotton smock and jeans. In this rig you are near enough spray-proof. The weight of the woollen underwear gives, hopefully, time enough for your body heat to combat the penetration of the outer garments. Of course it's not foolproof, if you're dull enough to be out on deck when she ships a green 'un, that's the end of that. Either way, if the water in the saucepan, on the stove, is now warm enough for ablutions, and you're beginning to stink, it's time to commence your toilet, and this is how to do it.

Pour a small amount of water from the saucepan, into a bucket, and make sure you have the right bucket.

Soap up, perhaps not as easy as it sounds - if you have a thick head of hair and a full beard you may find that you haven't enough fresh water in the bucket to raise a lather on your salty locks.

Discard the mud your original tub has been reduced to, and start again, using a *little* more fresh water.

A good lather now ?

Fine - discard what remains in the bucket - then stick your head in the bucket and pour what remains of the clean, warm water, from the saucepan, over your head.

Still soap in your hair ?

Remove head from bucket.

Empty contents of bucket into saucepan.

Replace head in bucket.

Rinse again.

Repeat 'til satisfied.

For those spoilt-rotten types who are used to taking a scalding chin-deep tub, followed by a refreshing rinse under a needle sharp shower, a 'yachtie' bath may sound pernickety, but it's top of the list as a morale raiser, and the feeling of well-being experienced by the once again body beautiful has only to be experienced to be appreciated.

I feel better, and sweeter too, as I dress in a set of dry gear after my successful ablutions. It's getting dark, and the unruffled ocean has taken the Folkboat and myself to its heart. We seem to be (fancifully, I must admit) equi-distant from all points, East and West, North and South of the ever-present compass.

The radio is an irritant, so I switch it off, then open a can of Guinness and dish out some bread and Danish cheese.

It's warm enough to sit in the cockpit, and even the rolling of the boat seems easier.

There's still no wind, but as well as a breeze, I want a ship.

Any old vessel will do, as long as she'll relay a message back home to my wife and family.

This is the first time I've thought realistically of home. My wife and children have often been in my mind, but now, I have time to speculate on what they mean to me, and I to them.

Looking eastward over the darkening sea, I'm prey to the uneasy feeling that I've been causing those at home anxiety. After another can of Guinness my conscience is at least somewhat assuaged; though still mindful of home, I view it from the singularly selfish attitude of a single-handed sailor.

I stand in the cockpit and search the horizon for a passing vessel.

A fine clear night, and not a light in sight.

Time to hit the sack, so after filling, lighting and then hoisting the 'steamboat scarer', I go below, wriggle into my sleeping bag and soon fall into a somewhat contrite sleep.

A good rest later, sometime in the small hours of this Wednesday morning, a shy little breeze chills the sleep from my eyes. I lie on the bunk, looking upward through the open hatch, wondering if the breeze will fill in to something worthwhile, or turn out to be a fickle tease. There's only one way to find out, so I get up on deck and cast a seaman's eye about the boat.

From the sou'easterly quadrant it comes - warm indeed, all the way from sunny Spain - without bothering to dress, I clamber out on the coachroof and after sweating up the main and genoa, soon have the breeze to proper use.

Back in the cockpit, fiddling about, bare-arsed, with the sheets and the self-steering vane - a good look round (all clear) then quickly into my still warm bag. I feel quite cocky as I punch my pillow into shape. At last I'm falling into step with the boat, and she's slipping easily over the merely rippled swell - within a minute her chuckling progress has prompted me to sleep.

Taking an A.M. sight the next morning, standing on the companionway steps, with my bum wedged firmly in the corner of the hatch, is a simple job. As she lifts, I have the sun, unencumbered by clouds or rain, beautifully balanced on a rule-straight horizon, a quick look at my wristwatch, then pop down below to work out the sums.

My wristwatch is my chronometer, and apart from a cheap, spun-brass yacht alarm, is the only timepiece on board, as I left my much loved, gimballed Waltham chronometer ashore in order to save stowage space.

The watch is a presentation from Peter Howells, a jeweller, of Haverfordwest, in the County of Pembroke (no relation) and I've come to take its accuracy for granted, as over the months its rate has remained the same, losing eight seconds per day. Peter had suggested that a Rolex self-wind Oyster could be brought down to finer limits; but I'm happy with it, not caring how large the rate, only that it remains the same.

If you can bring yourself to trust a wristwatch, you can save yourself a significant amount of time; opening lockers, raising lids of chronometer boxes, peering, eventually, into the face of the timepiece for a brief second, only to replace everything, before you make your way, still on hands and knees (if you're in a Folkboat) back from the 'chart table' which is merely a hollow plywood box holding a dozen or so charts that slides into place on top of the aforementioned chronometer box.

Bad planning?

Not necessarily so.

Aboard this hooker, the living space does not exceed six-feet long, by six-feet wide, by four-foot-ten inches high, And that is four-foot-ten inches low if you happen to be six-foot-three inches tall and tip the scales at more than two hundred avoirdupois. Into this aforementioned space must be fitted everything that's needed to sustain you and your boat for maybe two long months.

I know there's other stowage space available, but it's mostly in the wetter ends of the vessel, and spare sails, cordage, sea anchors, and their like live there.

Ever since earning my living at sea, I've enjoyed practising the art of navigation, particularly in small boats. Not only does it offer the immediate satisfaction of providing a neat cross on the chart, which represents *you*, but dealing with extraterrestrial objects is an excellent mental laxative, if you happen to be bound up in your own small world.

As I pinpoint the position on the chart, after the noon sight, 47° 11' north, 7° 52' west, log reading 195, on Wednesday 15th June, I realise that what's around me and my small boat is several thousand miles of encircling ocean, smudged occasionally by the distant smoke of a ship. A reminder that a passing steamer is the only means of getting a message back home. And I had promised to 'radio every other day', which now turns out to be the sort of optimistic statement that would have been better left unsaid.

This afternoon, what seems a reasonable opportunity hove into sight on the starboard bow. Through the binoculars he looks like a small trawler, on passage, unlikely to be bottom-fishing (not in two thousand fathoms), so maybe he's homeward bound from Irish grounds? Excitedly, I dig out the canvas roll of flags, hitch the message M.I.K. together, and hoist them close-up on the starboard yardarm.

By the time I've hoisted the signal, the vessel, a Spaniard by the cut of his jib, has me on his starboard beam and is passing less than a mile astern. Hopefully, I wait for him to alter course, but there's nothing doing.

Homeward bound, after a hard trip's fishing, there's probably only one man awake, and he perhaps dozing over the all too easily managed wheel. I don't blame them, but do feel disappointed as I haul my ineffectual signal down and re-stow it below, leaving the hoist 'made-up' in order to save time during the next attempt.

Adding slightly to my disappointment, the breeze veers during the late afternoon, and close-hauled now on port tack, we're hard put to make the necessary westerly course; but after another night, another sight, and another noon position, we've logged another sixty-three miles to the west'ard.

Then, on the evening of the 16th, Thursday, becalmed once more.

The sails lying in stitch-saving heaps on deck.

This is the second slack patch since leaving Plymouth, but instead of being welcome, as had the first, which I'd used to bring the boat and myself into a more shipshape condition, now, there's nothing that desperately needs doing and the delay proves irksome. As dusk draws in, so does the visibility, until by half-past eight in the evening, the boat, lying under a bare pole and rolling heavily, is shut in by a dense wall of fog.

Who does like fog?

Like the night, it can have an air of mystery, which suits some all the time, and everyone occasionally, but a thick fog holds more, and that is, menace. For the single-handed seaman, fog somehow brings the inescapable fact that *you are alone* in a manner which darkness, however oppressing, has not the power to muster. During a midnight gale, on a leaking barge, you can light a hurricane lamp and hope someone can see you - indeed, you are *sure* they will, before the vessel sinks.

In a dense fog, you can have no such illusions.

You are not only alone, because you have no companion.

You are alone *because nobody knows you are there.*

Zero visibility, combined with a lack of wind, is a dreary combination, apt to assail an emotional type with a series of depressing images that may only be countered by a glass of the very special beverage the Howells family know as 'Live Long'.

My wife and I made the stuff before the voyage started, and this is the first occasion I feel warrants the broaching of the jars. During the trials and tribulations in the English Channel (the problem with the battery) I'd certainly been in need of its morale boosting properties, but had been put off, at the time, by its sick-making propensity. However, surrounded by a fog that drifts damply through the boat, this seems the perfect time to sample the health giving liquid.

The stuff lives, and that's the right word, in two wicker-bound jars lashed to the spar ceiling abreast the mast. One jar contains a gallon of rum, the other a gallon of sherry, apart from half-a-hundred eggs, a dozen or so lemons, and pounds and pounds of demerara sugar.

Which to broach?

I can't remember which contains what, so, as it looks easier to unlash, I choose the nearest jar.

Remembering the difficulties encountered when bottling the stuff, I'm particularly careful with the corkscrew, and ease the stopper out of the neck undamaged, so that it can be efficiently replaced.

A powerful smell comes from the demijohn.

I put my nose to the neck, seems we picked the rum.

Solemnly, I shake the jar, though the stuff could not have been better prepared if it had spent the previous week in a cement mixer.

After pouring about a gill into a pint mug, I re-cork and re-stow the jar, leaving the corkscrew in place.

Taking the pot, I make myself comfortable on the edge of my bunk and view the brew. The greyish-yellow liquid slops to and fro, climbing the side of the off-white mug in time with the roll of the boat. Its consistency is such that, after most of it is on its journey to the other lip, some, containing peculiar darker spots, clings tenaciously to the higher side of the mug. It looks just about right for paper hanging, with shades of the sick in the bucket thrown in.

The fog, denser than ever, swirls about the open hatch, and seems a suitable companion for the witches brew in the cup.

Poised at the fateful moment, with the mug on its way to my lips, and my eyes shut, I hear the blast of a ship's siren, not loud, but oh so distinctly.

Shocked out of my wits, and forgetful of the limited headroom, I jump to my feet, crack my head on the coachroof and inadvertently shoot some of the goo on my face.

As I scramble up the companionway steps, mug still in hand, some of the powerful liquid runs off my moustache, and though not frugal by nature, I open my mouth and lick around (as any old tomcat would). The stuff is marvellous, a bit tacky perhaps, but none the worse for that.

As I wait for the newcomer to announce his progress, by another blast on his foghorn, I take a second gulp of 'Live Long', then wipe my beard, as another even louder blast on the siren reinforces my impression that this is a vessel, closing fast, somewhere on the starboard bow.

Without a breath of wind, and no steerage way on the boat, there's nothing for it, but another gulp of 'Live Long'.

Blast follows blast, punctuated by my own soft curses.

Finishing my morale booster, I get the boat's sheath knife, which is stowed handy-by in the cockpit, and run my thumb over the blade, to reassure myself that it wouldn't take long to cut the lashings that retain the liferaft on the coachroof.

The noise of the ship's siren has now reached raucous proportions, and after another ear-splitting blast, I can hear the sound of his engine (a motor vessel for sure).

I look at the oar lashed on the coachroof, but it's impossible to tell in which direction to attempt to scull the boat.

I think of my own foghorn, but dismiss its dismal squeak as nothing less than inconsequential to the situation that's developing.

Then, and only then, do I remember the radar reflector, stowed tidily away in the lazarette.

It's much too late to start rigging radar reflectors. He looms out of the fog, as a dark stem, topped by a white-painted fo'castle head. The vessel appears, then passes as one movement with the Folkboat being lifted and thankfully moved away from the menacing bow by its accompanying curl of a wave.

Looking up at the passing wall of steel, my eye is drawn to the wing of the bridge, over which leans a young mate. The comic look of surprise on his face turns, as I watch, to an angry snarl as he shouts down what surely must be an uncomplimentary comment on fool yachtsmen. I can't make out exactly what he said, and only have time to lift two fingers before he's past, disappearing into the pea soup with a finality which seems to raise doubts of his existence.

I lower myself on to the cockpit seat, feeling weak about the knees, with the hair on the back of my neck still bristling.

The dismal hoot of his receding foghorn prompts me to open the after hatch and search for the radar reflector, a job that so obviously should have been done some time ago. It's easy enough to find, more difficult to extricate from under the rope, tins of paraffin, spare shackles, smoke floats and the dozen and one other items that always seem to accumulate in a little-used locker. At length I get it out and assembled. Technically, an octahedral cluster, it's just an awkward shape to me, but I feel a lot better when it's suspended, as high as I can get it, between the standing backstays.

Down below, hesitating about what I'm going to have for supper, I think back and conjure up a mental picture of the ship sweeping past, a bare few feet clear of the boat.

Had I seen a radar scanner on his monkey island?

Almost certainly not.

I'm amused, and to celebrate such an auspicious occasion, as well as wet my bone-dry throat, have a hefty gin and lime to start the meal.

The next day is Friday and at the disenchanting hour of three o'clock in the morning I'm busy on deck, setting all available canvas in order to take advantage of a moderate sou'westerly breeze - pleased to be making progress again.

The westerly course means keeping the wind and weather fine on the port quarter and this, with the main and large genoa drawing well, proves rather too much for the self-steering gear. The principle reason is the luffing effect the squared-off mainsail has on the course of the boat. She'll settle happily at west sou'west, but as this is twenty degrees to the south'ard of what's required, I send Iron Mike below and take the tiller myself.

This is the first time I've done a turn at the helm for many a month, usually being satisfied with the performance of the uncomplaining gadget, or, if I have friends aboard, getting one of them to steer makes for room below.

First up, the trick at the tiller is pleasant enough.

I'm warmly dressed, with an outer covering of PVC which effectively eases the cut of the breeze.

I sit in the cockpit, making light of the steering, as she only needs a firm hand occasionally to check her tendency to luff to the south'ard.

An hour goes by, then it's hazarding dawn, the lightening sky drawing the eye to the eastern horizon, where the first silver tint is soon forgotten as the underbellies of clouds blush pink with embarrassment at their privileged position. The sea in turn is fully lit, and I can disregard yet another sunrise, but only after it has, as usual, held me spellbound by its beauty.

By the light of day, I can confirm that the mainsail is chafing against the starboard spreaders. I'd known it was taking place, but had put off the task of handing the main until there was a better light to work by. With the dawn, we're down to a genoa, boomed-out on a pole, and under this rig the boat moves well, offering a spread of canvas that helps her directional stability, so that Iron Mike is again up to the job. Allowing me to go below to whip up breakfast, wondering, as I do so, how Blondie and Francis are getting on - goodness only knows about David - and what about Jean Lacombe?

This is a lazy day. During the forenoon, just before the morning sight, the sky becomes overcast and remains that way, thus washing out the possibility of a noon position; as a result, I'm at something of a loose end, so I look for a book.

My friend Jack, one-time cook on the passage to Plymouth, had been entrusted with seeing the ship well-stocked for bread and literature. When he'd gone, whistling up the quay, I had perhaps foolishly assumed he would return with, say, four dozen books and two or three loaves of bread, but I'd forgotten he was a grocer.

As I rummage through the three waterproof bags he'd thrown on board, just before we cleared the quay at Plymouth, I come face to face with that omission, because while Jack has purchased plenty of bread (more than ten mildew-sprouting loaves) there are only six books, some of them displaying titles which prompt the thought that he may have missed his true vocation.

The first volume out of the bag turns out to be *The Overlanders*, which, arguably, does offer some sort of a diversion to a seaman embarked on an ocean passage. The next pick is *Sea Angling*, and this, combined with *Oceanic Birds* certainly looks useful. As indeed does *Cooking in Small Boats*, though the date of publication, 1909, could possibly compromise the menu.

This is followed by *The Farming Ladder,* and then, *Is Sex Really Necessary ?*

An adequate library for a single-handed ocean wanderer who can get through a 'Penguin' a day?

Nevertheless, it sounds as if the *Is Sex Really Necessary ?* argument might deal satisfactorily with at least some of my problems, and settling down to one of my favourite authors, I soon forgive Jack everything.

A few hours later, and more than halfway through Thurber, it comes to me that I had better husband my resources, so laying the book aside with a wry smile, I begin planning the evening meal.

Cooking in Small Boats is very little help (for lunching afloat, the Haybox is a desirable piece of equipment), jugged hare is highly recommended, as is the facility embraced by any 'good coal range', which would prove invaluable for heating an ample supply of savoury pasties, which the prudent owner will secure from his cook before he goes afloat.

Laying the charming anachronism aside, I light my gimballed primus, determined to show the Victorians that we, the present generation, know at least a thing or two about it as well.

Amongst the stores, hidden under quantities of beans and soup, are a few tins of smoked salmon, surely a must for a banquet.

Then there's the dehydrated food from the Min of Ag & Fish.

My choice falls on a meat and vegetable stew, helped out with sliced carrots and a few broad beans; cheese and biscuits will round it off, with perhaps a little cognac.

During the preparatory stages, I have, as an aperitif, an oversized tot of 'Tio Pepi' as being just the thing for a thirsty seaman afloat on an encircling ocean - could you get it any drier?

It turns out a good meal, and as I lie seal-like in my sleeping bag, delightfully full for the first time in a week, I think with gratitude of David, who had arranged the purchase of the dehydrated food from the Ministry of Ag & Fish.

Come to think of it, there had been a helpful exchange of ideas well before the race started.

Blondie had invited me to look over *Jester*, to see if there was anything I could usefully pick up (turned out to be the whole boat), but I certainly benefited from his ideas and advice, which he gave freely, keeping nothing back. He discussed the route, and talked of food, particularly an idea for sprouting grain on trays as he couldn't stand tinned vegetables. We also discussed the sort of music he intended to carry on tape.

With David, on the other hand, I was in a position to help him with his self-steering gear. After Blondie had seen the drawings (commenting, 'doesn't she oversteer?') I had given the plans to David, and they had formed the basis for his own self-steering mechanism. He had access to the dehydrated food, and had fixed me up with a supply. He'd also gone to endless trouble providing everyone in the race with a first aid kit, as well as giving encouragement to a bungler like myself by offering the sight of another lone mariner battling manfully to create order out of chaos.

Jean Lacombe had seemed glad to talk to a fellow sufferer at Pedro's, and kindly suggested the use of his New York flat, *'if you are there before me, mon ami.'* A generous thought, which prompted the offer of another drink.

Looking back on the pre-race activity, it seemed we had all done what we could to help each other.

And Francis?

When I went to visit him, he wanted to know all about my own and other people's preparations, but was careful when discussing his own.

As a parting gift he gave me a map of

Central London

6

a narrow squeak
a message home
an altered view of the sea

As darkness closes in on the boat, she's running hard before a fresh east sou'easterly breeze, which brings an overcast sky, out of which falls a drizzle of rain. The quartering seas are beginning to build, and the occasional crest, breaking just short of the transom sometimes slews the vessel off course. As this occurs, the vane of the self-steering gear feels a little more weight in the wind, moves the trim tab, and up comes the tiller to bring her back on the correct heading.

The night is just made for self-steering gears. Who in his right mind would sit out in the cockpit, enduring the maddening dollop of heavy spray that sooner or later seeps past your towelled neck; running in icy rivulets around and down your knuckled spine, eventually forming a damp pool in which you are forced to sit, one of the several uncomfortable challenges involved with small-boat ocean voyaging.

The people who come talking self-steering gears, and then conclude by remarking *'of course, I like a trick at the helm, that's half the fun of the game'*, are really talking about an estuary cruise, not an ocean passage. Those others, who do make ocean passages, writing gaily of how thankful they were when *'sweet little 'Idler'* had worked her way out of the variable westerlies, into the reliable Trades *'and so Meg and I were relieved of the tyrannies of the tiller, and could get some much-needed sleep'*. My heart bleeds for them - but why in the name of all that's nautically sensible don't they drop Blondie Hasler a line?

Eira's self-steering gear, which is my own design, is fair enough in its performance, but a veritable agricultural implement compared with Jester's sophisticated kit. And Blondie was right, she *is* inclined to oversteer. I have managed to get over the problem by rigging tiller yokes to limit the rudder action. Shock cords are also fitted to take out some of the snatch which occurs when the boat labours in a heavy seaway. Though the rig is far from perfect, I'm delighted with the progress the boat is making under the control of Iron Mike, while I keep warm and dry in the cabin, debating, with Thurber - if sex really is necessary? But being careful to take a quick look round the horizon, now and then, to make sure all's clear ahead.

By midnight I've finished the book, and stuck my head out of the hatch, yet again.

It's stopped raining; still a fresh sou'easterly breeze, cloudy, but with good visibility. We're well off the regular steamer lanes and the thought of my warm sleeping bag prompts me to get out the steamboat scarer, and as soon as it's rigged and lit, hit the sack and I'm gone.

I wake from a 'til then untroubled sleep with my body stiff and my ears cocked. A glance at my watch shows half-past-three - a good long caulk. How come I wake up so tense? *Get up on deck, lad, and have a look around, you've been horizontal long enough.*

Bare feet on the companionway steps are cold. Head and shoulders out of the hatch, and top and bottom are chilled - *but good job I got out.* There's a steamer crossing ahead, about two points on the starboard bow, showing a red sidelight. We should pass well astern of him, so it's nothing to worry about, *but that's a queer lot of lights he's got there.* Three whites, vertical, just abaft his sidelight - *three vertical whites.*

Three vertical whites. *Great Scott, that's a tug and tow.*

I scramble out of the hatch, into the cockpit, and kneel on the afterdeck to undo the locknut on the self-steering vane. As I crouch there, she sticks her arse into a sizeable crest and gives me a good soaking.

Helm hard up, and jibe the genoa, which is boomed out, as soon as the sail is taken-aback way comes off the boat.

Looking down to leeward, I catch the last of his red sidelight before it blacks-out and he's showing me a white.

A distance astern of him, there's an indistinct shape, which must be the vessel being towed.

By the light of his afterdeck clusters I can see the heavy towing wire, leaving its hook and disappearing into the murk. *A massive ocean-going tug, towing something that looks like a gigantic floating dock.*

And I'd been about to sail between them.

As the tow draws abeam, I can see a light of sorts, exhibited aft, but it's a poor affair and barely visible. As soon as we're clear, I fill her away again, having to let-go the genoa sheet to get her out of irons.

Going below, I strip off my wet gear and try to stop myself shivering by towelling away like mad. You don't get over a fright like this so easily, and it takes a good many reassuring looks out of the hatch, together with a mug of sweet tea, spiked with a hefty slurp of Scotch before I can recover my composure. I also stay awake for the remainder of the night and have no difficulty playing the very model of a lookout.

By ten o'clock in the morning, I've obtained a good A.M. sight, written the log, breakfast under belt, and exactly one whole week at sea from the time they fired the gun.

I can't say I hold any rapturous view of my progress or performance to date. The noon position, 46° 51' North, 13° 28' West, log 359, indicates we are four hundred and twenty five miles out of Plymouth, but not, unfortunately, the same distance nearer New York.

A week out of Plymouth, and I haven't been able to get a message to my wife, with this rapidly becoming the uppermost thought in my mind. The first few days of the passage had been such absolute hell that I had not thought of anybody (with the exception, of course, of poor little me) not, I hasten to add, without a twinge of conscience.

Now that the weather has moderated, and the boat and myself survived some unexpected difficulties, I feel a little more receptive to what may be happening elsewhere - so it would seem that not having a link with home has begun to have an effect. Not that I think my wife would be driven, by lack of news, hysterically to the conclusion that she should search for weeds. I know her better than that - if personality counted for more than experience, she could have been in the boat, and would have put up a performance that would certainly equal my own.

Neither would she reproach me for the failure of the radio.

The hard fact of the matter turns out to be, that I'm reduced to three methods of communicating with passing vessels.

The International Code of Signals, using flags.

An ineffectual shout.

And lastly, but universally understood, the time-honoured two-finger exercise which, while giving a certain childish satisfaction, is in itself a limited form of expression. Who but a single-hander would deny his chosen method of transport may tempt him to adopt the sort of self-centred stance that an impartial observer would interpret as unbecoming egotism?

We can only hope to grow out of it.

Regarding ship to ship communications. It seems, remembering my ineffectual attempts to speak to the trawler, that it will be necessary to keep a sharp lookout in order to gain sight of a crossing vessel, in time to alter course, and bring the point of nearest approach well within half a nautical mile. Bearing in mind the probable relative speeds of our cockleshell and an ocean liner, together with my range of vision, which is limited by my height of eye, I calculate that given ship's speed twenty knots, boat speed four knots, sighting ten miles distant, an approaching vessel would have to be heading within fifteen degrees of the Folkboat if we are to close within half-mile signalling range, which the size of the flags, a diminutive eighteen inches, dictates.

To further complicate the issue. A great deal depends on the direction of the wind, whether or not the passing steamer is to windward or leeward. If the latter, the signal hoist might be masked by the mainsail.

As with many other arithmetical calculations of the degree of probability of one thing or another, I find the result depressing, so having finished my off-putting mental exercise I go on deck for a blow.

A nice day, but the breeze has dropped to little more than a light air, and Iron Mike is having difficulty with his steering because not enough puff is passing his vane.

Out of habit I search the horizon.

Smoke to the south'ard.

Clear astern, and to the nor'ard.

There's a smudge ahead.

Remembering my recent calculations, I do not immediately cry Sail Ho and hoist the signal M.I.K., but wait, as patiently as I'm able, and for a while retire to my virtuous couch.

In a few minutes I must pop up again.

The smudge has become the funnel and topmast of a ship, all in one glorious straight line. What better phallic emblem? Pregnant with possibilities, as she rises over the heave of the ocean's swell.

Down again to Thurber.

Up again, to confirm she's still heading our way.

Down again to get the flags out.

Up again to hoist them.

I have to admit I'm excited. The prospect of being able to pass a message home is the only thing in the world. And the distant vessel seems to be altering course in order to pass close-to.

As she draws near, I can make out the name on her bow.

Brunseck

Her watch-keeping officer is leaning over the wing of the bridge, looking through his binoculars, at me. I feel shy under the scrutiny, nevertheless, I wave, slowly, so as not to give the impression of excitement.

He waves back.

I point to my signal hoist, M.I.K., please report me to Lloyds of London.

He waves again, gives me the 'thumbs-up', and is past.
I look at his stern.

Brunseck of Hamburg

Sitting in the cockpit, limp as a rag, now it's all over, my feelings, a mixture of sadness and relief are vaguely disturbing, and I'm slightly ashamed of such emotional turbulence.

Below once more, in my cosy little world, where everything is still within reach, I feel at home and start preparing the evening meal.

After supper, the breeze eases away and by ten o'clock we're near enough becalmed, with just the odd zephyr drifting temptingly about. I try to make the best of it by giving Mike a spell at the tiller; by midnight there's nothing else for it, but to down the genny and the mainsail. During the night it stays the same, an overcast sky, smooth sea, slight swell, with an occasional drizzle of rain. Lying in my bunk I toss and turn, but can't sleep.

Come morning, and I don't feel well, suffering from a heaviness about the head and eyes, very much as if recovering from the influence of drugs. So take this as a well timed prompt to see what's in the first aid kit which David has generously provided, complete with detailed instructions.

Every type of ailment or disaster that might plague the single-handed mariner is dealt with competently and at length, down to, and including sea serpent's bites. It is also, despite David's vein of humour, a catalogue of horrid things to avoid, particularly a fractured pelvis. However, not yet confronted with that ultimate disaster, I reach for the liquid paraffin, confident that its well-advertised powers will provide the necessary movement.

Fear of injury, as well as ill-health, had been constantly in my mind during my first single-handed passage (a trip down to Spain, just to see if I could come to terms with the problems involved with this type of challenge).

During that experience, I found that someone with an active imagination, and time enough alone in a small boat, can work himself into a sweat about the risks involved, if he's foolish enough to do so.

It really is a fruitless exercise, best ignored.

After my experience of the previous year, I just watch my step, eat and drink in moderation, carry plenty of liquid paraffin and let it go at that.

If you do suffer a major disaster, the best thing out of the box would be a shot of morphine, and then try to make contact with the next vessel in sight. In this context, signalling flags can't always be relied on and possibly the method of choice, as well as a few parachute rockets, would be an Aldis lamp. Effective both by day and by night, on surface ships or aircraft, it's a useful item of equipment. Like a fool, I've left mine behind, along with my Waltham chronometer, supposedly to save stowage space.

If I had used my head, I would have altered the boat's lighting system from six volts to twelve, thus halving the consumption of my low-wattage bulbs. And this decision would have allowed me to use the Aldis on the boat's permanent accumulator. It would also have provided a reserve power supply for the radio transmitter, which is now completely useless.

How short sighted can you get?

A Sunday spent idle, mostly sitting in the cockpit, which gets harder and more angular by the hour. The barometer is high and steady, in contrast to my morale which, though flipped by the thumb of the German mate, is on its way down once more.

During the early afternoon, the surface of the sea is darkened. Patched here and there by the seemingly unconnected movements of small air masses as they wander at will o'er the ocean - looking maybe for a gradient to marshal them as a front. One such metnomad passes over the boat and in an instant covers both it and me with a host of small black flies. I am utterly revolted, slapping, sweeping, brushing, cursing them away. They are in my hair, crawling down my neck, at the corners of my mouth, creeping about my eyes. Revolting little insects that seem completely foreign to the 'til-then spotless ocean. Their presence turns my boat into a rotting carcass which they seem loath to leave.

Then I notice they seem incapable of flight, so I launch my own offensive. With the same old plastic bucket dipping over the side, I cascade the boarders off the deck, drowning them in thousands. Those few that gain entry to the cabin, I sweep into bits of screwed-up paper and hurl them overboard; those not vulnerable to the brush remain as disgusting little blobs which are swabbed up later in a general shipshape turn out.

Up again on deck, I spit into the sea which, when I look at it closely, is covered with the filthy things.

I could be sailing through a graveyard.

There's no prospect of a breeze, but I'm so determined to quit this bit of ocean that I unlash the sweep and scull away, discarding clothing as I warm to the task. Naked at the oar, feet wide apart on the cockpit seats, body, balls and boat moving rhythmically to the surge of physical effort.

Out of breath, but composed once more, I lay-to, spend a minute or two combing my hair, hopefully getting rid of the last of the blasted insects.

Then, after balancing precariously on the pushpit, jump with a joyful shout into the sea - to hell with the crazy arthropod-laden anomalies!

I'm enjoying my trip into and particularly under the 'oggin, but the boat still has way on her after my exertions with the sweep, and she's moved slightly down wind by the time I regain the surface.

I'm now anxious to get back on board. With a few nervous strokes I can get a hand on the rudder and rise, seal-like from the sea, shaking the water out of my beard as any old dog would choose to.

Climbing the rudder is easy, I've done it a hundred times before, yet I'm glad to regain the deck, prompted by the fear of every single-hander. And added to that subconscious niggle, there's also the fact that my cleansing dip means I will be salt-tacky until my next freshwater bath; nevertheless, I feel it's all been worthwhile as I towel off below.

It's Sunday, and another evening meal is washed down with a spot of gin and lime, while the mind rotates about the seemingly central pillar of existence (what food is available aboard the boat). With the reassuring thought being, there's stacks of tinned stuff, plenty of biscuits and butter, more than enough tea, sugar, cocoa, chocolate, boiled sweets and the like.

Water is the main concern; my attention is also drawn to the dehydrated foods that have been designed to constitute thirty-eight complete meals. The limiting fact had been the pricey nature of the supplies purchased from the ministry of Agriculture, Fisheries, and Food. With this leading to the decision to restrict the use of the dehydrated meals to every other day, making do, in the meantime, with tinned stuff, cheese and biscuits, together with the occasional self-heating tin for a quick but lazy meal.

It may sound Spartan - in practice, it means very little hardship.

I've already found I don't need the quantities of food that would normally be eaten ashore. Probably explained by the fact that I'm conserving my energy by spending a large proportion of the day, as well as all the night in a horizontal position.

This again, is not as tedious as it may sound.

The headroom available below limits my choice to sitting, sometimes head bent, or crouching uncomfortably over the galley or the chart table.

By far the best alternative is stretched full-length on a bunk, where I can concentrate on the really important conundrums.

My supply of ales and spirits are limited. Two dozen cans each of Guinness and Pale Ale. A bottle of Scotch. A bottle of brandy, and a further two of gin. My requirements are modest by shore based standards because a 'spot of gin', really is a very small spot indeed, with my previous experience reinforced by the effects of the liquor drunk so far.

Possibly because of my reduced diet, particularly its limited bulk, I have found that everything I drink, even including a light ale, rushes immediately to my head. Not a feeling to be sought after in a small boat, moving quickly in response to an ever changing ocean.

Reassured that I'm not short of victuals, fly and fancy free, I can now look forward to another good night's reinvigorating sleep.

For the next twenty-four hours weather conditions remain the same. A light nor'westerly air arrives a chance time, but no sooner have I the main and genny hoisted than it fades away, leaving me wondering if the canvas should be on deck again.

Putting off the decision until the chafing gets on my conscience, then going forward with a grumble which, if overheard by the Clerk of the Weather would certainly be as damning as the slaying of any blasted albatross.

Comes the dawn, it has breezed-up from the sou'west and during the forenoon blows a moderate gale, necessitating close-hauled work, yet infinitely better than sitting on my broad backside with the only wind my own.

Now there's work to be done.

Double-reef the mainsail, then hand it, struggling for a while under the small staysail, but still managing to get a good noon sight.

A moderation in the weather, and it's possible to reset the double-reefed main.

Wind goes westerly.

Tack ship; after four hours on starboard tack, I think it's time to go-about, not wanting to get any further to the south'ard.

Tack ship again - just one damned thing after another.

However, things do change. Two days becalmed have made me as lazy as an adder and quite forgetful of the rattles, groans and spray-throwing thumps that are the normal accompaniment of this particular beat.

How now the sea?

After only twelve hours of moderate winds, the calmly hibernating giant has risen to billowing proportions with the ease of a judge being ostentatiously re-robed. I stay in my bunk, confident the boat can face whatever trial's in store. She might be labouring, but not, I hope, in labour.

The short steep seas, smacking against the thin larch planking, seem to be knocking for admittance, only denied by the skill that put the hull together. I feel safe enough, close tiled, not a prying eye in three degrees, supported by a vessel that lists two thousand in its crafted title. One fathom more and some will know the tight-knit feeling that brothers-all can face the flood, an inner guard 'gainst apprehension.

The moderation comes at midnight, freeing a point as it does so. Before going on deck, I light the primus under the ever-ready kettle, measure cocoa, milk and sugar, then out on deck to lend a hand.

'… *ahoy there, for'ard.*'

'… *set up the lift. Look lively there. A hand to the clew tackle, two more to the points. Take the fall of the halyard to the winch, bosun; let's have a good taut luff.*'

'…*Aye Aye, sir.*'

' … *now then boys, you heard the mate, lay-into-it, 'earty now.*'

' … *that's it, 'vast heaving, make fast. Ease the topping-lift; handsomely now, handsomely.*'

'… *how's your ship's head, quartermaster ?*'

'… *west nor' west, sir.*'

'… *make it West by North.*'

'… *Aye Aye, sir; west by north, West by North it is.*'

'… *well done lads. They're going well for you tonight, bosun.*'

'… *Aye, they are that Sir. Makes all the difference when they know there's a good hot broth in waiting.*'

'… *stand-down the watch below.*'

'… *we got a good cook, Sir.*'

'… *not bad, bosun - not bad at all.*'

This morning, after a dream-filled sleep, I shot the sun, a left and right, both barrels, that brought a school of porpoise leaping from the sea, all bubbling with laughter. I smile back, and swear to God they eye me with amusement.

For half-an-hour more they ring the boat, timing their surface-breaking grunts so our eyes are on a level and, if I cared to, I could lean outboard and touch them.

Captivated by their size, their merrymaking company, by their interest in this sea/man, labouring his way across an ocean they roam at will. It seems my bumbling presence has them chuckling.

Then a smaller porp breaks surface, his glistening body scarred, his skin the worse for wear. He looks me straight in the eye, grins, then winks. He seems a little squarer than the rest; re-enters the ocean with a resounding splash, and on that signal, with one accord, they turn and make off west'ard at something in excess of fifteen knots.

The rest of the day seems uneventful. After the noon sight, I help drive a herd of cattle across the plains of Central Australia (guided by *The Overlanders*), but between the lines of white faced Herefords and the clouds of choking dust, my little porp will persist in sticking in his smiling snout.

In the end I get the message.

During evening, the breeze backs a point or two and it's time to tack again. A few more chores and it's Thursday morning, with a sou'westerly breeze, Beaufort four to five, the sky heavily overcast, with a moderate sea and swell; but, fine and clear.

Just after dawn, my friends the porps draw close aboard once more, as I had been certain they would. They don't bother me with questions, merely pass the time of day, to which I, in a gentlemanly manner, reply as best I can.

The unfavourable weather makes it impossible to get a fix. This is hardly cause for alarm, but it does give rise to what is, for me, a new complaint. For the first time in the passage I suffer a twinge of boredom. That imagined endemic complaint of solitary travellers, but surely not beyond the wit of man to cure.

I remember the questions after my first single-handed voyage, when so often people used the phrase 'boring', when they meant 'lonely'. All their lives labouring under a delusion, not having the time, lost in a world of self-centred events.

' ... what can we do now ?'

Cry their children, when a hundred yards away there's a river to ford, a hill to climb, a corner to turn. All leading to that crowded scene which, if they're not careful, may devolve to little more than a host of aimless crickets chirruping noisily away while trying vainly to divert attention to themselves.

While I'm sometimes annoyed at being held susceptible to boredom, I can't help feeling flattered when asked if I'm ever lonely. The first implying that you should be able to, but can't; while the second leads to the conclusion

photo: **author**

just after dawn, my friends the porps draw close-aboard once more
as I had been certain they would
they don't bother me with questions
merely pass the time of day
to which I
in a well-mannered way
reply as best I can

that you can, and have, but miss it. None of which helps me avoid the fact that, at four o'clock in the afternoon of Thursday, the twenty-third of June, I feel a little isolated.

Who could honestly blame me?

Alone in a small boat, equidistant from the Azores, South West Ireland, the Isles of Scilly, Ushant, and Cabo Villano, with the bias naturally towards the Cape with the supposedly villainous countenance.

As with most people troubled with having nothing to do, I'm surrounded with a host of things all screaming for attention.

One of the working staysails is badly worn where it's continually rubbing on the shrouds. Searching for some chafe-protecting material that I can stitch on the synthetic sailcloth, I happily remember that in the first aid kit there's a quantity of self-adhesive elastic bandage. Assuming, perhaps rashly, that this will not be needed to splint a shattered limb, it makes excellent chafing gear, first stuck, then stitched to those portions of the sail that are subject to the most destructive wear.

Being struck by the novelty of the idea, it's only the matter of a moment before anything that impinges on anything else, rattling cups, vibrating glasses, the odd pencil, ropes, sheets, halyards of various sorts, all are insulated from their immediate surroundings, with the boat and her equipment taking on the appearance of a battered pugilist.

Fired now as a practical do-gooder, I scour pans, coil ropes, clean jets, sweep up blanket fluff, oil the log, keeping on and on - but still bored as the devil, being ultimately reduced to that mirage of a panacea, a stiffer than usual snort.

This evening, as I adopt my favourite stance - shoulders wedged in the companionway, one foot on the cabin sole - the other raised on the steps. I look moodily to leeward, and for the first time feel a little disgruntled, perhaps a little drunk, somewhat dismayed that my enthusiasm for single-handed sailing seems less resilient than I had led myself to expect.

And ain't that, in itself, a significant admission?

It's not that I'm downhearted.

I firmly believe that the boat and myself will ultimately arrive in New York, being satisfied that my experience, and perhaps a little luck, should put the outcome beyond reasonable doubt. However, I am disappointed at the rate of progress.

Viewed from the hatch, the ocean stretches as far as the eye can see. Beyond that, its immensity is limited merely by my imagination; when that imagination is aided by a glance at the chart, then, the thousands of miles yet to be sailed can be related to the distance that has been currently made good.

It's then that the prospect of being alone for so many more weeks begins to nibble at morale.

During the evening, I listen to the radio with more pleasure than I can previously recall, which is perhaps another indication that my isolation is beginning to have an effect.

The next day my spirits zoom once more, due entirely to the appearance over the southern horizon of two dashing patrol vessels, which turn out to be Yanks. They come romping over the ocean in the high spirited manner of terriers over a burrow and I watch, fascinated, as they carry out a series of complicated manoeuvres which seem to be the other half of a sub-hunting exercise.

The game over for the time being, they dash towards me at high speed, their lean hulls cutting easily through the swell, pointing muzzled guns in my direction. If I was a rabbit, I would run. They reduce speed and circle at a distance, with the circumspection an experienced dog pays to a balled-up hedgehog, until one of them cuts out of ring a'ring a'rosy and comes alongside for the nautical equivalent of a sniff.

'... Hi there.'

Answered with a wave.

'... you're a long way out.'

'Yes.'

' ... everything O.K. ?'

'Sure.'

By this time his rail is lined with gaping gobs, sunburned youngsters who could be the pride of anybody's navy, if they hadn't all been chewing gum.

'... where are you bound ?'

'New York.' (murmured, as a nonchalant aside).

They all stop chewing, smile, and on the instant, row upon row of gleaming white teeth grace the vessel's side rail.

' .... sure is a long way, in that little boat.'

Photo: **author**

dashing patrol vessels
which turn out to be
Yanks

There isn't much I can say in reply to this round-robin, which seems complete in itself, but I'm becoming fascinated by all these people, and have to make what I hope is not a visible effort to bring myself to attend the Skipper's next remark.

'... *anything you want ?'*

'Well, yes; as a matter of fact there is. Will you send a message to the U.K. for me, please ?'

'... *why sure, be glad to.'*

So I give them details of the boat, and ask them to relay the information to the Royal Western at Plymouth. They are very kind, and shout cheerful remarks as they draw away, with gums once more a-go-go (we've been told that an army marches on its stomach) but it seems the US Navy's content to wriggle along - with an appreciative nod to Mr Wrigley's Spearmint.

This material contact with the outside world gives me tremendous encouragement, no doubt prompted by the absolute certainty that those at home will get another message; perhaps their first, as I have never managed to rid myself of the doubt that the signal through the German merchantman may have bogged down somewhere along the line.

Does it matter that the sky is overcast?

The cabin cramped.

The reading material limited.

Great Scott, why hadn't I asked the smiling gobs for a few more magazines and books?

Never mind, Thurber can stand re-reading, and I can make a detailed study of oceanic birds.

This afternoon sees the boat broad reaching under a full mainsail and the big genoa, before a sou'sou'easterly breeze that freshens imperceptibly, to the point where I spend an hour debating whether or not it's time to reduce the amount of white stuff held aloft by the wavering arc of a stick.

In the evening, the breeze grows tired of havering and backs easterly, forcing me on deck to hand the main and boom out the genoa, making things easier all round - Mike said it was about time too.

Then it's Saturday once more, and at ten o'clock precisely, we have been at sea for

two whole weeks.

take your time
you may miss it
when it's gone

This weekend turns out dull with occasional rain and drizzle, the heavy overcast makes sights impossible, so at noon the D.R. position is 45° 39′ North, 21° 09′ West, log reading 768.

After my fit of depression, but while still in the state of enthusiasm sparked by the naval patrol, I decide to curb my imagination, hoping at the same time to put a floor under my mood swings, by dividing the distance to New York into more easily managed 'bits'. Thus, I have 30° West, and 50° West marked on the chart, as significant hurdles to be negotiated en route.

This little subterfuge alters my perspective. With 30° West as the immediate goal I feel much better, knowing it's attainable, having recognised that this 'shoot for the moon' stuff is all very well, as the medieval aviator must have said, when plunging with his paper wings from a death-defying pinnacle. Isn't it sometimes better to phase your effort more in keeping with your limited capabilities?

In some fields, such foresight is a rigorous necessity.

I have only six cans of beer in the booze locker, planning to consume two before 30° West, two before 50° West, and two on arrival in the good old U.S. of A.

This is logistics, the application of a dedicated mind to the intricate problems of supply. So I can turn-in happy enough as I have managed to tune to the B.B.C. Light Programme and get Big Ben striking the hour, not a perfect time signal, in the scientific sense, but plenty good enough for me.

During the last few days, prompted by a minor failure of its metal strap, I have kept my Rolex wristwatch in a padded cocoa tin, on a convenient shelf, but since leaving my wrist its rate has gone to the devil, and I feel obliged to fix the strap, which isn't difficult, and wear the watch once more.

Its variable rate in the tin I put down to fluctuating ambient temperature, instead of the just about level delivery of a healthy person's body. When worn again, it settles down immediately but leaves me with a twinge of regret, that my Waltham chronometer has been left somewhat foolishly astern.

Getting up during the night to help swell the ocean's roar on some distant strand, I'm surprised to see, a bare mile astern, a vessel bound nor'westerly. I'm delighted with his brightly lit appearance, and soon bring to mind what I assume to be the goings-on amongst those darker patches on his boat deck. As he passes, too close astern for comfort, I find his presence annoying - three ships in two days, the place is getting crowded.

It would be an exaggeration to say I caught a whiff of perfume as she passed, but I thought I did, and that's just the sort of ticket to more than tickle my fancy.

I'm a young lad, healthy enough to look with some resentment at the disappearing lights of the liner. I think of the rhythmic music, the soft lights, the peachy cheeks, she just smiling as your hand slips casually from the small of her back to the thrill of her rippling hips.

'... whoa up there, boy, time to call a halt.'

But ain't that easier said than done?

Two lonely weeks at sea have been preceded by another period of discipline, made necessary by the happy event that kept my wife at home when, under normal circumstances, she would have been on the quay at Plymouth.

So it's time for another session with Thurber, but not really hoping to be offered anything other than a comic slant that may or may not assuage the age-old problem of abstinence.

Sunday passes, with a freshening breeze continually building the height of the seas, which the boat, on occasion, seems to be attempting to flatten.

This is ill-advised work.

As I lie in my bunk, my teeth rattle as she hits a bigger one. The boat shivering as she's swept by a dollop of angry Western Ocean, with the breeze just moderating in time to be able to hold on to a fully reefed mainsail and spitfire jib.

At noon it's still heavily overcast, sights impossible, passing rain squalls ringing down curtain after curtain on Neptune's endless play.

Yet strangely enough, as the wind moderates, the swell begins to mount. An awe-inspiring undulation which lowers the boat into the belly of the ocean, where the breeze grows faint 'til the boat soars again to breast the height of yet another crest.

Not the slightest worry to the boat, but a less than gentle prod to the seaman, that these monstrous ripples are the muscular spasm of an ocean, over which you have the temerity to crawl.

And they are endless.

A mighty demonstration that no man can resist, which persists until the shallows of the Continental Shelf reach out, disturbing the travelled equilibrium of the tottering giant 'til he falls, grumbling, on the strand of the trembling shore.

All this afternoon, this evening, and during the night, the play continues to a spellbound audience of one, needlessly emphasising that the small-boat voyager is merely there on sufferance, and he forgets it at his peril.

Another great thrill this next forenoon, a ship, soon passing to the nor'ard.

Wyoming

registered at

Le Havre

Although I can't say I feel blasé at the prospect, I'm not experiencing the same mad pounding of the blood brought on by earlier sightings. Nevertheless, this is an opportunity to check my D.R. position, which is bound to be considerably adrift as the last celestial observation was obtained five days ago.

This is something I would normally be reluctant to descend to, but the prospect of another week of heavily overcast skies does much to sooth my pride, so I hoist, in addition to the code group M.I.K. another group of flags which enquire.

' … what is your present position ?'

The vessel passes at tremendous speed, something in excess of eighteen knots. Yet he does the decent thing, takes a round turn out of her and steams past again; but he's still going too fast to enable me to make out the megaphoned shout that drifts across the water.

It's my turn now to play the game; with an eloquence a Parisienne might envy I hunch my shoulders and raise my arms. A demonstration that indicates to the watching Frenchman that I can't make out a sea-blown word he's hollering.

As with every other merchantman, he's reluctant to reduce speed. Having rung the telegraph 'full-away' when leaving the New World, to ring down 'stop', abruptly in the middle of the Western Ocean would cause consternation on the platform and bring an anxious Chief Engineer hurrying to the bridge, so he steams around the Folkboat while the Officer of the Watch makes up a signal.

And there they go, close-up on the triatic stay.

' … 44° North; 26° West; is there anything you require ?'

Nice friendly chap, think I, waving my thanks, while he makes a last round turn and then departs, with an undisturbed engine room department.

Now I can go below and compare positions.

The fix he gave is obviously to the nearest degree, but even allowing for this simplification, it seems I'm further along than I'd reckoned. So hurrah for that, which comes of not being starry-eyed of miles and courses hopefully made good. So much better than living in a fool's paradise, and then finding yourself a hundred miles astern of your optimistic reckoning.

So up goes my morale.

The sixteen days of slogging to windward is at last showing up as progress to the west'ard. Another few days and we will be north of Fayal, so if the worst comes to the best of endeavours a bolt-hole is available. Also, the magic hurdle of thirty degrees West is slowly shading the horizon.

Will there be much of a bump as we cross it?

Only the impact of a tin opener on one of the six cans of ale that must last, merely another thousand nautical miles.

This Monday night it blows fresh from the sou'west, with occasional rain squalls lashing the surface of the ocean, so it's once more, slog, slog, slog, to the all-prevailing breeze.

Then she veers a point, necessitating going-about in order to maintain the major tack, seeking more hard won miles that are reeled up slowly on the dial of the log. Tough on the boat, but easy, physically, on the crew, provided Iron Mike doesn't rust-up under the continuous deluge of salt-laden spray.

The well-being of the crew has facets other than the obvious.

The head-popping exercises that began at Plymouth, and have continued ever since, resulting in a reasonably careful lookout, now have a further chore added to them.

Approximately every hour, a few strokes of the pump are needed to keep the bilges dry. Nothing to worry about yet, but a significant departure from the previous status quo.

Being close-hauled for week after week, with the boat well heeled and occasionally labouring, must be imposing a tremendous strain on the hull. The ton of iron ballast fighting a continuous battle with the ever-varying pressure delivered by the thrust of the spar held sails.

Tuesday comes and goes; an A.M. sight is possible, but at noon nothing remains of the sun but a barely distinguishable orb, blanketed by a pale grey coverlet - 44° North, the latitude of sunny Spain, but also Nova Scotia and forbidding Sable Island.

I'm continually hoping for an improvement in the weather; not expecting too much of the wind, which will probably stay westerly, but the sun - surely it's time for the sun to appear again?

The continual windward work, with its spray-swept decks and slopping cockpit has led to the inevitable erosion of the carefully stowed dry rigs, which are removed from spray-proof plastic bags, to be worn for a few days, and then, when wet, discarded. As a result of this oceanic onslaught, the fo'c'sle now contains a miserable pile of soaking woollens, which bear more resemblance to a reef born sponge than the springing back of a mountain ewe.

A mouldy smell permeates the boat.

Small patches of green fungus have established themselves on the deckhead, in those awkward corners safe from the occasional wipe of an antiseptic rag.

Opened tins of biscuits soften faster than they can be eaten, to be partially restored by toasting under the busy stove.

All the blankets are damp, some of them have joined the stinking pile of gear for'ard, others I use to fend off the continual drip from the hatch which, as I sleep to leeward, falls persistently on my upturned shoulder.

I've done everything I can to stop this irritating leak, which is caused by a poor joint at the for'ard end of the companionway scuttle, but to no avail. It remains a saline drip, after drip, after drip, that feeds my variable temper, erupting as a vulgar oath when a heavier cascade on deck pisses on my face as it finds its way below.

The obvious solution, sleeping in the windward berth, has been tried, but this has proved a failure, as the angle of heel is more than the canvas leeboard can comfortably contain. It has got to be the lee berth, otherwise the sleeping seaman risks, when she hits a big one, being unceremoniously tipped out of his bunk to end up cursing on the cabin sole.

Most of the paper aboard is too damply tired to resist the prodding of a sharpened pencil.

Holes are appearing in my plotting charts.

The log book has been soaked.

Even Thurber's pages lie limply between sodden covers.

The dusty plains of the *Overlanders* now turn to stinking bogs, effectively holding up the arrival, at the railhead, of a thousand head of white-faced Herefords - on their way, let's not forget, to an unforgiving abattoir.

It takes longer to get a good stum down in a wet sleeping bag, if you've been out of it long enough for your body heat to have been dissipated. When you return, it has the feeling of a winding sheet, clinging to your lower limbs with a sterile caress, quite foreign to the expected pleasures of bed.

The dampness enters your muscles.

You wake stiff necked and sore shouldered; aware of your joints, as they creakily complain of the penetrating vapour that reproaches the mind, a little every day, eventually condensing as a salty trickle which runs down your knuckle-rubbed cheeks.

... tears of self-pity?

Probably best to deny it.

Midnight, for the solitary individual, alone in a small boat, can be a trysting time for memories. They come crowding in, swamping the emotions of those susceptible individuals who are usually ashamed to admit it.

This night, as I lie in my damp bunk, I dwindle; my mind slowly rotating around my physical being, then swinging out on a tangent so that I can look back on myself, and my boat, from a superior elevation.

The efforts of the past week lie spread, as if on a table, and I look down on them with the strange capacity of seeing each individually, but at the same time in their natural progression; my home and family join the curving tail, and then my cup is full.

It's then that I cry; not from pity, but from passion. The acceptance of those things past running as a stream into my consciousness, not diverted by everyday reserve, but flooding out of sightless eyes.

It is, unlikely though it may seem, an enjoyable feeling, and my mind rebels. I think it wrong to take pleasure in a mental aberration, which I bring, as quickly as I'm able, under firm control.

I get up, and make a cup of tea.

This morning, of Wednesday, the 29th of June, after struggling to get a woolly looking sun down to a dirty grey horizon, I look at my watch, and just can't believe my eyes.

'... Good God: it's stopped.'

The failure of a wristwatch ashore may not be of earth-moving significance. But to lose a vital navigational tool when a waste away from land?

I think the bottom has fallen out of my world.

After I've put the sextant away, I look at the watch again, but the sweep second-hand has remained in the same spot. I put it to my ear, with the faint hope that, even though the second-hand has stopped, the guts of the thing will still be in working order - there's not even the suspicion of a tick.

I shake it again, and listen.

... silence.

I feel incredibly depressed.

... no watch - no time - no longitude.

My descending thoughts do nothing to remove the feeling that I have been an absolute idiot to leave my chronometer ashore. I sit glumly on the edge of my bunk, elbows on knees, chin cupped in upturned palms, while my fingers absentmindedly scratch my bearded cheeks.

I look at the ship's clock, screwed to the coachroof coaming alongside the matching barometer. Although the case of the timepiece is made of polished brass, the movement is a replica of the cheapest bedside alarm, it's devoid of a second-hand and has a wildly varying rate compared with even the poorest chronometer.

So I take my pride and joy off my wrist, and shake it yet again.

... not even the suspicion of a tick.

There doesn't seem much I can do. The Rolex has worked well throughout the voyage, the rate has been good, and as it's a self-winding type I only take note of it when Greenwich Time is needed to enter a navigation table.

Should I poke around inside?

Although I have tools aboard, they are more suited to chopping down masts, cropping bottlescrews and sawing bits of timber than prodding life into a delicate contrivance. I put the timepiece back into its previous home (the padded cocoa tin) and try to forget about it.

The forenoon passes with my mind continually returning to the problem, even the freeing of the moderate breeze from nor'west to north-by-west does little to cheer me up. The loud tick of the cheap alarm seems determined to capture my attention, so I go on deck for a spell, to try to climb out of the hole I feel myself slipping into.

It's a reasonably decent day.

The boat is making good use of the breeze. It's only patchily overcast and there seems every prospect of obtaining a meridian altitude, which can be obtained without bothering about the loss of the Rolex. The cheap alarm keeping Apparent Time as well as it knows how.

I look around the cockpit.

At the gaily-spinning log, with my eyes following the log line into the water, noting there's a shadow in the wake; a disturbance on the surface of the sea, perhaps 50 yards astern of the boat.

There it is again.

A fin.

And astern of the fin, perhaps forty feet astern of the fin, an immense tail.

It doesn't look like a whale, so I stand on the afterdeck of the boat to get a better view, holding on to the standing backstays.

Whatever it is, cruises back and forth, crossing and re-crossing the wake of the vessel.

The more I look, the more impressed I become - this beast is so much bigger than the boat.

And it's coming closer.

What to do?

'... *you needn't be shy.*' (bawls I).

For want of something better to say, and to give my tongue, with which I'm nervously licking my lips, something better to do.

Leviathan comes to within a dozen yards of the boat.

... a Basking Shark ?

Harmless? Yes (I know it: but does the beast know it?).

Big Boy looks placid enough. A huge body propelled by the languid sweep of an enormous slate-grey tail.

We look at one another for twenty minutes, I can't say with any feeling of intimacy on my part, but certainly with respect, which eventually gives way to slight annoyance.

'... *go away, Beastie, pick on someone your own size.*'

He still follows the boat - an elephant, being led by a diminutive mahout.

'… *shoo* ! … *Shoo* ! … *Shoo* !'

It's no good: some Celts can talk the hind leg off a donkey, but I fail fair on a fish.

My belly tells me that it's lunchtime, reminding me that life goes on without the need of a machine to measure passing hours. I go below with a feeling of relief - who likes being dominated by a denizen of the deep?

There's only one remedy to a situation like this, a large glass of Live Long, which does me a power of good.

I choose corned beef for the meal, which goes down well with a few pickled onions and thickly buttered ship's biscuits. The morale-raiser does its work, and I feel fit enough to look the monster in the eye once more, if he's still there.

He is !

Back below I go.

There still remains half a tin of meat, but I'm reluctant to share it with Tiny Tim (do basking sharks eat bully-beef ?). In any case, this cold grub is my supper, as it's one of the alternate days and I'm doing without a cooked meal.

Nevertheless (referring to Tim) a beast this size can't be too fussy.

Can it?

All it must want is a lot.

Turning out what remains of the meat on a plate, I think, being a generous fellow, that I might as well offer it to my neighbour, so up I go on deck, and when there, hold on firmly to the standing backstays.

'… *here, Fido* … *here, boy.*'

'… *sit up and beg, there's a good dog.*'

I wish I could say that he came when he was called, but he didn't, he just swam along as lazily as ever.

'… *you won't grow into a big strong fish, if you don't eat your vittles.*'

He wasn't interested, so I threw the empty tin at him and retired below.

The Live Long has not only emboldened me to face the mysteries of the deep, but also prompted me to have another look at my Rolex, so I get it out of its tin and glance at the second-hand.

Motionless.

I flick it several times, to try and free whatever it is that's stuck - no luck.

I then debate whether to open up the back and prod, or give it a tentative tap on the companionway ladder, either way, there doesn't seem much to lose.

Helped on by another tot of the fortified eggs, I come down in favour of the steps.

Have you ever held your one and only chronometer by its damaged strap, trying to decide how hard to bang it on the rung of a ladder? It requires an inner compulsion that may only arise if you went out of a morning and found a dinosaur grazing your lawn.

After that, anything may happen?

Without bothering about the finer points of the watchmaker's art, I raise the watch, then bring it cautiously down on the varnished mahogany tread.

After I've done the dirty deed, I put the timepiece to my ear, I must admit without much hope, and listen.

Not a sound.

Another treatment?

Why not?

Bang (it has a slightly firmer ring to it).

As I'm holding the watch by the folded metal strap, its face is difficult to see.

Is it worth bothering to look?

Just one more tap for luck?

'… Bang.'

Is it worth looking now?

I have to, if only to find out if the hands are still gracing the face, so as casually as I know how, I turn the timepiece over.

'… praise the Lord … it's going.'

96

And so it is.

So help me if I never sail another boat. My expensive wristlet chronometer, self-winding, waterproof, anti-magnetic and *shockproof*, has been stopped for several hours, but has now restarted.

'… you want to know how ?'

So, my friend, do I.

The breeze holds to the nor'ard throughout the afternoon. As evening falls I fiddle with the Direction Finding Radio, searching the airwaves for a signal. I have a reasonable idea of Greenwich Time, from the cheap and cheerful tick tock, and after a while manage to obtain the necessary 'pips' and can accurately set up the chronometer. This accomplished, I turn-in with a peaceful mind (Tiny Tim departed during the later part of the afternoon).

The next morning dawns fine and clear. My morale, when I'm taking the A.M. sight, couldn't be better. I find she's merely three miles astern of the reckoning, and this small success, after so many days of overcast skies, gives me a new found energy which keeps me working, even though the breeze fails in the afternoon and once again the sails come down on deck.

It's a marvellously fine day.

The still air gives play to the sun's rays and I'm soon down to a pair of shorts, dipping up buckets of 'oggin and scrubbing the deck with a long-handled brush. The sea is calm, and after the boat is shipshape - I sit on the coachroof admiring my oceanic world.

What appears a watery waste is, when you look closely, amazingly alive with creatures, with my attention drawn to the sails of Portuguese Men O'War. They must have been present for some time, but the mirror-like surface of the sea is now accentuating the height of their rig, which, as they aren't bothered with chafe, they have confidently let stand.

We are all becalmed, and several of the Men O'War are close to the boat, their translucent bodies floating in a blue sea, trailing red tentacles. Skeins of translucent lace, the sort of stuff that could be rendered in watercolour, but never, ever, in oil.

Using the friendly end of the scrubber I give one of the 'Men' a gentle prod. It has the consistency of jelly and could be easily damaged, but although I know the tentacles are capable of paralysing small creatures, and of giving a man a nasty sting, I have no intention of causing them harm. I'm aware of a fellow feeling for the inhabitants of this particular part of the ocean.

It's been growing in me for some time. Even the previous day's alarm (the appearance of my oversized visitor) has done nothing to disturb it. My friends the porps were the first to trigger it off, and I now look into the depths of Neptune's kingdom with a companionable gaze.

There are millions of tiny creatures here.

By far the most common are transparent pencil-sized wrigglers, about an inch long, sporting one black eye in the middle of their bodies. I scoop some up in a glass and have fun watching them perform.

Higher up the social scale are small fish, the size of an olive, and just as green. They're quick, and scatter before the dipping hand.

The boat casts a long shadow into the endless deep, and in it larger fish circulate, guests at a garden party, strolling flowered lawns.

I enjoy being a parasol.

Shading my eyes from the sun's reflection, in order to have a better view, I wonder if I can lean outboard far enough to put my head under the surface of the 'oggin, then open my eyes for an undisturbed look. When I do so, a dark shape moves gracefully across my watery field of vision, a small shark, his back a brilliant blue, his underbelly white.

I don't feel anxious, and he looks perfectly at ease, so I sit up without a sudden movement in order not to scare him.

He comes to the surface. Fin and tail out of the water. Glistening in the sun. About six feet long and purposefully lean. As he turns away I can see his curving mouth, and when he passes close-to, a row of neat white teeth.

... they look purposeful too.

At noon, sights put her at 43° 28′ North, 30° 08′ West, log reading 1,155 miles (we have negotiated the 30° West hurdle, without even a tremor) so I have one of the cans of beer that were scheduled to last another thousand nautical miles. The booze is warm, but acceptable, and when the can is empty, I throw it overboard.

After a pause, Jack the Knife recovers from his nervous flight, cruises quietly around it (the can) and then comes up for a really good look.

... but it's only a tin.

During the afternoon, I get the bedding out on deck and festoon the boat with blankets, pillows, and sleeping bags. As one side dries, I turn them over, and long before sundown they are warm to the touch.

As night falls, more fish come about the boat, and until the breeze arrives, in the early hours of the morning, I'm entertained by plops and splashes; a sure indication that it's not only Man who likes an occasional night out.

Only seventeen miles are made good during the next twenty-four hours, and I wonder, dispiritedly, how much more Francis and the others have made good on this particular day. It's all very well getting a good suntan, but the name of the game is getting to New York in the shortest possible time, with this sombre assessment of my position beginning to affect my morale.

As the voyage has progressed, it's noticeable that my feelings are fluctuating at an increasing rate. To help myself along, I have the second good wash of the voyage, out in the cockpit, stripped off, and soaped all over.

It's amazing how little water you need to lather a large body. And quite staggering how long it takes to remove the suds when you're limited to a rinse of two and three-quarter pints of fresh water.

As before, the ablution works wonders, with the effort, as well as the necessary hoarding of supplies being judged so very much worthwhile.

The breeze arrives during the afternoon, and we sail close-hauled on starboard tack over the Friday night, until Saturday noon, when she's at 42° 31'North, 30° 42' West, with the log reading

1,243 nautical miles out of Plymouth

sail on
past temptation
and the dismal thought
so many rocks to be avoided

Still slogging to the west'ard.

Still close-hauled.

Fluctuating feelings, mostly lonely.

Right up to this present minute, I've done a similar chore every day (filled in the British Medical Research Council's questionnaire), one of the other competitors taking part in this little jaunt turned the job down, and I wonder now if he was right.

'… how do you feel ?' (it asks).

The sort of remark you shoot at a colleague, the morning after a night spent out on the town, and in those circumstances expect little more than a cliché.

Not bad, awful, never better (almost anything will do).

But not here, for this intimate appraisal they want you to unzip your guts and expose the writhing mess for their beady-eyed assessment.

I'm lonely, I'm scared, I'll be glad when the trip's over.

Is this stuff of any value to anyone?

' … how often do you masturbate ?'

Can it get more personal than that? But I think I know, now, why Sheila Chichester threw such a fit when she saw what was being included.

In any case, why bother to reveal this information to some inquisitive medico who will dissect it, and what he judges to be me, in a smoky London office. Yet I keep on, religiously filling the thing in, and after the time spent at sea, it's beginning to exert a malign influence on a reluctant, even if determinedly conscientious subject.

In this regard, I have got into the habit of trying to stand back and look at myself objectively. Sometimes wondering - can I really be such a puff ball that my morale's affected by the slightest change in the weather?

We have made the position north of the Azores and must now head as close to west as we can make. A northerly breeze would be just what the doctor ordered, but although we were fortunate yesterday, it has gradually backed, through west, until by noon today we've got a steady west sou'westerly. Near enough a dead header, and my spirits slump once more.

The weather could be worse.

The visibility is good.

The breeze and swell moderate, it's just the direction of the whining wind that twists your (my) miserable gut.

Close-hauled all the time.

Beating.

Beating.

Beating.

I was once told that windward work in a small boat is *'little more than a vanity.'*

But what does this cynical remark really mean?

Fruitless desire ? Empty pleasure ? Vain pursuit ?

Mere ostentation ?

Or better still.

An empty pride, from over-weaning self-conceit ?

It may all be true: none of it diminishes the fact that you can get a small boat to make progress when she's close-hauled, if you stick at it, with the old expression being a good one - *working* a boat to windward.

You can try coaxing; but in the end, it won't do.

When the sun is halfway between his zenith and the western horizon, the good old orb bears roughly sou'west, and that's where we're bound. But the wind blows from the same quarter; steadily, persistently, relentlessly, bringing a buildup of sea and swell as an endless fluctuating wall, which you can butt your head against without the slightest prospect of success. That's the size of the problem, which the boat is so much better suited to than I am.

I get depressed, when I look at the chart and see the limitless expanse of ocean; the size of it deluges and floods the mind. The old tub is much more sensible, she tackles it, drop, by drop, by drop.

Wave, by wave, by wave.

Taking the rough with the smooth. Displaying a persistence that I would like to possess. While I'm dejected, she may grumble, and at times groan at the length of the task, but she does keep going.

The sheets are hard in, not tight enough to hinder her, just taut enough to flatten the main; similarly with the staysail.

The weather shrouds are fiddle-tight, as are the forestays, but the other rigging flops uselessly about, giving little support to the mast as it leans heavily to leeward.

The straining terylene mainsail is setting well.

The lower panels are glistening where dollops of spray strike with a drum roll rattle, then run towards the foot of the sail, to be carried aft and fall off the end of the boom - back from whence they came.

The reef points flap about, and it seems their endless flicking must eventually lead to wear at the belaboured spots, but so far there's no sign of it. What does draw the eye is the luff of the mainsail, which is held to the mast by stainless steel slides, one of these slides, halfway up, has come adrift and the sail is inclined to sag away from the mast.

Should I repair it now?

It means getting wet *(let's leave it a'while, 'til the next spell of reasonable weather)*.

These slides are also causing other trouble. They have sharp edges, which are chafing away at the taped edge of the sailcloth. The rawhide preventors are also showing signs of wear, and will require attention soon.

Iron Mike is still manfully at it, the hardest worked man on board, but right now he needs a helping hand, as the short steep sea is doing its best to knock way off the boat, and Mike is inclined to keep her too close-winded.

Shall I get out to adjust the vane?

It means getting wet *(to the devil with it)*.

Let's wait and see how often the spray comes aboard, then, when we're familiar with the wetting rhythm, just lean out of the companionway hatch and shorten the tiller shock cord in order to provide a little more strength to Mike's persistent elbow.

As she lifts to the sea, the rudder, which has a slightly greater area than that of a standard Folkboat, bangs about on its pintles and bids fair to shake itself to pieces.

The tiller restraining lines, which are necessary to prevent her over-steering, are aggravating the problem. This liveliness at the tiller would be of no concern to a human helmsman, whose arm would move unconsciously, reacting to the buck and thrust of the boat. But here, the lines limit the swing and as she kicks against the restraint, the whole after end of the vessel shudders - one more thing to worry about.

There are others.

She's making water.

Not the modest, bilge-sweetening amount, the once a week pump a clinker built vessel always makes, even when lying at a mooring.

After weeks of slogging to windward, the hard worked seagoing hull requires clearing at much more frequent intervals.

I do it when I think about it. Not making a regular logbook entry. Just a dozen strokes on the pump whenever it's convenient - before the afternoon nap, while cooking supper, waiting for the kettle to boil, when up during the night for a look round the horizon. A regular chore that's become an accepted part of cautious shipboard routine.

And who could wonder at it?

As she mounts a steep sea, she's buffeted by the crest, with an accompanying deluge of spray. For an instant she hangs, free as she will ever be, while floating on an ocean. Both ends clear, balancing about her midship's section (and it's then that she creaks), she's only allowed a moment, poised, as the sea moves aft, leaving her forepart unsupported.

Down goes the bow, slamming into the trough in a way that rattles glasses, even though they're securely held in their carefully constructed through-shelf storage.

As she plunges, her deeply vee'd forefoot hurls the sea, port and starboard, low and far, reminiscent of a man sowing corn by hand; but the old orb and Nep between them have added their own delightful sparkle.

She's not allowed time for recovery.

The bow is lifted, suffers another clout from a crest that reduces her speed through the water. If it's been a bad error on Mike's part, the mainsail will give several complaining flaps before she once again pays off and is footing as before.

It sounds endless?

It is, my friend.

It is.

Down below, lying in my sleeping bag, with nothing fresh to read (even Thurber's inclined to tire after the third uproarious round, apart from a wry smile when asked about the toss-off) I'm very much part of the boat.

I know every rattle, every thump, every creak tells me how she's doing (that particular shudder) is caused by a tremble in the weather runner, which is set up hard in order to keep the inner forestay taut.

There's not the slightest need to sit in the cockpit, looking under the foot of the mainsail, to watch the luff of the jib.

When she's too close to the wind, the head of the staysail lifts and starts its telltale flutter.

As I lie, full-stretched on the windward bunk, cradling my head on my arm, I'm as sensitive as a compass needle, my feet to the nor'east, my head sou'westerly. By just lifting my foot, to touch the through bolts that hold the runner sheave to the deck, I can feel them tremble as Mike pinches a bit, then bears away to correct it.

If the breeze backs a point, she'll follow it down to the south'ard, and the motion of the boat will become easier. As I lie motionless, while being carried ten feet in the air, and moving headfirst yet another ten, I can hear the water moving past the hull. Chuckling as a mountain stream, running over and around a rock.

The planking is a bare three-quarters of an inch thick, and if I put my sensitive fingertips to the hull, as a cracksman might approach a safe, I can *feel* the passage of the sea. Since the voyage began, one thousand three hundred miles of 'oggin have passed that particular point.

It sounds endless?

it is
my friend
it is

As I lie, not needing sleep, merely the passage of time, I can stare at the planking as a chicken may be mesmerized by a line of eye-crossing chalk. Fascinated by the rows of rivets and roves that are clenched to secure the hull.

Everything depends on these slender bits of copper.

The planking is perforated by these russet-coloured spikes, in the manner of a nautical pin cushion; yet what they're tasked to hold together, the mast and rigging strive to tear apart.

I'm aware of these tensions, so much part of the boat that when the hatch is closed, I'm not oriented, as a gimballed kettle.

I'm an intestine
contained by what may look like a boat
but is actually nothing other than a smoothly enveloping skin

From noon to noon on Saturday/Sunday we've logged seventy-eight very nautical miles, and by Monday midday, another hard-earned sixty-two. The last day's run has been close-hauled to the south'ard and not much more than half the distance can be counted as genuinely made good; the rest has been squandered by the cursed necessity to tack, tack, and tack again, working the boat to windward until you are convinced she's bound to rattle your brains out.

This morning, a ship hove into sight, broad on the starboard bow, passing not much more than three miles to the nor'ard, without giving any indication that she'd seen the Folkboat. It's quite amazing how close you must necessarily be, before you can depend on a sighting (if you ever have to bet on it, don't put it at more than a mile).

You think that a white sail, prominently held aloft amidst the blue of an encircling ocean would prove a certain eyecatcher?

The trouble is, half the time the boat is hull down in a trough. And when on the top of a swell, the sail is camouflaged by a thousand flashing crests that sparkle as far as the eye can see. The only exception to this rule lies in a flat calm, when the mast and limply hanging sails, if you've been rash enough to leave them aloft, stand out as so much trivial washing.

The feeling of disappointment left by the passing ship is swept away by the drone of a high-flying aeroplane, just a silver spot, which even through the binoculars I fail to identify, regarding type and nationality.

He flies in large circles around the boat and I kid myself he's aware of our presence (I'm feeling so isolated, that even such a tenuous link is not to be thrown carelessly aside). As he passes overhead I speculated on his base. Almost certainly the Azores, and wonder just how far away they are.

A little elementary work with the dividers, and up comes the surprising answer.

Seventy-five miles (this has been in the back of my mind for several days) but I've been quietly shutting it out.

Seventy-five miles.

only a day's sail
how tempting it is
a hot bath

fresh food
a message home to Eira and the children
the more I think about it, the more attractive it becomes

It's twenty-three days since leaving Plymouth, and during that time we've sailed one thousand four hundred miles, but that's all over and done with now. It's the next two thousand miles I can't drive out of my mind. It

106

seems unbelievable that we're not yet halfway to New York. I just can't accept the fact, until I force myself to look at the chart and note the extent of the wide white spaces.

What would happen if we did put into the Azores?

I needn't kid myself that I'd be sailing the very next day. At every port I've ever entered, I get involved in something or other. No matter how outwardly quiet the place may seem, it's always hard to leave, and the distance to New York would remain formidably the same. The temptation to pack the whole thing in may become irresistible.

While I'm debating this cherry on a stick, the breeze has backed a point and as I stand in the hatchway, looking to the south'ard, it backs a little more. It's now sou'westerly, so with the boat on starboard, she's heading straight for the Azores, could be Flores, or any one of a host of off-lying islands.

just seventy-five miles
not Pygmalion likely
all hands on deck

Tack ship, de-clutch the self-steering gear, take over from Mike, steer for a minute to get the feel of the tiller, then helm hard down, let fly the sheets, round she comes (I've judged it badly) there's a big sea bearing down on her, just as she's in the eye of the wind.

Up goes the bow, but fails to clear the crest, which curls over the foredeck as a breaker on a reef.

For one wet second the scene is frozen in my eye. Then the action recommences. Another crest comes, breaking as it does so in a spraying roar over the foredeck. Flooding abreast the mast. Brimming the coachroof. Cascading as a waterfall into the cockpit, where I'm crouching, trying to avoid the worst of it.

stone me

I'm soaked to the skin - not all that serious, as I'm only wearing shorts and a smock - but it's colder than imagined, and the salt from the 'oggin will tack-up my hair and beard again.

As the water sluices off the sidedeck and gurgles out of the cockpit drains, I stand up and see that she's 'in irons' (lost her nautical way) with the main and staysail flapping uselessly about.

Without any flow passing the blade, the rudder and the self-steering gear are useless, allowing Mike to indulge in a complacent squeak. He seldom makes such a prunes of it himself, so there's nothing else for it, I must get out on the foredeck and back the blistering staysail.

Devoid of the steadying influence of the breeze on the canvas, she's not only bobbing to the passing seas, but rearing uneasily, not a bit like her usual, easily leaned gait. So I have to be careful as I move for'ard, and keep my head down to avoid being hit by the wildly-swinging boom. My bare feet feeling their way over the side deck, as I keep my body well in-board until I reach the liferaft box, which is halfway along the coachroof.

When that's been grasped, I can move for'ard, soon getting another hand-hold at the mast.

She's still 'in irons', so when I reach for the sheet, I will have to be careful the madly flapping sail doesn't catch me in the eye with a wicked flick of its heavy brass thimble.

It's difficult to get hold of this animated item, which has a mind of its own, and after several ineffectual attempts, it seems best to wait for a calmer moment.

Got you, you monkey.

Then 'back the staysail', holding it outboard, so she can blow off to the nor'ard.

Is she going to behave ?

It takes a little time, with the wind pressing hard on the hand-held sheet. She's still hanging, and doesn't want to pay off, so I may have to go aft and put the rudder over in order to use the stern board she's now making.

Now she's coming.

Hold on to the staysail a little longer, to make sure she's well round, even though the mainsail is starting to fill.

I could let go the sheet now, but she's still not gathered enough way. As an all but stationary object, the hull is being hove down by the pressure of the breeze on the mainsail, so I had better get back to the cockpit via the weather side deck. It's not only higher and drier, but if I use the leeward side I'll have to dodge carefully under the boom.

As I shuffle along, facing inboard and leaning over the coachroof, a crest playfully slaps against the ship's side and shoots a jet of water into the air, which not only soaks my back and head, but splashes up the leg of my shorts with the unbounded enthusiasm of a well-directed fire hose.

Have a heart.

Back in the cockpit again.

Helm hard up, and keep it there with my knee. Sheet the jib in order to help her along. No need to bother with the mainsail, the boom has come over on its self-tacking slide.

She's moving nicely now, so I can bring her close-hauled, then move to the after end of the cockpit in order to adjust the windvane.

Below once more, I sit on the edge of the bunk and peel off my soaking cotton smock, which can be thrown up for'ard to join the other wet gear. By lifting my bum just clear of the settee cushion, when she's nice and steady in a trough, I wriggle out of my shorts. They are the 'beach' variety, manufactured of a man-made fibre that doesn't absorb water in the manner of cotton or wool, so if left long enough, they drip dry.

Towel off, not as rough and warming as it could be, because the towel is wet, but better than nothing, and lastly, attend to hair and beard again.

The sleeping bag has got to be moved from what was previously the lee berth, to what has become, because the boat's on the other tack, the problematical berth to lie in.

Before I make the change, I attack the starboard mattress, encased in its plastic waterproof cover. The foam rubber filling has the annoying habit of arranging itself into what feels like a tightly rolled tube, so you find yourself lying alongside this unfriendly thing, instead of 'on' it in the normal way. It's worth spending twenty minutes trying to flatten it out, with the job not being as easy as it appears.

At length, I give up on the unsatisfactory upholstery, because it is, after all, my fault. I well remember the person (it was my sister-in-law Pat) who was making the mattress, asking if I wanted it buttoned? ... or un-buttoned?

Buttoned ? ... un-buttoned ?

There were so many things under discussion at the time, I didn't give the problem the attention it warranted (result, no buttons) so I'm now lumbered with what amounts to a roll of rubber, masquerading as a mattress, encased in a plastic bag.

Nevertheless, I'm glad to hit the sack.

When in the sleeping bag, I bring the logbook up to date, not with navigational information, which is done at the time of routine sights, but I'm keeping a personal journal at the back of the book, which accepts without embarrassment information the medical questionnaire doesn't seem to require.

Now that the temptation to visit the Azores has been resisted, I feel justified in making a cocky entry. As I scribble the note with a stub of pencil, I'm assailed by the notion that I've turned down the opportunity of sending a message home, so accompanying the feeling of guilt comes a hope that a ship may soon pass close enough to take note of another M.I.K.

The day passes, and another long night.

The breeze keeps varying between nor'west and sou'west, and that means frequent trips on deck to make sure we're holding the profitable tack.

In these latitudes, it's warm enough to do away with all clothing, except a pair of bum and ball protecting shorts, and this reduction in kit does at least offer the prospect of being able to stop adding to the pile of mouldering items cluttering the for'ard stowage spaces.

On one of my trips on deck I notice a smudge of smoke ahead, and stand for a long time, straining my eyes for the steamer; but he's hull down.

After a fidgeting spell below, I have another look.

This time his upperworks are visible. He's bound to the south'ard and will pass a long way ahead. With a sense of regret I watch him getting smaller, eventually fading to no more than a smudge of smoke once more.

Then it's midday and time for sights, lunch, and the long afternoon stretches before me as an unwelcome task.

I have nothing to do.

Anything readable has been read, and re-read, until I can close my eyes and carry the gist of the narrative.

When the urge to do something becomes overpowering, I go on deck, heedless of the occasional spray, to lower the masthead burgee and the Welsh Ensign. They show signs of wear, and as I think the passage is not yet halfway over, I take them below and roll them up, carefully stowing them away in order that they will be fit to fly again in New York.

Then comes Thursday, the seventh of July.

Although it's easier to sleep during the night, particularly if the day is hot and sunny, the hours of darkness offer better radio reception - the conditions when the rudimentary DF set can pull a variety of broadcasting stations into the boat.

I lie in my sleeping bag, with the box of tricks conveniently balanced on my stomach, twiddling the knobs, feeding a variety of crackles, bangs and squeaks into the headphones.

The B.B.C. comes in, very faint, and only for half-an-hour before it fades, but long enough to get a time signal, which cheers me up no end (my watch is still keeping good time), then come the news.

'... this is the B.B.C., London. It is with regret that we have to announce the death of Aneurin Bevan.'

Not even the crackle of atmospheric hash that accompanies the announcement can hide the depth of feeling in the voice of the announcer. I feel immensely saddened. Although I've never met him, and do not entirely agree with his political stance - wasn't he a powerful orator?

A great Parliamentarian?

The person with a lead role in the establishment of the United Kingdom's much admired (but, oddly enough) not always popular National Health Service.

I have a lump in my throat. Here am I, lying in my own little wooden box, so many miles from home, and this arrow has been launched while I turned an inconsequential knob.

a shaft of knowledge
barbed with poignancy
twanged from the bow by the passing of a fellow Celt

I have tears in my eyes
they brim my cheeks
as a display of daft emotion ?

(my excuse would be) that I'm unable to share this knowledge. It has entered my mind, and there it has stayed. I can't pass it on.

chatting to a neighbour
over a pint in the pub
to the wife in bed

illustrating the fact that
doesn't just talking
help spread the miserable load?

The middle of a night that boasts a full moon, shrouded by a layer of cloud; the hatch tight-shut 'gainst stray falling spray. It seems only what can be felt, exists; beyond that lies infinity, stars, then a merciful Creator.

It's a strange feeling - Aneurin Bevan.

dead.
ashes to ashes
dust to dust

I should be used to darkness in the cabin.

To conserve the ship's 6-volt battery, I've confined my reading to daylight hours; but now the cabin's not only dark, it's *black*. There seems more light when I close my eyes. Before the BBC News is over I switch the radio off and get up from my bunk, to sit crouched before the stove.

Although I can't see it, I know it supports not only the half-full kettle, but also a clean pint mug. So my hand goes out and grasps the wicker-bound jar of Live Long.

an egg in a shell ?
an embryo
in a womb

My surrounding yolk is the sadness conveyed by the news that Bevan has passed away. It seems a weight, not only on my shoulders but all over my body; squeezing from all sides, as if the atmosphere itself bears heavily upon me.

but it's just that
I am
sad

Time to take a good long gulp of the eggs and rum, finish it, replace the mug and wipe my hair-fringed mouth with the back of a salt-laden hand. Then go back to my bunk and the radio, thinking, if there's bad news about the ether, there should also be some comfort, if only I can find it.

The B.B.C. has faded beyond the reach of my small receiver, all I can find is a haranguing Egyptian and a wailing Arab dance. Then a further turn of the knob brings something that captures my attention. A drawling nasal voice that can only have come from North America.

'... this is station W.N.E.W; bringing you The News, on the hour, every hour.'

It fades in and out of the air waves, which does nothing to lessen my excitement. I feel we're really getting somewhere if we can tune in the good old U. S. of A.

The first bit I manage to decipher concerns a U.S. Navy blimp, which has crashed with the loss of all on board, while searching for missing yachtsmen - who later turn up unharmed.

I lose the transmission for a moment, then it comes again.

'... Mr Max Aitken's yacht, 'Drumbeat' was dismasted this morning, off

the Newfoundland coast.'

I switch the damned set off quickly, before another tragedy occurs. I don't think I can stand another major setback, as it is, I have another large tot of Live Long to ease my jangling nerves.

I hardly sleep throughout the rest of the night. While my body lies rigid and motionless in the boat, my mind roams uncontrollably about the continents. At last, dawn comes, and Glory Be To God it's a fine sunny day; such a day that you would want for a Saturday afternoon's cruise, so I determine to make the best of it.

The nor'westerly deals lightly with the boat, enabling me to change the working staysail for the large genoa. Then come A.M. sights, and I'm delighted to be able to move about the vessel. The depression of the previous night evaporating as the forenoon arches towards its zenith.

The main sheet carries away.

The first real gear failure since the debacle of the battery.

I'm delighted - it gives me something to do.

I spend an hour repairing it, when I could have the whole job done in twenty minutes - but feel I have all the time in the world.

With the impetus of work leaving a satisfying glow, I haul out the water jars, taste every one for sweetness, measure the supply. Twenty gallons remain. This means I have used ten gallons in twenty-eight days, which works out at less than three pints of fresh water every day, for all purposes - I reckon it an achievement.

Then comes the noon position, eighty miles reeled up, cause for another celebration.

The atmospheric pressure is high and steady, with the barometer recording one thousand and forty-five millibars. As this is an uncorrected reading, it's probably some distance from the truth, yet the fact that it's steady means more than the actual reading. It makes me wonder if the breeze is going to hold, and, of course, it doesn't.

During the afternoon it folds, and we're becalmed once more. This does little to deflate my elation, which I keep longer aloft by digging out a tin of boiled linseed oil and spend a useful hour 'dressing' parts of the standing rigging. Only their second season, and already showing signs of rust.

Over supper, while still becalmed, I wonder why it has been such a successful day.

After the depressing radio news, I felt low as I had ever been, but the returning pendulum has carried me to unusual heights, which even the lack of progress has done nothing to let drop.

Is it perhaps the fact that the Azores lies a couple of hundred miles *astern*, and can be treated as a *diminishing* temptation?

It could well be.

Yet more than that, I think it's the drawling American voice heard over the radio that has given me the nudge. A lift, that has lasted throughout the day; but there's another night.

> *becalmed*
> *black water*
> *under a snow-white moon*

> *sails lying in white-mounted heaps*
> *sitting in the cockpit*
> *enjoying a mug of scalding cocoa*

> *liquid mud*
> *steaming*
> *under the light of the silvery moon*

> *and the silence*
> *it's deep*
> *wrapping sea and sky in Neptune's sloppy kitbag*

> *who holds the neck*
> *has yet to draw it tight*
> *and I'm in the bottom of the bag*

> *cowering*
> *in an effort to avoid the noose*

The boat rolls, the surrounding ocean makes sucking noises as it leaves the wooden planking; on the leeward side of the hull, the immersing lands tinkle - as bells, while she moves, slowly, easily, without any sign of tension - as a satisfied woman in bed.

> *not only is there no wind*
> *there's no atmosphere*
> *no varying pressure, warm and cold*

> *an airless ocean, centred in my eye*
> *pale beneath the moon*
> *I shiver,*
> *and the spell is broken*

114

photo: **author**

an airless ocean, centred in my eye
pale beneath the moon

Hell's delight, here I am, supposed to be *racing* to New York.

It's more than time to go below, to fiddle about with the radio, and soon the music of Edward Elgar is floating me off to yet another planet.

I cry again
why bother to control my emotions?
nobody can see

or hear
nobody will ever know
what other outlet can I use?

stand up,
and sing to the stars ?
talk to the silent boat?

(get up you silly bastard, or you'll soon be going crazy)

Exercises in the cockpit, stark naked under the moon. White man, black man. Knees bend, swinging arms. Up-down, up-down, up-down.

feeling better

Down below for shorts and a sweater. Light the stove for a cup of tea. Grateful for the purposeful roar of the primus, that displays a blue flame which draws the darker ends of the cabin together.

While standing in the companionway, drinking the sweet tea, looking to the south'ard at the unfamiliar stars, something fondles the back of my neck, and is gone - but if it's coming, it'll come again soon.

and here it is again
a delicious tickle
a breeze

Down with the tea, climb on the coachroof, heaving away like a madman. Up go the silvery sheets. Back to the cockpit; take hold of the tiller to coax her through a flat patch. A quick trip below for extra clothing, then settle down for hour after hour of cat and mouse play with a zephyr of a breeze; an air that Mike's rough and ready vane can barely register, let alone master.

I like the feel of the tiller in my hand.

It's made of oak, solid and comforting.

Under the cloudless sky, through what remains of the night, we sail

116

tauntingly along.

It's not as dark as previously, just the time, before the time it starts to silver up the dawn. The moon is lower now and the rippling water has spread a path, with my eye drawn to, and by, the glint of dancing moonbeams.

Suddenly, I'm alert, all sleepiness gone, because there's a shadow in the moon's reflection, low against the glitter.

It's gone again, swallowed by the still dark sea, but I'm certain it's a ship, and near enough on the same course as ourselves.

It's noticeably lighter, and I can swear there's the shadow of a vessel, two points on the port bow.

Another ten minutes pass and the eastern horizon has paled the dawn, but it's still dark overhead.

However, I'm sure there's a vessel, not showing a light.

I can hear a low rumble of machinery, which sounds strange and menacing after the entertaining dream of a night. I'm standing in the cockpit, straining my eyes to identify the stranger. I must fetch the binoculars, but by the time I've gone below, cleaned the eyepieces and the object glass, it is halfway light astern, yet just glim enough for'ard to shroud the detail ahead.

The rumble has stopped and I have to sweep the optics from side to side in an endeavour to pick up, whatever it is.

Got it.

Can't be a ship (too low in the water, and not a sign of a light).

It can't be a whale (that low rumble has just restarted).

Another look through the glasses, and I know what it is.

It's a ruddy submarine.

It comes as a complete surprise.

I haven't seen one at sea for years.

During the war (World War 2) I grew to hate the damned things and the endlessly freezing stand-to watches that their threatening presence required. Staring, hour after hour, for the telltale track of an approaching torpedo. All those years of looking for the threatening bubbles; and then, when you are blown arse over head, it comes as a complete surprise, because the vessel concerned, the *Ascanious*, was not blown up by a torpedo, but a stray magnetic mine.

Taking note now of the low shape, with its characteristic fin, all the old revulsion comes flooding back.

I remember some of my shipmates.

The voyage after I had left to join another vessel, they had been caught in the Indian Ocean by a patrolling submarine. After the ship had been torpedoed and sunk, with the surviving members of the crew scrambling into the lifeboats, the sub had surfaced and gunned them in a leisurely, but agonising manner. So I feel no affection at all for the thing I can see on the port bow.

Whose is it, anyway ?

American?

British ?

Even a Russian?

Having popped the question, I'm looking at the vessel with a little more interest. The breeze is still light and we're only making a bare knot through the water, so the sub must be stopped because we're definitely closing it.

It's lying motionless in the grey sea, hull black and glistening where the plates are wet. I can see two heads sticking out, just above the top of the fin, almost within hailing distance.

A few minutes more, and we are.

'Ahoy there.'

No reply (but we're closer now).

'Ahoy there !'

There's an answering wave from the sub.

Now I'm in a hell of a pickle (what am I going to say?).

What *do* you say to a submarine, when you meet it in the middle of the North Atlantic Ocean, by the first light of dawn, after you've spent a month or so alone?

'Good Morning.'

Another answering wave.

What am I going to say now? I feel, crazily, that I've exhausted my conversational gambits, but we've passed, and he's some fifty yards abaft the port beam, so I'll have to think of something damn quick or it's going to be too late, he'll be out of hailing distance.

'It's a fine day.'

I feel a proper idiot (it isn't broad daylight, anyway).

Another answering wave.

He isn't helping me much.
Why in the name of all that's nautical and friendly, doesn't he actually *say* something?

We're too far apart now for even a shouted conversation, with the fin silhouetted against the brightening eastern horizon, black, and menacing as ever - there's a brightly flashing light winking at me.

Dear God, he's Morsing me.

So I'm dashing below to get the torch, wondering if it will be bright enough to answer in the now rapidly advancing daylight. When I regain the deck he's still flashing away.

' ... short-long, short-long, short-long (AA, AA, AA).'

That's one thing you never forget (the general call sign) however long since you practised your Morse Code, so I give him an answering flash from the torch, which prompts him to stop calling, and start transmitting a message. I now find I'm so excited that beads of perspiration are forming on my forehead - he's sending much too quickly.

Slow down, Jack, slow down.

Yet he keeps on.

What the devil's the matter with me? I can read Morse (at least, I *could* read Morse). He's still on the first word, repeating it over and over again, and I still can't get it, my eyes starting to water with the strain.

' ... s-l-o-w-l-y ... p-l-e-a-s-e' (tapped out on my torch).

So he starts again, the light flicking on and off, off and on, on and off, sending out the code at less than half the normal speed, yet regardless of the care he's taking, it still doesn't mean a thing. I could burn with exasperation, while I give him another flash, hoping to get him started on the next word. I can't read it (sweating, having difficulty with my sight) it's hard to tell whether my eyes are watering from the strain of trying to decipher the message, or filling with tears of exasperation.

I make one last effort, but it's no good, and after a while the signaller on the sub packs it in.

I'm mortified.

I wish the ocean would swallow me up. I'm the one who keeps floating; he's the one who slowly sinks beneath the surface, offering the aspect of a judgement - and who could blame him?

I'm bitterly ashamed of my performance.

Can't read a simple Morse message.

I think I should be shot. Postpone the fatal moment by throwing the torch down on my bunk. There's a satisfying thud as it bounces off the mattress and hits the for'ard bulkhead.

And I don't care if it has broken the glass.

It's breakfast time: who the hell wants breakfast? Not me. My mouth's as dry as a cork, indicating (signalling?) it's time for a slug of gin, spiced with lime and just a little water. What a time to start drinking. I've never done it before in my life, not even after the wildest party have I ever taken a slug of the 'hair of the dog' the next morning.

Nevertheless, I swallow a long pull of the gin - it tastes bitter, yet not as bitter as I feel.

I'm sure those on board the sub must think me a proper prat. [1]

Can't read baby-talk Morse !

Another uplifted tipple of gin, and down goes the mug with a bang on the cast-iron stove. The handle comes off and is left dangling from my index finger as an oversize and somewhat embarrassing ring.

The gin is burning my empty stomach, quickening my blood.

My neck is getting warm, my ears are tingling, my head is gettinglighter, starting to spin; must get quickly into my sleeping bag, worming down to the bottom, pulling the hood over my head.

(1) *Rough seafaring types will know that a 'prat is some way between a prick and a twat, but not necessarily indicative of the sexual orientation of the person being described.*

Who cares if we suffocate?

Let's have a good stum-down.

In a few minutes I'm floating in an alcoholic haze; and after a few more, I'm asleep.

It's the same day, still Friday morning.

I have a head on me the size of a bucket, only just managed to get up before the sun is too high for a reliable longitude. And when I do make the observation, it takes three times as long as it normally does to complete the simple mathematics.

Back to the bunk during the forenoon, and by midday feeling a little better. Reliable Mike has managed fairly well on his own during my drunken slumber, and the poor day's run of merely fifty-six miles can hardly be laid at his door.

After the noon sights 37° 56′ North, 34° 38′ West, log reading 1,670 miles, the breeze, which has held nor'westerly, falls light and variable again. So I give Mike a much needed spell, and while at the tiller take a look around the horizon (no sign of the sub, thank God).

The breeze, which has given signs of not knowing from which point to blow, eventually settles in the sou'west, so I tack ship. Twenty minutes later the breeze flies up to the nor'west, and I have to fly up on deck myself to put the boat about again (no good sailing in the wrong direction). Half-an-hour later back it goes to the south'ard again.

'… why can't you make up your mind.'

By seven in the evening the Old Man seems to have done so. Eventually deciding on sou'west by south, which is fine and dandy because it allows us to make due west.

Another fine night, clear skies, full moon (no submarine) and no radio, because for some reason or other, all the English language programmes are escaping the ionosphere and what we are left with, in this particular spot, is a jangling wail of stuff from the other side of Suez.

I feel I'm better off without it.

All I ever had from that part of the world was a bad case of athlete's foot. An irritation of skin lice, known to the cognoscente as 'crabs'. And a debilitating fungus colonizing my inner ear as the result of swimming too often in the polluted waters of the shit laden Suez Canal; but apart from that, the moon is full, the breeze holds steady, the swell is long and comfortably low.

Who wants canned music?

The sea and boat between them are constructing their own concerto.

The broad 'cello of the swell provides the depth and feeling into which the pleasant tenor of the bow can rise and fall; with this encouragement, the rigging sighs a rich contralto, vocal to the passage of the mild night air - all we lack is a bit of Welsh harmony.

I sing

nothing more, 'nor anything less
than a bold Jack-donkey
peeing loud and long on a corrugated drum of reverberating tin

I blush
and henceforth
resolve to keep my mouth tight shut

I've not been sleeping at all well this past week, but lie awake, hour after hour, with nothing to do except think. Then think a little more, finding my imagination running wild, and have to spend more time than I should trying to control these escalating thoughts.

I've noticed that I sleep better after a good hot meal. Unfortunately those culinary highlights are only appearing every other day, due to the shortage of the dehydrated foodstuffs (sometimes the cook can only get it together every third day). No matter, it's noticeable that after a bellyful of grub I can hit the sack and sleep a good six hours.

During the early part of this passage, the first time I enjoyed a really long zizz, I worried about it for the best (worst?) part of the following day, being concerned about the likelihood of being run down during the long night watches.

When did we last see a ship (is it eleven days or twelve?). It's a considerable time gone by, and many, many miles ago.

What are the chances of sighting a vessel today?

During this night?

During, say, the next six hours?

Even if there *is* a sighting, the chances of passing close-to are remote, so let's have a bellyful of grub and then make sure we get our collective heads down.

As a matter of fact, the catering staff on this old hooker are reasonably well up to the job.

'... it's nice of you to say so.'

(think nothing of it) did you put those sliced potatoes into the half-pint of boiling water, coming-up to twenty minutes ago?

'… of course I did.'

I hope you remembered to use a third salt water.

'… do you think I'm daft ?'

What are we having now?

'… minced beef, sliced carrots, broad beans, and of course the spuds.'

Sounds great.

'… don't worry; it will be - even if the deck wallahs on this old tub can't read Morse - the cook's a long way from being a bum.'

Can I give you a hand?

'… well, yes. Catering sometimes does present a problem for a single-handed sailor. For starters, you can open that packet of dehydrated beef.'

What shall I do with it?

'… (shove it up your) well, better not. Just put the stuff into a saucepan of cold water, then place it on the stove and let it come to the boil.'

Why cold water?

'… don't ask me; write to the Min of Ag & Fish.'

What else can I do?

'… put the beans and carrots into the pan of boiling water.'

What else?

'… take the pan off the stove, and let it stand for five minutes.'

Good God, it's complicated, isn't it?

'… we're not halfway there yet. Is the beef bubbling ?'

Coming to the boil - how long does it have to simmer?

'… about ten minutes. Don't turn the stove down, just push the saucepan to the back burner.'

Is it time to put the beans and carrots on?

'... just about. Stick 'em on the front of the stove, so they'll come quickly.'

Isn't it a good job I'm giving you a hand.

'... for heaven's sake, stop talking, you're breaking my concentration.'

Are they done yet?

'... no.'

How much longer?

'... not long now.'

Another two minutes?

'... if you keep bothering me, how in hell do you expect me to turn out a good meal ?'

Sorry.

'... if you want to make yourself useful, you can open that packet of diced apple. This other stuff is nearly ready. As soon as there's a free saucepan, put an ounce of apple in it, and just cover it with fresh water.'

You're using quite a lot of fresh water aren't you?

'... yes; but for hell's sake, keep quiet while I dish up. Just pass me that perforated spoon.'

Those carrots look good, and the beans are a nice colour.

'... I'm glad you approve.'

Here's my plate.

'... wait your turn, you greedy bastard.'

Great Scott - you're not going to eat all that !

'... I am, you know. And the diced apple. And a tot of brandy later.'

What about me? There'll be none left for me !

'... you ? Who the devil are you ?'

There's only one of us aboard this hooker, mate.

'… and that happens to be.'

Me/*me*

9

alone
all, all alone
but are you sure ?

Still the wind holds westerly, up four points to nor'west, down four points to sou'west, but always the same quadrant.

It's driving me mad.

Close-hauled to windward, day after day after day.

And then the nights.

Lying as a mummy in my sleeping bag, body jammed against the vessel's side, not stirring for hour after hour after hour.

I can't persuade myself it's worthwhile getting up to look for a passing hooker. It's thirteen days since we saw another vessel.

There *are* no other ships.

Only mine, and me, in it.

This is a little-used part of the ocean, three hundred miles west of the Azores, out of the major shipping lanes. Yet wouldn't it be reasonable to assume that some east-west traffic would pass this companionable way, say on passage from Gibraltar to New York?

Possibly eastbound commercials, from Nova Scotia to the sunnier shores of the Med? There *must* be other traffic, particularly between the U.K. and South America. There are thousands of ships plying their trade about the oceans of this world. Millions of tons of shipping, criss-crossing from port to port. Giving jobs to their crews. Making money for their owners. Providing work for their builders.

And the necessary maintenance. Refitting in dry dock, scaling, painting, prettying 'em up for passengers. There are armies of people traversing the ocean right this very minute, yet none pass this excruciating point. There's only me, crawling to the west'ard in my five-ton tomb. Bidding fair to join the Flying Dutchman; condemned to sail this stretch of water 'til the world shudders to a halt. Spins its oceans to the heavens; leaving the poor old universe with the wizened face of a monkey, from whence we all can start again.

but not me
I'll be sailing on
on and on to the moon
where there's no welcoming harbour

nevertheless, on I drive
depart the planet's swirling orb
and after an aeons sail
I'll be becalmed

within a day's sail of the shores of eternity
but, search though I may, having made the landfall
fail to find a sheltered bay in which to set the vessel's hook
so I sit, forlorn, hugging my body with my mind

... what's my wife doing in Saundersfoot ?

... happy ?

... sad ?

... thinks I'm drowned (too level-headed for that).

... looking after the children.

... how are the children?

... that delightful little nipper, Christopher; what a difficult confinement for Eira, caused by nervous tension the Doc said.

... yes, me. I'm the bum that brought it all about; could have been a blue baby; Rhesus Factor all *wrong.*

... shouldn't have come on this damned silly trip.

... what am I doing here?

Great jumping catfish, we're all at it now.

Only part of the trouble is the feeling of guilt at leaving my wife ('what am I doing here' is open to so many interpretations), more to the point is - what am I doing in *this* particular spot?

Three hundred miles west of the Azores, taking the low-powered steamer route from Plymouth to New York, while I am supposed to be *racing* across the Western Ocean.

Blondie, Francis and David are going north-about, and everyone thinks it's possible to do the trip in thirty days.

Hell, I've been at sea thirty days already, and only have not much more than half the distance made good.

Another thirty days to go.

Not only will I be tail-end Charlie
 I'll be fit to be tied when I dock.
If I dock.

… you'll dock all right.

How can you be so sure?
There's a devil of a long way to sail. The best part of two thousand miles. A lot can go wrong; even now, the tinned grub is getting low.
We only stocked the ship for forty-five days, with a couple of odds and ends thrown in at the last minute. Thank God there's plenty of water, you can go a long time without food. You've had it in five days without water.
And the wind.
It's stuck in the west all the miserable time.
Westerly, always westerly.
It's blowing my nerves to tatters.
 I'd rather it blew a screaming gale from any direction than this Beaufort force 4 to 6 the whole of this close-hauled slog.
We haven't had anything approaching a severe gale during the passage, which is, presumably, the one advantage of the low-powered route; headwinds, but moderate conditions and time to lounge in the sun.

'… the trouble is, we're not a low-powered steamer.'

Just beating our brains out, while the other guys are doing well. No doubt having their share of adverse weather, but they'll be encountering greater variety up north. Look how many times we've been becalmed.

There are only two sorts of wind down here .

' … Paddy's hurricane (up and down the mast) or the same blasted westerly.'

How far to New York?

'… nearly two thousand miles.'

Good God, another month at sea.

' … why don't we put into Bermuda ?'

What's that?

' *... put into Bermuda: we're not far from that latitude, and you've got to take note of the Gulf Stream.'*

Isn't it a bit like giving up?

' *... not at all, we're passing the place, you deserve a look in.'*

It's not a bad idea, though we should keep going to New York.

' *... don't bother to decide right now; see what the weather does.'*

You may be right.

'*... you persuasive, devious, weak-willed, gutlesss, snivelling bastard.'*

The next day is Sunday, the tenth of July; moderate sea, moderate to heavy swell, overcast, with a light drizzle, reasonably good visibility.

After being horizontal all night, it takes some seventy strokes of the pump to clear the bilge, and that's a lot of water in a small boat.

We're still close-hauled to the westerly breeze (surprise, surprise) yet I'm not quite so depressed as previously. The task of attempting to get a sight under adverse conditions has taken me out of myself, and not before time.

I spent the best part of an hour over the A.M. observation.

The gaps in the heavy overcast being few and far between, the sun only appears for a second or two, and we seem fated to be in a trough when he does. Or a crest interferes with the horizon. Or I'm just not quick enough to get the old orb down where he should be. However, even these failures have a bright side because - it's given me something to do.

Though it's overcast, it's warm; 38 ° North (the latitude of sunny Seville).

The sea is noticeably warmer, with the spray just bearable on my skin as I stand in the hatchway, sheltering my sextant, waiting for another elusive shot at the sun.

During the afternoon, as I carefully digest my frugal lunch, while lying as usual on the bunk, I hear what sounds like a hand, slapping its palm on the surface of the ocean. It doesn't sound threatening, could even have been an unruly dollop striking the topside of the boat.

I keep to my bunk, with my ears pinned back.

Hear it again (difficult to identify) the same watery slap, not in or about the boat - something concerned with the sea itself.

Out on deck to have a look.

Not a thing in sight.

The breeze has eased, leaving a moderate sea to enhance the westerly swell.

The sky is clearing, allowing the sun to shine through a broken panoply of cloud.

The sea looks grand as ever. A brilliant blue, with the usual crests flashing self-satisfied smiles at each other as they curl and curtsy to the roll of the oncoming swell.

Another good look round the horizon, then back below.

... there it goes again

... something slapping the surface of the ocean

I might be hearing things (mustn't forget to put it down in the medical log).

... climb out of the companionway, on to the coachroof

... it's amazing how much further you can see, if you increase your height of eye, even by six feet

There is something ahead, my ears haven't deceived me (hard luck the medical log). There are several large shapes, half-a-mile away, fine on the starboard bow.

... easily recognisable

They are whales (great whales for a Welshman). There must be a dozen or more. They don't seem to be going anywhere, just cruising around, blowing away, mucking about as fountains in a fairground; practicing keeping ping-pong balls aloft for us country lads to shoot at.

They're moving to the nor'ard and drawing ahead, so we'd better ease off a point, to give 'em a little more sea room. As they come abreast our starboard beam, must keep a sharp eye lifted.

I thought the shark was big.

My God, these lads are gigantic. Some of them are hove-to, maybe sleeping, their immense bulk lying carelessly awash, others are cruising around.

They look harmless enough. And it's fortunate they're docile, if one of them swam in our direction and opened his mouth, that would be the end of Howells boat and all.

Two of them, a little distant from the rest, lie in the water facing one another, their heads overlapping, seemingly whispering in each other's ear.

The nearest raises an immense tail, flukes as big as the Folkboat, brings it down on the water with what for him or her is just a gentle tap (that's probably what I heard in the first instance).

Up goes his/her tail again, then down, a good firm slap.

Up in the air again, held longer aloft, then down it comes, crashing on the passing swell with the noise of a cracking whip.

Great founts of water are being thrown in the air.

His/her mate raises her/his tail - up it goes.

Down.

Two great kids, splashing water at each other, spooning (slap, bang, make love to me Sam).

They're not far away. I could disturb them with a well-thrown stone. They're oblivious of our passage. Not so with the others; one in particular, who has left the school is cruising quietly abeam, and unless I'm very much mistaken has been detailed-off to look-see and report to the rest of the pod.

What can you do, or say, when ten (twenty?) (thirty?) (forty?) tons of inquisitive mammal, decides to ascertain you friend or foe?

'… good afternoon.'

Loud and clear. We don't want to mumble it, and give him an excuse for an even closer look do we?

'… ain't it a fine sunny day ?'

And it is.

I'm getting nervous. He's much too close and quietly closing the range. So I start edging the boat down to the south'ard; a point, then another, freeing sheet, so she picks up speed until we're near enough running downwind. And it seems to have done the trick. He's dropping astern, turning, giving me the rear view of a huge body, tapering, then widening again to that gigantic tail. I breathe a sigh of relief as we leave him clear astern.

The lovebirds are still at it, slapping and banging away, sending spray high in the air (who knows, maybe they're just married, and this is their first disagreement?). I just hope I'm not around for their first real fight. Although I wouldn't mind a peek at

'… let's kiss and be friends.'

The breeze has shifted sou'westerly and we've tacked ship. It's another bright moonlight night, moderate breeze with a slight sea and the inevitable swell. We're making good just north of west and it's peaceful enough (no whales, just noises as before) still slogging to windward, still close-hauled, fiddling about with the radio.

The reception is variable; sometimes the Arabs have the monopoly of the airwaves, then they're driven back by the infidels of the Western world, even a couple of Canadian stations come in.

No newscasts, for which I am profoundly glad, just a little light music, which is acceptable. However, before I get emotionally involved, the Arabs are back, caterwauling away and that's the end of that.

Many strokes of the pump to clear the bilge, and it's only an hour or two since it was previously pumped.

An increase in the rate?

Could be, hard to tell. There's only one way to make sure, and that's to start logging times and the number of strokes.

Why bother?

Even if I measured the exact amount put back in its place, it wouldn't do a thing to arrest the 'oggin's entry. There'll just be another thing to worry about - mustn't make a fetish of it, just keep the boat as dry as we can.

'… but it's in the back of your mind, isn't it ?'

Yes, I suppose it is, along with a lot of other worries.

'… such as ?'

Oh, I don't know. All this started while we were lying here in the dark (not the same temptation to morose-about in the day) it's the nights that are long.

'… what else have you got on your mind ?'

Just wondering where the others are.

'… you're always on about them. Give it a rest for a while. They've probably got problems of their own.'

That's true, one of them may bump into a 'berg.

'… do I detect a note of hope in your voice ? That sounded a very naughty little thought to me.'

No: I honestly hope to God nobody comes unstuck. If they do, it will put an end to this race for another twenty years.

'... *you think so ?'*

Certain of it: mustn't have a fatality at this stage in the game.

'... *if that's the case, you'd better pull your finger out sunny-boy; get up and see if it's clear ahead.'*

You do it, it's your turn.

'... *you lazy bastard.'*

Up on deck, I find, with relief, the darkness in retreat. The sea peeling dawn. The speckled night skin forced back by the finger that set the spinning top in motion. The hands are busy with a brush. Whitening the canvas. Lazily applying a pale pink wash (why hurry, when you've got all the time in the world?). Applying a quicker stroke. Plashing brilliant blue about an ocean that's reflected in the arch and reach of the sky. More colour now. Daubs of startling hues, squirted with Neptune-like relief, spreading with the speed of light to the final.

Eye-dazzling.

'... *click.'*

The sun has risen.

Only the tantalizing, rapidly enlarging lip of the upper limb, yet signalling it's time for breakfast.

' ... *then on with the chores of the day.'*

It's two weeks to the day we last spoke a ship.

Two weeks, during which I've grown more anxious with each passing hour. Spending more time in the cockpit. Keeping an eye open for shipping. Once in a while, a faint smudge on the horizon indicates a vessel hull down, but so few of these have materialised that though I note their presence, they hardly raise much hope.

Very occasionally, perhaps twice during the past fourteen days, a ship has been in sight, maybe seven miles distant, tantalisingly on a track nearly parallel with our own and moving in the same direction. It's hopeless trying to attract the attention of the watchkeepers on these vessels, intent as they are on their own commercial business.

What mate, the second officer of any ocean-going steamship, keeps to the wing of the bridge while in the middle of the Western Ocean, searching the horizon for a small boat's sail?

Not one: during the night, and in thick weather, the radar is scanning, and that device is being relied on.

What chance does a small wooden boat stand of being identified, on a twelve-mile radar range scale, displaying the usual clutter conditions of ocean-going sea and swell?

None.

'… what chance have I, of sighting a passing ship? During the next twelve hours?'

If I had asked myself this question during the night, the answer would have come out pat.

'… absolutely zero.'

It's daylight, after an inspiring dawn, a cup of tea, an empty bilge and a satisfactory sight (all substantial morale boosters). I feel, although the chances of seeing a vessel are slight, they are still there; hanging in my mind as a curtain of doubt between the forces of hope and despondency.

During the forenoon I'm up and down in the cockpit, full of an unwanted expectancy, while at the same time knowing I would be far better off if I could take it slow and easy below.

The breeze is moderate. A small amount of spray is being thrown for'ard of the companionway hatch, which means the afterdeck remains dry and I can sit out in shorts and sunglasses.

As we're crawling to the south'ard, the sun is climbing, presenting, as it does so, a dazzling reflection on and off the flash and glint of the sea.

The cabin soon gets hot and stuffy. Most of the below deck kit is wet or covered with salt, and this, acting as a special sort of Neptunian wick, is boosting the humidity, even though the hatches are open in an effort to maintain a draft of cooler air.

When the sun's height reaches respectable proportions, the cabin seems to get smaller, more demanding of its space, forcing me, the interloper, out on the zephyr-swept deck.

This 'out in the fresh air' requirement, as well as the duty of keeping a sharp lookout for a steamer, gets me sitting in the cockpit, usually down to leeward, long legs stretched out on the seat, feet up against the after-coaming.

One of the things to watch for is sunburn - it won't do to get blistered out here, skin unwashed for days on end. Whenever I think of it, I'm reminded of the scourge of saltwater boils I once experienced in the tropics. That would be a diabolical complaint while sailing single-handed, but so far, my skin seems healthy, with my body much nearer normality than my winkle picking mind.

During the day, I can sit out, dream, and speculate with an outward appearance of calm. The eye providing some sort of balm to the brain.

The sea, fascinating as ever, is an unwearying blue. I notice it has floating in it brownish patches of something or other.

It's difficult to identify.

As we sail past, the bow wave throws an irritating mixture of spray and bubbles which camouflage the stuff.

As the blobs are left astern, supported by the blue of the ocean and the sparkle of the sea, they look brown and not very attractive; reminding me of circular pats of cow dung on a well-cropped pasture at home. Not out of place, but hardly to be sought after.

Nevertheless, I'm soon fishing with the boathook, to the alarm of those small fish which have been following the boat for so many half-forgotten days they've become an accepted part of the scene.

As I stab the dark brown blobs, which are about the size of footballs, little fish dart away.

leaves
before a breeze
being blown away

yet
still retaining
an attractive pattern of their own

It's more difficult than first imagined to spear one of these strange clumps. Part of the trouble lies in the boat's movement through the water. Not so much the speed - even those that lie in our path are moved, by the bow wave, beyond what amounts to 'spearable' reach.

It's exasperating.

Time and time again, when I see a nice brown patch directly ahead of the boat, I stand by, boathook at the ready, as a pikeman poised for battle. Then, on every occasion, as the boat cleaves her way through the 'oggin, she moves the tempting stuff either just out of reach or sucked below the surface.

There seems little hope of success from the after end of the boat, so

I move up for'ard, first taking off my clothes and throwing them down below.

It's not much fun sitting in damp gear, and anyway, I'm a real nature boy - now I'm free of critical eyes.

Up for'ard I go, lying on the foredeck, legs each side of the coachroof. Head and shoulders cantilevered over the stem. One hand grasping the pulpit for steadying support, the other holding the boathook as a pig-sticking spear ahead.

'... *if anyone was watching now.*'

If anyone *was* watching, say from an accompanying boat, I would be a hairy figurehead, imitating Neptune himself, advancing his trident expectantly ahead of the vessel.

'... *so.*'

Exhilarating !

Being carried over the surface of the ocean, which is swept astern at surprising speed. The dark blobs are passing more frequently, and I start fishing in earnest, lunging at them as a lancer at a peg.

When the boathook enters the water, it's pushed hard against my arm and is difficult to hold (after a little practise, I learn to aim-off). Although I think I'm scoring hits, I realise that the phenomena of refraction is distorting the line of sight I'm relying on.

How do I allow for that?

Must take a rest and think it out (my arm is tired anyway).

Put the boathook down on deck, alongside my right leg, and move astern a little (now only have my head ahead of the Folkboat's stem).

It really is the most marvellous place to lie.

The movement of the hull is accentuated - we rise and fall as if on the end of a see-saw.

'... *not a common or garden see-saw.*'

One of Neptune's Sea Saws.

'... *up and over the swell.*'

Tracing out a sine wave.

'... *with the splash and surge of the briny.*'

Where, previously, I had lain on my bunk, hardly conscious of the motion, which on many occasions has been far greater than at present.

'… now I'm lying on the foredeck.'

My life is *all* motion.

'… continually forward.'

Astride these cantering horses.

'… over the welcoming blue of the sea.'

I feel very much part of my surroundings (is the fact that I'm naked, anything to do with this stroke of nautical intimacy?).

'… I think it probably is.'

The sun on my back is warm. At regular intervals she dips a little quicker and throws a cloud of fine bright spray. My head and shoulders stay dry, some of the drops, instead of falling as they normally would on the foredeck, touch the small of my back as a more than cool caress.

'… they also land on the upturned curve of my bum.'

The spots tapping playfully as a score of fun-tipped fingers.

'… while the sun warms me, she sprays more of the cool blue sea.'

My shoulders are getting hot, so I turn over, wriggling a little further aft 'til my head is inboard of the stem.

The sun is hard in my eyes, and I have to shield them with a forearm raised, not in anger, but delight. The good old orb is marvellously warm on my belly.

She dips again, up goes the spray, and now I can see it, my pleasure is immensely heightened.

The slam of the bow spouts the drops above the gunwale and as the sun catches them, these gems sparkle as they form a small but brilliant rainbow.

Some are carried over the boat, others fall on my belly and my groin. It seems impossible that anything so colourfully vivacious could feel so cool and, I must admit, at the same time, stimulating (*what would Thurber say now?*).

I'm completely relaxed for the first time in days, perhaps weeks.

Who knows?

My emotions are fluctuating with such alarming frequency that I lose count of phase and inclination.

My body feels fine, taut, and leanly fit.

After twenty minutes of this ocean-going caress, I'm starting to feel cold. Regretfully get up and, with the boathook, make my way aft, having to recognise that here, as everywhere, nature balances her gifts with meticulous care.

'... give a little.'

Take a little.

'... emulating the seductive movement of the sea caressing boat - boat caressing sea ?'

I still haven't managed to spear any of the tantalising flora, past which we're still sailing. So I make one more determined attack, a'midships this time, feet on the gunwale, one leg inside and one leg outside the lifelines. A hand securely gripping the main shroud. Leaning outboard now, intent on capturing one of these balls of maritime mystery.

Leaning outboard?

Yes: I know I should be wearing safety harness, but somehow, feeling as I do so much at one with the boat, it hardly seems worth the trouble of going below and rigging myself out. In any case, you look a bit of a mug, stark naked but for a safety harness.

The nylon retaining cord is inclined to dangle embarrassingly past your belly button, brushing the tip of your dick. I must keep a firm grip on the rigging *(and myself)* with one hand for the ship, and another *(perhaps not quite such a virtuous one?)* for Howells.

'... we're still passing the dark-brown blobs.'

I have yet to capture the stuff, but can identify it.

'... nothing more, nor less, than very ordinary.'

Weed.

I've spent an enjoyable, even if frustrating morning, and now it's time to do the navigational chores. When I look at the log, to read the distance run between sights, I notice it's stopped spinning.

The line is still there, trailing astern of the boat, but no rotation, so I unhitch the inboard end and haul the line in, hand-over-hand, over-hand.

It seems heavier than usual.

I can see the spinner, which has been brought to the surface, so keep pulling until it's within a few feet of the boat and I can identify what's wrapped around it.

' ... *it's foul with.'*

Guess what?

' ... weed.'

Hauling the quarry aboard, I can indulge in a quiet smile. A whole morning spent hunting the stuff, even to the extent of hanging outboard at risk of life and limb (not really) and all the time there's a log-clogging bundle being towed astern of the boat.

Clearing the spinner, I re-stream it, and then have a good look at the strange stuff which lies on the cockpit sole.

It is weed, but with a difference.

Not as dark brown as it looks in the water, more of a lime green.

There's no colour graduation between the stem and the leaf of the plant, its body seems to serve both needs, while here and there are grape-like clusters.

Trying to tear the stuff apart, I find it tough and wiry. The explanation for its clinging presence on the rotator of the log.

I hang it in the rigging to dry, emulating the feeling of a person who may press a commemorating flower between the leaves of a well-loved book.

Then down below to find out where we are.

Another small step has been made to the west'ard, the thirty-first day of the voyage and the fourteenth since the last message home. However, I must admit the pleasures of the morning have almost driven that thought from my head.

Is this short freedom from guilt, the springboard that prompted my feeling of well-being?

No matter, I'm now back in the same old rut, head out of the companionway hatch, looking for a steamer.

Nothing in sight.

I feel certain there's a vessel around somewhere.

But perhaps I'm confusing this with the new feeling of confidence, which is so rare I seem virtually a new man.

Everything feels right this afternoon.

Everything, that is, except the wind, but as that's been in the same quarter for a month or more, give or take a few favourable spells, I now regard it as more or less a fixture.

It's the middle of a scorching afternoon, so I can do a little more sunbathing, keeping a weather-eye lifted, and while lounged on the deck become aware there's a faint smudge of smoke on the horizon, yet at the same time not being in the least surprised that it's there.

As I look, it disappears.

Perhaps this is a clue to the source of the feeling, that we would sight a ship today?

'*... maybe you have already seen a trace of smoke, out of the corner of your unconscious eye ?'*

How else explain it?

'*what about the occasion, during the earlier part of the passage, when you got up just in time to avoid the tug and its tow.'*

I think maybe this solitary experience is sharpening my senses, which are now able to make better use of.

'*... extra-sensory perception ?'*

Or was it just luck, when I woke in time to avoid the tug?

'*... maybe you heard the rumble of her engine, or the cascade of water as she cleared her deck of a sea ?'*

Who knows?

'*... the only certainty is, you've been expecting a vessel all morning, and now there is one, right astern, but still not in sight.'*

I can wait.

While doing so, I get the flags out (good old M.I.K., still ready and willing), pull on a pair of clean blue jeans (can't have them seeing me looking scruffy).

Another look astern. More smoke, fine on the port quarter; the vessel herself is still hull down, maybe over twelve miles distant.

Now let's see, he's the overtaking ship, let's say he's doing fourteen knots, we are doing four, giving him a closing speed of ten knots (a mile every six minutes if you prefer).

I judge him to be about thirteen miles astern, that puts his E.T.A. abeam at about one hour and eighteen minutes from now.

'... how can you be so sure ?'

Shutup and stick to the catering. I'm doing the navigating aboard this hooker. Go below and make a cup of tea, we've still got plenty of time.

Twenty minutes go by, while we enjoy a nice pot of tea and a chat, concerning the accuracy or otherwise of the visitor's E.T.A.

'... how much do you bet, on half-an-hour either way ?'

Don't bother me, for heaven's sake. Be quiet. I never gamble, you know that.

After another look out of the hatch, I can see that he's still hull down. Topmasts and the upper part of a funnel are visible - by the angle between his masts, he's going to pass a mile or two to the south'ard, so we'd better alter course now, to make sure of speaking to him.

After another twenty minutes, I can just make out the whole of his upperworks, and even more when I stand on the coachroof. Our alteration of course has brought him on our port beam, he's still seven miles off. I can see that he's a tanker - we couldn't have been far out when estimating his speed, and we're closing nicely, everything going according to plan.

'... don't be so cocky.'

(the next ten minutes are spent looking for a comb and a mirror)

'... when did you last use them ?'

When we had a bath, remember?

'... I do, but how long ago was that ?'

Too long, mate, far too ruddy long.

Eventually I find the comb. The mirror seems lost forever (and I'm the guy who boasts he's completely at one with the boat) someone who knows every little quiver, every subtle movement, and I can't find the blasted mirror.

'... like a lot of men, mate: you think you know, but there's one hell of a lot

you don't know, right ?'

Right.

At length, after getting into a bit of a flap, because I don't want them to catch me with my beard and hair all tangled, I get the sextant out and look in the index mirror (a little small, but very accurate) experiencing the shock of a lifetime when I see my own reflection.

Great Scott, can that be me?

'... see what I have to put up with, mate ? Having to live with that gargoyle as a constant and complaining companion.'

I really am a fright (needed a haircut and a beard trim before the passage started, over a month ago). But how did I get like this? Come to think of it, after the two baths of the trip so far, I didn't bother to view the body beautiful, just pulled a comb through my locks and left it at that. Even when I trimmed my moustache I did it by 'feel'.

'... and nearly cut the end off your nose, when she lurched at that awkward moment.'

Nothing daunted, I spruce myself up and get out on deck for this State Occasion. He's only three miles away, and through the binoculars I can make out his colours. A light grey hull, white upperworks and a jazzy yellow funnel - a pound to a penny he's a Scandinavian.

'... taken.'

I reckon we're just about dead ahead of him now, time to alter course, back to our original heading, this puts him fine on the port quarter, just as it should be.

She's a grand sight, swept bow creaming through the ocean, what she can't cleave, she rolls ahead, spilling out on either bow as a tumbling froth of wave. On the upper part of her stem she has a well-designed and brightly painted motif. A nice thing this, which the Swedes and Norwegians are very fond of doing; not as good as a generously busted figurehead, yet still well worth the effort.

Now I'm itching to get those three little flags close-up on the halyard. I must wait, no sense doing it too soon, *must* wait 'til he can see them going up, so he'll know it's a signal and not a line of washing.

He's within half-a-mile. There's the second mate out on the wing of the bridge.

Strewth, he's bringing her even closer (hold on, mate, not too close) up go the flags, fluttering gaily, happy to be out of their canvas roll.

He's having a damned good look.

Hell's delight, he's coming even closer. The quartermaster has given her too much helm and she's swung to starboard. The mate is turning his head and giving the quartermaster a bollocking, and even though I can't hear what he's saying, I've no doubt about the gist of it.

He's right up on us now.

Her name is.

T.S. Peterson

Named after a person. I'm not keen on surnames for ships, preferring the wider application of a Christian (given?) name. And it's got to be a woman's.

. Who ever heard of a ship called Bert?

He's got the message.

He's going to wave. There's something in his hand, it looks like a loudhailer.

'… we have your message.'

The voice booms out. It seems the ship herself is speaking; very impressive, while I must be content with a wave.

'… anything you require?'

' Another wave (this time two hands crossing).

'… good luck.'

Another accepting wave, and he's passed.

A great feeling, sitting in the cockpit, having given and received a cheery wave from those members of the crew who are leaning over his taffrail.

He passed so close that we're now sailing in his wake. The sea strangely smooth on the surface, but seething just below.

I watch it for some time.

The clumps of weed are swirling around as if boiling in a cauldron, brought to the surface for a moment and then sucked down, out of sight in an instant.

I wonder idly whether it would be possible to swim in the wake of a fast ship. Offhand, I would say it might be a dodgy sort of a do, nevertheless, intend to try one day.

Damnation take it. I've been so absorbed by the movement of the sea in his wake I forgot to read the Port of Registry on his stern, and now he's gone too far, even with the aid of binoculars. Blast it, it will make a poor log entry. I feel even glummer as I watch him slide buoyantly hull down.

He took time to come up from astern, now seems to be receding at twice the rate of knots. Never mind, it's another message to Eira and the children back home.

Hurrah for The Observer (and that's the first hurrah for a month).

They (the owners of the paper) are paying the fee required by Lloyds of London for reporting through a ship.

I've always been an Observer reader, now I'm an addict.

how nice to be an addict
does it mean
that you have too much of something?

good or bad ?
if so
I'm addicted to single-handed ocean racing

oh brother, am I addicted
but I'm looking for a cure
what I need is movement

movement to the west'ard
westerly movement
sail through this coming night,

to turn back the page
on yet another day
the other side of turmoil

Night falls as the entrance to a tunnel: the days have become interludes that spread apart the dark.

The days have names and numbers - the nights are trackless wastes of time.

I hardly know which day it is, regardless of the fact that I'm careful to cross off the pages in the Almanac. It wouldn't do to lose track of the date, but the days, Monday, Tuesday, Wed'nes'day, Thuuursday, Friiiiidaaaay, Saaatuuuurdaaaay - what day is it now ?

145

I hardly know
what counts with me
is not the day

but those periods of darkness
which fall between the gridlock
of the hours

I attack the night as a swimmer, attempting underwater lengths of an immense pool. Drive myself to the end that's halfway (turns out to be little more than midnight). Then the lung-bursting return, gasping for air as my mind is for light. It seems an improbable task (lungs must burst) can't carry on. Coming up for air, I find a sheet of ice sealing off the surface, struggling and kicking (*must* carry on) swim, swim, swim, and then, at last, having passed the point of impossible achievement, struggle to the surface.

and it's dawn once more

Dawn, to another day, with the wind still westerly. The boat struggling to overcome this idiotic zephyr of a breeze that shuffles to the east'ard as if there never was another quarter of the world to plot a vessel's course to.

Only one thing relieves this rather special day. At seven o'clock in the evening, the log registers two thousand miles made good, and that's a long way to wind'ard in any man's mumbled use of language.

Then, again, it's night.

While sleeping, I'm sailing a ship that has masts as an endless road has telegraph poles. On each there sets a sail. They disappear into the distance, progressively smaller 'til they're but dots at the further point of an endless curve of decking. And I'm reefing these sails; working like a madman before a gathering storm (she carries too much canvas).

The deck's awash (I work waist-deep in water).

Out of the corner of my fractious eye I can see the sails I've reefed, maybe a hundred or more, being blown to ribbons before the advancing gale. We're overcome by darkness, and I'm awake (or am I awake?).

The cabin's as black as ever.

I'm a bug in the centre of a sack of soot (am I awake?). I can hear the wind (but the dream had wind) and the sound of water amid the flapping of a sail and the endless tear of canvas.

Dear God, I drift between conscious doubt and doubtful dream, while the sweat I lie in is not derived from the cabin's close embrace.

it's breaking dawn
I'm an Inca, worshipping the sun
shine down on me this day and never set

Whose turn is it to make breakfast?

'... you do it, while I pump the bilge.'

How many strokes was that?'

'... fifty-two.'

The sun's well up, and it's hot in the cabin. Out on deck, naked in the cockpit, I'm cutting toenails with the occasional drift of spray leaving a crackling rime of salt. Move to coachroof, lie on back, looking up at the boom and the curl of twisting sail.

... feeling stiff.

Back to the cockpit (sitting in it, as you would a bath) legs in the air, backside supported by elbow-propped hands in order to drive around the feet. Pedalling, round and around and around. Round and around and around. One hundred round, Two hundred round. Two hundred and fifty round. Two hundred and seventy-five round. Two hundred and eighty-five round. Two hundred and ninety, around, around, around and around. Two hundred and ninety-five, around, around, around and around. Ninety-six, ninety-seven, ninety-eight, ninety-nine, around and around and around.

three hundred, around and around and around

Sweating rivulets, off forehead, into beard, off chest, on to belly, from just about everywhere into crotch. All tacky with salt, but tired, thank God, tired. Kneel in the cockpit, grasping coamings, port and starboard, now.

heave
shining muscles
creaking tension
pounding ears
eyes shut
eyeballs red
belly straining
hamstrings twanging
let go

sun still shining
breeze still blowing
sea still running
man still living
boat still sailing
sun still shining
breeze still blowing

I know this sort of thing just will not do.

Although I'm short of physical exercise, I'm also suffering from a type of intellectual boil-up. My mind is buzzing like a bee and just as apt to land where it's not entirely welcome. So I'm stung to sharp awareness, that unless I bring myself up with a round turn, with or without the two half hitches, I run the risk of emulating the foo-foo bird, and you know what happened to him.

'… didn't he disappear up his own arse ?'

right first time

As I sit on the starboard cockpit seat, waiting for my better half (?) to return to what passes aboard this hooker as 'earth', I decide that I would be far better employed giving the boat a minute examination, rather than myself. So for'ard I go and start running a seaman's eye over the pulpit and various other items.

The inner and outer forestay anchorages are sound, although the threads of the bottlescrews are showing signs of rust, as are the lower parts of the stays themselves, particularly where the piston hanks have rubbed the galvanising off the mild steel wire by their passage up and down the stays.

The staysail we're using now is in reasonable repair, but not in very good shape. There's nothing we can do about that, apart from making a mental note to finish stitching the spare sail down below.

The for'ard hatch is still showing the split in the coaming caused by the enthusiasm of the naval type in Plymouth (and ain't that an age gone by?). Constantly deluged by spray, the crack shows dark, and this disfiguring patch is spreading under the varnish.

The coachroof coamings have also lost their shine.

The mast gleams dully white, covered by a spray-delivered, then sun-evaporated rather attractive crystalline layer of salt.

The stick looks good, together with its supporting shrouds; however, they are starting to rust at their deck ends and I must remember to wash them off and give them a coat of boiled linseed oil during the next spell of decent weather.

The side decks, having been sluiced hourly for thirty days on end are clean enough; here and there they carry a brown stain from the rusting iron fittings.

It's very pleasant out here on the coachroof.

A sunny afternoon.

We're still close-hauled, it's true, but now the march of pleasant air and rising temperatures have taken much of the sting out of this beat, and beat again. I suppose you can get used to anything in the end.

Mike is doing well, windward work is child's play to him, he's much better at it than I am, never dozes, and during the night he'll follow the wind shifts as a hound follows the scent of a fox. Just one snag, of course, they both follow regardless, and occasionally have to be whipped into their work.

I can stand now, admiring the way Mike keeps her footing, as I lean against the mast and look down into the sea.

The fish are still there, assorted shapes and sizes escorting me through, and in, their oceanic manor (manner?).

Some prefer swimming close to the hull; others keep an apparently respectful distance, nothing I can see keeps station ahead of the boat.

Looking for'ard, there are no fish. As she rises to the swell, I can see, directly ahead, a large object in the water.

Mike's limitations are now painfully exposed. If I don't go aft and take over the tiller we're going to ram this baulk of timber.

It's so pleasant out in the sun.

Maybe the breeze will back a shade, and we'll pass just clear of the log, or maybe Mike will pinch a bit, and we'll leave it on our port hand, either way we could miss it.

I can see it plainly now.

It just rose on the top of the swell, one end clear of the water for an instant.

It's a big piece of timber, wallowing sullenly in the sea.

There's a bird sitting on it.

'… what a pretty bird !'

Haven't seen many birds during this passage.

The first week, the usual gulls; then, as we made the most of our departure they seemed to lose interest, and for a long time we were without, apart from just a few when passing north of the Azores.

Now we have this bird, sitting on the end of this baulk of timber.

Mike hasn't done a damn thing about it, he's steering straight for the thing, the silly ass.

He'd better watch what he's doing.

Goodness me, that *is* an attractive bird. Some kind of gull, of a variety that doesn't visit the shores of Wales.

There are other, much smaller, darker birds fluttering around the log, tiny creatures. I know them well enough; they are Mother Carey's chickens.

Storm petrels, very attractive.

If we don't alter course soon, we're going to run them down and spoil their oceanic playground.

> *not far now*
> *the helm must go up soon*
> *or it'll be too late*
> **Mike**

Mike

> *great suffering catfish, Howells*
> *get your finger out of your arse*
> *and alter course*

I have to rush aft like a madman, stubbing toes on cleats, half-falling into the cockpit, fumbling with a fistful of thumbs to undo the tiller yoke (can't get the lee-side undone, so it's got to be the other line) that means must run her up to wind'ard. Hell's bells and buckets of blood, the damned log is lying athwart our course, anyway, here goes.

> *down goes the helm*
> *the bow swings to starboard*
> *(can't see the log)*

> *must be right under her forefoot*
> *the wait seems endless: now I can see it*
> *(missed it by inches)*

The sea lifts the boat, and for one agonised second it seems it's going to set her squarely on the end of the baulk.

A giant matchstick, thirty-five feet long if it's an inch; three foot square. A battering ram that would go through planking as a spoon would destroy the fragile shell of an egg.

The boat comes down, only a foot away, thankfully with sufficient way on her to clear the log. In a second it's on the quarter and I can pay off and refill the upset sails.

It's not only the sails that are disquieted. There are beads of sweat on my forehead and the back of my neck is prickling.

'… only by the Grace of God there, Howells.'

I know.

'… you must have been mad. Dreaming out there on the foredeck.'

I know.

'… you'd better come below and have a can of ale.'

At noon we are four minutes west of 40° West, so I'm due a can of beer and sit down to it with enjoyment. I also have a little cheese and the very last onion.

The passage has been started with a good pile of onions, however the fracas with the battery and the resulting spill of acid has damaged some, and I'm down to the lone survivor.

I look at it with regret (isn't just *one* of something a sad business?). It's a good onion, with a fair skin, a swelling orb, terminating in a tidy tip. Yet one of something, *one* of something, is just not a damned bit of good.

'… what about that baulk of timber ?'

That's just what I mean.

Did you notice how sullen it looked?

All on its own, being carried about the ocean by a current intent upon its business.

'… even wandering tree trunks have a useful purpose; it was at least providing a home for barnacles.'

Did you notice how numerous they were?

'… they covered every inch of space, except the side that floated uppermost to the sun. Thousands upon thousands of them - only one onion.'

It seems a pity to put it to the knife. The razor-sharp edge touching the golden skin. The clean cut, the first, crisp, peeling layer; off comes the hairy root, then the excruciating agony of its decapitated tit.

'*... now eat it.*'
You eat it.

'*... it's like biting a bit out of a breast.*'

It's only an onion.

The meal is a tear-drawn affair, during which I give thirty-five strokes on the pump - even though we're alone, there seems to be plenty wanting to join us (or maybe they want *us* to join them?).
I just lie on the bunk, my mind an unreconstructed blank.

'*... what about those Indian mystics who can sit on a bed of nails for a month.*'

That's the sort of mental attitude I require.

'*... what do they do ?*'

Just leave the body behind, sit on the spikes while the mind abdicates for the period of trial.

'*... stroll through a perfumed garden, while ignoring their predicament, which, to a normal person, would be absolute purgatory.*'

I wonder if I can do that?

'*... no need too wonder, lad; you've just done it.*'

So I have.

The beer can is rolling about the cabin sole. As she lifts and dips, it strikes, first to port, then to starboard, clinking and clunking, tipping and tapping, bonking and banging, rattling away with the persistence of clicking dice to a compulsive gambler.
At the beginning of the voyage, I would have been up like a shot and thrown it overboard within ten seconds. Even those noises from the bottom of a poorly-stowed locker used to get on my nerves. Now, I lie on my bunk and listen to the can roll from side to side, working its passage as a bubble in a builder's level.
It doesn't irritate me.
How can it?
I'm not actually *in* this length of skin and bone.

How is it possible for that stupid can to imagine it can bring awareness to this hulking body?

It's wasting its time. It can knock 'til eternity open the door and then refuse admittance. There'll be no need for me to knock.

I'll slide under the door
pour myself through a keyhole
enter in the oil for the lamps
shine round the room as an incandescent eye
nothing can keep me in this boat

I can leave it any time I like
it may be nice to see what it looks like
all these miles, and I've never seen the boat sail
I should have two boats. I could sleep alternate nights
admire one from the other

shout across when something needs doing
stroll over and invite myself below for a drink.
look back, and point out just how a boat should be sailed
if I wished, I could depart this labouring tub
it might be useful: can't you sometimes see things

from a distance
that remain blurred
to the nearer
astigmatic
eye?

Up on deck, I see, without surprise, there's a steamer a mile ahead and bearing down, with a two-flag signal close-up on his triatic. No need to look it up in the code book, I know what it means.

'… do you require assistance ?'

What a joke - of course I don't.
What a liberty to suggest such a thing.
I have a mind to ignore him altogether.
How *dare* he suggest that I need anything (in the meantime, M.I.K is sullenly hoisted).
I don't want anything from you mate.

'… nevertheless, I would like you to report me to Lloyds of London.'

153

He's a Frenchman, the **Bayeux.**

'… I watch him leave me astern with a feeling of relief.'

I'm going below to listen to my can, roll its way from one side of my light-headed head to the other.

The next morning, Thursday, the fourteenth of July, I feel more myself.

The wind still westerly, up and down a point or two, and the same distance remains to be sailed to New York, less the miles made good during the interval from the last sights taken.

While lying in my bunk, I have definitely made up my mind that we're bound for Bermuda - to hell with New York.

This capitulation is strangely acceptable.

I've been gnawing over the decision for days, yet have avoided it as bitter medicine promoted by an over-eager nurse. Once swallowed, I've relaxed for the first time in a week; have been able to sleep, six blessed hours of dream-free rest that has served me so much better than the previously unending nights as a rigidly shelved automaton.

Another sunny day, so I spend the forenoon in the cockpit, watching the sea (yes: after thirty-four days battling against it, I can still get immense pleasure just watching it) and those fellowtravellers *in* it; and, now and again, those attractive creatures that venture to fly *over* it. Strangely enough, we seem to be the only thing that is actually *on* it.

The fish still follow the boat.

Impossible to tell if they are those of yore. They look the same and I'm prepared to accept a possible previous acquaintance, so we treat each other as old friends, not suspicious strangers.

While I surprise them by leaning outboard, watching their antics, they pay me in kind, by getting their flighty cousins to mount a zooming aerial display.

The first time it occurs, I only catch a glimpse from the corner of my eye, yet it's sufficient for me to neglect my merely swimming escort.

I'm sure I've not been mistaken, and wait.

Soon I see another (just what I've been waiting for) indeed, what you could reasonably expect to see in these tropic lower latitudes.

Flying fish.

At first the chance one, then a group of half-a-dozen, now an extensive flight, winging their way close to the surface of the sea.

They are about the size of a useful mackerel, daubed with brilliant colouring, layered over an even brighter blue. Their blur of silver wings hang feather-light as they make their darting exits with nautical precision.

Thirty or more burst from the sea, hard-by the starboard beam. They 'fly' fifty yards to the west'ard then dive below. An entry that would gain an appreciative cheer from an audience seated poolside at an Olympian event.

I try hard to see if they're beating their wings (impossible to tell with the naked eye) like attempting to arrest the support offered by those of a dragonfly. You are certain there's movement taking place - but all the *eye* can see, is the dazzling blur of reciprocating motion.

I have the binoculars out, and spend an hour trying to pick them (the fish) up. It's an impossible task. They are much too quick, and every damned time they appear in a new and irritatingly different place.

If I look to port.

A host arise to starboard.

If I stay glued to that quadrant.

I'm exasperated to see a dozen rise from under the bow of the boat, on a similar course and speeding well ahead.

How fast?

Difficult to say, fifteen knots, twenty knots?

Their flight, arrested by the eye, gives the impression that it's the Folkboat that's stationary and they're moving with the urgency of starlings.

I wonder why.

It seems our movement through the water is disturbing them. They break surface in alarm, dashing off on either hand, as couchant rabbits rise before a walking man, aided by a casting hound; waiting, 'til the very last second, before breaking cover in a madly scattering dash.

Occasionally they fly towards the boat, apparently pursued by something they fear even more than our old hooker.

I can see the suspicion of a school of fish, shadowing their headlong flight. It's all happening so quickly against a background of moving water, dazzling sun, flashing crests, it's impossible to pick out the details of the act.

I'm a privileged audience, having the very best seat in the house, before an impossibly difficult play.

What's hunting them has given rise to mouth watering desire.

Can I ignore such succulent feed?

It's obvious we're sailing over what amounts to a battlefield, from the smallest tiddler to the largest whale, they *(we)* all prey on each other. And given that I'm part of this gladiatorial bloodbath, I feel inevitably drawn to this catch-as-catch-can ocean-going circus.

For us predatorial lads, even now, this minute, some hunter is ripping the guts out of his quarry, and then enjoying the meal; oblivious of the fact that gliding up behind him is his natural enemy, and before what's being eaten has been digested, he/she, will be joining the agonising stream of death that sustains all life.

In the evening, I feel bold enough to try a little fishing. Nothing too obvious, like a hook on the end of a line. I just get the steamboat scarer out and fireup the lamp.

It hasn't been in use for many a long night. As darkness falls, the yellow light pools it's way out and about from the boat; spreading over the surface of the sea. A welcoming attraction, perhaps, for a careless scud of flying fish?

I feel like a wrecker, exhibiting a light on a rock-bound coast. Hoping to entice a passing merchantman ashore, not without guilt, fobbed off with the thought that, if they (the flying fish) don't provide *me* with a meal, they will no doubt fall into the jaws of some other equally fatal trap.

The night draws on.

It's strange, after so many previous hours spent in total darkness, and happy enough to do so; now, it seems odd to be under the light of a gently swinging lamp.

I feel sorry for the lantern.

It's doing its best to challenge the night. The enormity of the task absorbs its effort with a finality that casts, not a shadow, but a doubt on the efficiency of its glow-worm of a wick.

If ever a light *gleamed* - this is the one that's doing it.

Down below, the cabin brings it into even better perspective.

I can lie on my bunk, as a spider may retire to the corner of his web, while waiting the arrival of an unsuspecting fly. Once, I'm sure I hear the soft thud of something that could have been a fish, landing on deck (and up I jump, with the enthusiasm of a boy visiting his set-for-rabbits snares). But though I search the cockpit, and go up for'ard, there's no sign of a fish.

When I'm in the bow of the hooker, sitting in the pulpit, with a moderate breeze sighing past my ears, it's strange, to look aft and see the glow of the hurricane lamp swinging from the backstays.

It seems the length of a football field away from where I'm sitting. Something remote and unconnected with my world; and yet, it's only twenty-five feet from one end of the tub to the other.

She's reaching now to a northerly breeze. The first freeing puff for a month, and moving at something approaching her best boat speed, say six knots, give or take an onion.

It's effortless movement. The sheets are well-eased and she leans comfortably on the breeze, slipping without fuss through the lap and slap of an ocean.

From where I stand, right in the bow of the boat, leaning my arse on the pulpit, looking aft, the squared-away boom holds the sail away from the hull, masking the source of light still swinging from the backstays.

Under it, and to the weather side of the mast, the yellow glow seems sucked out of the lantern. Offering a silhouette; a novelty that fascinates the eye, until the moon rises and does its best to all but dowse the light, leaving me wondering if it will still be possible to tempt a fish aboard.

Going below, I feel strong enough and sufficiently composed to listen to the radio, which provides a programme of music, and then, The News, on the hour, every hour, with the regular chime of a bell.

The information offered consists primarily of a catalogue of disasters, both natural and man-made. Our earth-bound activities apparently centre about riots, forest fires, earthquakes, plummeting aeroplanes, rape, murder and flood. All announced in a style biased towards the dramatic impact of the news, rather than the content.

As I lie, hardly able to bear the grief of a mother whose child has just been murdered by a maniac in Central Park, I hope that one day the responsible (irresponsible?) people would think it worthwhile to give at least a modicum of air time to publicising some of the better things in life.

The newsreader finishes his dirge and gives a brief recap of the weather situation in his area. As an afterthought, he mentions that the first hurricane of the season has formed down Cuba way.

I turn the radio off with a sharp click.

'… the first hurricane of the season.'

What a pronouncement. I imagine the announcer putting a skullcap on his head as he intones the fatal words.

'… what happens to these West Indian hurricanes ?'

Some of them sweep up the eastern seaboard of the 'States, others travel inland (only for a short, ocean starved, reducing windspeed distance), others, after they've done a powerful lot of damage in the Caribbean, re-curve into the North Atlantic and may come this way.

'… could this boat survive a hurricane ?'

The short and absolute answer to that is - no. There are so many variables, wind speeds, the rate of advance of the storm, its developing intensity, whether you are in, or out of the navigable semicircle - but the short answer still is - no.

'... what's the likelihood of a hurricane re-curving this year, over Bermuda and continuing to the east'ard ?'

Who the devil knows. But the news has shocked me. It's the sort of thing that lodges in the back of your mind.

'... tropical revolving storms.'

Months of greatest incidence?

'... July, August and September.'

How many a year?

'... probably less than ten.'

And they have the whole of the western side of the North Atlantic to roam over. However, there's always the chance.

'... Holy mackerel, Howells; you have plenty of other things to worry about. Dismiss it from your mind, it may never happen.'

It might.

I feel myself being sucked down to the level of depression which I had only the day before climbed out of. The news weighs on me as an additional burden. I feel now that I had been a fool to listen to the radio, would have been better off without it.

It is useful for time signals; right now seems more trouble than it's worth. It's tempting to throw the whole bag of tricks over the side.

What if I *do* know there's a tropical storm coming my way?

What can I do to avoid it?

The short and sweet answer to that is, absolutely nothing.

A hurricane may be only travelling at thirty knots, but developing wind speeds well in excess of a hundred miles an hour. Imagine the seas that would raise; and after the horrific advent, entering the eye of the storm (always provided you've survived thus far) to encounter masses of water, towering over the boat, falling out of a windless sky - the eye of the storm itself.

I have a cold sweat on my brow just lying in my bunk thinking about it, with the funk effectively keeping sleep away for the rest of the restless night.

I toss and turn in a bath of hideous possibilities.

Drowned a dozen times. Succumbed to exposure on several occasions. Twice torn limb from limb by the fiercest goddamned sharks I have ever seen in a long and adventurous life.

Long before dawn I've renounced my role as spider to the fly and taken in and doused my small oil lamp (back to a feeling of compassion for the fish), once again, I'm small, vulnerable, and *frightened*.

With the dawn, I'm up, examining the for'ard hatch, anxiously testing the coaming. Try as I might I can't convince myself the weather will remain moderate, that the hurricane is more than two thousand miles away, and probably moving in another direction. Yet I tackle the job of reinforcing the hatch as if the arrival of the ultimate storm in the whole of maritime history is imminent.

' *... and not only imminent.'*

Inevitable: a gigantic sword that's not poised above my head - has actually started on its downward path.

'*... you're doing the right thing; the hurricane is certain to re-curve.'*

I need no convincing.

The question has left the realm of rational debate, it's become an emotional problem.

It's not if, but *when*, the catastrophic storm will strike.

The for'ard hatch is now reinforced with battens and lashed tight shut. Impossible to open without the attention of a razor-sharp knife or a fireman's axe.

The task complete, I sit on my bunk, convinced I've done a seamanlike job, nevertheless spend the rest of the morning popping up and down as a maniacal yo-yo, from below, to a position perched anxiously on the coachroof - looking to the sou'west, oblivious of the fact that the glass remains high, the swell low, the breeze moderate, the weather fine, the visibility excellent, yet

absolutely certain
this is only the calm
before the devastating storm

I damn near tap a hole in the barometer in my anxiety to see it drop.

It remains obstinately lodged at one thousand and forty-five millibars.

of course it's stuck
it must be stuck
how can the weather possibly remain set fair?

The necessity of taking and working up an A.M. sight, followed by the fore-noon's run-up to the Meridian Altitude, helps control my imagination (it seems that even the slightest mental discipline helps stabilize a fractious mind) with the product being a Noon Position that reads 35 degrees and 36 minutes North, 43 degrees and 32 minutes West, with the log reading 2,296 nautical miles.

and this is Saturday, the 16th of July

10

and so
you think you know yourself

This trip is really taking the skin off Howells, one more slash of the knife
and the next time he gets up from his bunk, only the outer shell will come
away, his guts will be left behind, quiveringly exposed.

Will he be surprised?

Nothing can surprise him now !

He's always been fascinated by the sea, now he's in it up to his neck,
on the point of believing it's only a matter of time before it'll close over his
head, that he's been decoyed into being

*... invited to spend the evening at the home of an admired friend. Having
arrived, the door's slammed shut and the visitor discovers, to his horror, that this is
the house of a demented being.*

*The trap has closed, but when all seems lost, an avenue appears which
though detestable, offers the only possible choice.*

*I'm in a field, an immense field, a ploughed field, brown furrowed earth
under a blood red moon.*

*I'm wandering about, aimlessly fingering my body, astonished to find it's
still complete; wishing some of it away, smelling, sniffing, scuffling amongst the
garbage that's been dumped here.*

What can I smell ?

I'm searching, retracing my steps, finding a patch where I once sat.

I pause, squatting on my haunches.

The scent is overpowering.

A vile stench.

Then I know.

My spirit has at last an odour.

*I have the neck and nose of a giraffe, long enough to sniff out anybody's
conscience.*

The sickening smell is quite familiar.

I know it well, it's the fear that accompanies the stench of death.

*Beneath the plough-turned furrow rots a layer of dung, smearing my body
with a foetid slime.*

Worms coil about me.

I no longer evade their blind caress.

My torn back, caked with blood, is stung by urine as I lie between the four

hard hooves of a rampant stallion.
The fount of this demeaning deluge.
Pissed on by a horse.
I'm sick, and as a cow consumes her own afterbirth, I follow suit and re-
digest my disgusting self.

This Saturday afternoon, I wake from the post-lunch nightmare, hot, sweaty, and with an overpowering desire to get out of the cabin into the cleaner air on deck.

It's a bright day. The scattering of cumulus does nothing to temper the heat of the sun and I sit, panting, alternately wiping the sweat from my forehead, drying my eyebrows, while plucking at my tattered shorts which are coming apart at the seams. The material is sound, though torn in places. The stitching on which the garment depends has rotted and the whole thing is disintegrating.

I toy with the idea of getting to work with a needle, but such a tedious task seems irritating, so, as the panels are only retained by the barest thread, I pull them off and throw them overboard.

Under my shorts, and integral with the waistband, is a cotton jockstrap, and soon all that remains is the elasticised top, two buttock hugging straps, and the tidying cotton cup. I feel, at last, that my body is down to the irreducible minimum of clothing, what remains is not demanded by modesty, but by convenience. If only I could rid my mind of similar impedimenta, while retaining what's still serviceable.

Isn't that a much more difficult task?

While I'm idling my time, the breeze has gone easterly, a faint air that hardly passes the boat. Mike is completely befuddled and after booming out the genoa, squaring off the main boom and tightening it with a preventor, I take a turn at the helm.

It really is a glorious afternoon.

Under my more anticipatory hand, the boat holds better to her task and is slipping quietly through the water, making good, perhaps two knots or more.

As ever, I don't bother to steer a compass course, it's not in any way necessary.

I have become familiar with the sun's altering bearing throughout the day, and can hold the boat to her work within five degrees of the required heading without the slightest mental effort.

The ocean remains blue and undisturbed by wind.

Astern and sometimes close to the quarter, fly Mother Carey's

Chickens, which I watch with friendly interest.

They've been here for days.

Almost certainly the same birds. No bigger than a sparrow and apparently tireless. Quite unlike the concept of a seabird, they constantly beat their wings, seem incapable of the soaring flight one associates with creatures that measure their roaming by the passage of an ocean.

They keep close to the surface of the sea, sometimes hovering over a favourite spot, all the while so intimate with the ocean they seem to be walking on its surface, paddling with practiced ease on the dip and dab of the briny.

They never alight. I've watched them for hours, and they never once renounced flight to take a well-earned rest.

They busy themselves endlessly in the boat's wake. Darting off perhaps twenty yards on either beam to investigate some of the still-present weed, then, after a few quick stabs with needle-sharp beaks, they rejoin our nautical caravan on its endless journey west'ard.

All this late afternoon and evening I've been steering under the broiling sun. Heedless of sunburn. Determined to remain on deck as long as possible. With the fore hatch battened down, the temperature below is unbearable, and I only venture into the cabin to get myself a cup of water and sometimes a boiled sweet. In this way the day has passed and I find, with a deal of thankfulness, that I'm getting tired.

I don't turn in, prefer to keep working about the boat.

Hand the mainsail, which is chafing badly on the starboard spreader.

Gybe the genoa, then boom it out to starboard.

Take the mainsail off the track, and during the cooler evening, while it's still light, set about re-stitching the luff of the sail and renewing the rawhide chafing pieces.

Some of the slides are cracked, badly manufactured items that have been cold-formed out of stainless sheet. I rouse out new ones from the bosun's store, and feel quite pleased with myself when the job's completed.

While hunting for the spare slides I come across the Saundersfoot Sailing Club burgee, together with the well-worn Welsh Ensign that has been taken down days previously.

After a quiet think, I determinedly re-hoist them. One to the masthead, the other to the starboard yardarm.

They look good, fluttering in the light breeze, against a dark blue sky, mottled with a scattering of clouds.

The night passes, not easily, but as a protesting creak of time that plunges a sided gorge, displacing melancholy boulders which disturb the introverted current.

Because I'm tired, after the enervating exposure to the sun and the prolonged activity about the boat, I enjoy a priceless natural sleep, which brings me to the dawn of yet another day with more confidence than I had hoped to experience.

What is the solitary traveller to do concerning rest?

If you find, as I am doing, that physical and mental limitations give rise to a heightened emotional switchback, which allows the mind to ride wild to distant parts, peopled by an imagination prompted by the weeks of solitude - what's the solution?

The first aid box and a powerful sleeping draught?

Here we may have a cure more deadly than the complaint. I feel the need to sustain my faculties; that they should remain as unimpaired as possible.

What I need is natural sleep.

On the one hand, I begrudge my declining awareness, while on the other wish for oblivion. So I'm profoundly glad when dawn breaks and I can escape the terrors of the night, to embark on a more rational day.

The weather's fine.

The breeze still easterly, the second day of this favourable slant.

The boat running to the west'ard under the boomed out genoa, with the furled mainsail preserved by its gaskets from any further chafe.

I spend an hour rigging the working staysail, which is held out with the boathook, pressed into service as a makeshift pole.

We sail goose-winged now, and with the extra one hundred square feet of added canvas, she picks up half-a-knot, satisfying progress, as restful as an hour's sleep.

A.M. sights, then breakfast, the forenoon spent rigging an awning over the coachroof.

The cabin is now unbearably hot, partly because the sun in these latitudes strikes fiercely on the boat, partly because the breeze, before which we're sailing, has had it's apparent speed decreased as we carry our own private patch of air forward to accompany the vessel.

I've been unable to conquer the unreasonable fear of what I'm convinced is an approaching storm, with the result that the for'ard hatch remains tight shut, and this mixture of unavoidable fact and inescapable fiction, which in my case carries the same conviction, drives me to action.

But not to the most reasonable and obvious solution.

I merely rig an awning.

A blanket, stretched over the boom gallows and carried for'ard over the coachroof, held at its dog-eared corners by handy pieces of codline.

It's worth doing.

The sun no longer beats directly on the plywood deck, and is prevented from shining through the open companionway hatch to pressure-cook the cabin.

The sea has completely changed its attitude towards the presence of the boat.

The five previous weeks of stubborn hammering have accompanied the disappearance of the westerly wind, and now, what sea there is moves in the direction the boat is sailing.

The difference is inspiring.

What was previously a battle, has become peaceful co-existence.

It seems the ocean's had a change of heart.

Though the swell hails westerly, a reminder of the relative permanence of oceans, the wind-marshalled waves now form astern of the boat, lifting, then allowing her to slip before the curl and crest of overtaking seas.

The decks are dry, beginning to shrink under the cracking attention of the sun, yet so easily is the boat accepted by the 'oggin, that most of her topside planking remains dry - the yellow painted hull is bleaching in the orb's reflected glare.

As I walk for'ard, the deck is hot under my bare feet, and the reflected heat scorches my body as I lie full length on the foredeck. The only place aboard, apart from the over-hot bunks, that I can go full stretch.

The noises are different.

Gone are the thumps, bangs, rattles and groans of the previous engagement.

No spray shocks, then delights the eye by its passage over the boat. I can hang my head outboard, to watch the yellow stem cleave the sea with male approval. The ocean parts, then rolls away on either beam to leave the wake, while at the eager prow a rise of water lips the hull with delightful indecision, turns back the sheets to an endlessly inviting bed.

Along the waterline, barnacles and weed are sticking to the planking, and because the boat's immersed below her normal marks, they have been able to set up home on a part of the hull devoid of antifouling.

Amongst the cone shaped barnacles are long stemmed mushrooms, waving a surprise of well-domed heads. They look too fragile to stand against the foam of water surging past the hull - but it seems they are well attached and more resilient than they look.

They are brown. Sprouting from the yellow planking. Waving in a blue sea, they delight the eye as daffodils enhance a forest glade.

The fish are with us.

Under the overhanging stem swims a fine creature, five feet long and beautifully proportioned. Mostly silver, some blue, and not content with that, flaunting a bold bright yellow tail.

He acts as guide to our dripping caravan.

At eye-attentive intervals, flyingfish zip … zip … zip … and zip again out of the ocean ahead and abeam of the boat.

I wonder if they're disturbed by our presence - or that of our formidable escort?

Some to port, some to starboard; an endlessly unfolding Neptunian fan that marks our fascinating ocean-going progress.

'… it's so hot, I must go aft for water (half-a-cup: no more).'

These last few days have been noticeable, not only for the rise in ambient temperature, but for a significant increase in my water intake.

I'm keeping careful note of every drop - with the dawn drink, and the pot of tea at breakfast - it stands at a little over two pints so far today. What I'm going aft for will bring it up to three, and this is only the forenoon.

The cabin, though hot, offers some relief from the sun, which is now approaching noon and nearly overhead.

Our position, 35° 21' North, 45° 00' West, log reading 2,365, seems encouraging enough to justify one of the last remaining cans of beer. And because the distance to be sailed, before arriving at Bermuda, turns out to be only twenty miles more than a thousand, this is a good excuse for a celebration.

But not yet. Let's stoically wait until the log has reeled up those twenty missing miles - sometime during this coming evening we'll enjoy this lukewarm drink.

During the afternoon, the failing breeze makes it necessary to take over the tiller from Mike, emphasising, yet again, that when running before a light air he's inclined to wander all over the ocean.

I also have to keep going below for more water.

My lips are drying out, and I have a tender feeling about the eyes and the corners of my mouth.

When I run my tongue over my lips, I can swear they're cracked. And on one of my trips below, I take the trouble to examine them in the sextant mirror, only to find the skin is unbroken, merely sore to the touch.

Nevertheless, I rouse up some salve from the first aid kit, and that helps. I also transfer the last half-dozen ascorbic acid tablets from the main stock, place them in the screw topped jar that holds the daily use supply.

Back again on deck, under the still-high sun, I wonder if I should cover myself with clothes (construct an Arab's nautical burnouse?) hoping to prevent, or at least slow down my dehydration by adopting an insulating layer?

It seems like sacrilege.

Weeks of overcast skies, cascading decks, soaking clothes and damp bunks have left me with a hunger for warmth and sunshine; so I lie, supine, content to frizzle in the sun, my eyes shut, steering merely by the feel of the breeze on my neck.

The sun's now fine on the starboard bow and nearing the dazzling horizon, getting on time for that long looked forward to beer.

'… what does the log say ?'

The damned thing's stopped.

'… caught up with weed again ?'

I'm the one who has to haul the thing inboard (he's much too lazy) but it's a good job he noticed it, the spinner *was* foul with weed.

'… what's the log reading ?'

Two thousand, three hundred and eighty-two miles.

'… but it's been stopped for a couple of miles.'

Get the beer out.

'… you do it, you're nearest the cabin.'

Where did you leave the can opener?

'… it's on the port side of the radio shelf.'

It's not.

'… that's where I left it.'

(he finds it, in the cutlery drawer, and we enjoy a drink together)

'… I wonder what the lads are doing back in Saundersfoot ?'

Same as we're doing right now, supping ale, but what they'll be having will be in pint pots and in rather larger quantities.

'... what time is it, in the U.K. right now ?'

About ten o'clock; another half of beer and we could be going home to the kids. I expect they'll be up late this summer evening, probably swimming and sailing most of the day.

'... wonder how Christopher is ?'

Doing well (you can trust his mum).

'... be nice to get a message through to them, wouldn't it ?'

It sure would.

'... why don't you try that ship over there ?'

What ship? ... over where?

'... that chap, fine on the port bow.'

Good grief, I didn't see him.

'... it's a damned good job I'm keeping a weather-eye lifted.'

Shut up and get the flags out, he's going to pass close-to.

'... he's bound easterly, making between fifteen and twenty knots, a tanker by the look of him, and not far away.'

Time to get those flags up.

'... there they go, M.I.K., he's bound to see them. Hell, he's less than half-a-mile away, and passing even closer than that.'

I can see his name.

'... what is it ?'

Dea Brovic

'... can you see anyone on the bridge ?'

No.

'... anyone on deck ?'

No.

'… do you think he's going to see us ?'

Good God, you mean to say he can pass this close, and *not* see us?

'… come evening, and I just can't stand his company any longer. I think, if I don't get away, even for an hour, he'll drive me mad.

I made him a decent meal, but while I slaved over the stove he stood watching me, then just picked over the grub (the fastidious bastard) and I had to put up with his grumbles.

It even put me off my *meal.*

A person can only stand just so much of this sort of thing, then they're off. I left him.

I told him straight, I couldn't stand it for another bloody minute.

It wasn't only the grumbling; it's that hulking great body of his, so damned awkward about the boat.

It doesn't suit me at all.

I'm neat, quick, like to get things done.

He just moons around, admiring his suntan.

He'll be sorry, if he isn't careful.

And what about his gangling body anyway ?

Does it serve him any better than me ?

Look at all the years I've been with him.

Has he ever had a gracious word for me ?

I've forgotten when I had a decent pat on the back. It's laughable really: there he is, prancing about, near enough nude; that thing he's wearing is sparse enough to make me sick.

Nature boy indeed !

Only a few weeks ago he wouldn't have been seen dead in that sort of kit.

He's always had a thing about his legs, y'know.

Oh yes, as long as I can remember, and they are rather funny, but if I just so much as smile when I mention them, he goes off at the deep end.

Isn't it silly ?

Who cares about his stupid old legs ?

But what riles me even more is his language. I just can't stand profanity, and he has a really foul mouth.

I don't like that in a man.

There's no need for it.

I can express my thoughts quite adequately without those filthy words; and it isn't as if he was being completely honest.

Look at him now .
Lounging in the starboard bunk, on top of our sleeping bag.
See how he's sweating ?
I have to go back to that and lie alongside it
The way he tosses and turns all night, it's so irritating, spoils my rest. When
I get up in the morning, after a dreadful night, I look and feel a fright.
Yes I do; and it's not fair !
And not only that. He dreams you know. Not those amusing little things
we used to enjoy together. He doesn't seem satisfied with those. It's got to be on a
gigantic scale and in full colour.
Sometimes he wakes me up by the absolute frenzy he works himself into.
Nothing I can say seems to be any good.
He won't believe anything I tell him.
What's the use of a man like that ?
There are other things too; nasty little beast that he is.
Just lately his dreams have been taking on a queer twist.
(I can tell you now).
He can't fool me.
Him and his brown body.
I think it's getting the better of him.
(you know what I mean ?).
Those dreams of his, they're becoming very erotic.
In the beginning they worried him, but he seems to be enjoying them now
and it's me who's getting worried.
Whatever I say, he just laughs.
I told him I'd leave him. Straight-up I told him. Right from the shoulder.
And all he did was laugh.
Until the tears rolled down his cheeks.
Just look at him now.
Lying on his bunk, thinking he should get up and have a look around.
You'll have to excuse me. I have to go below.
He just can't do a thing without me.

Unlikely though it may seem - it's a fine night, the breeze has veered a point, and has now fallen away to little more than a light air.

We sail before it, light as thistledown, not keeping a good course, just wandering away to the west'ard.

I can hardly complain to Mike. I'm finding it difficult enough to concentrate on the essential tasks myself. Sometimes feel incapable of movement, as if some essential cog is missing. Then, whatever was missing returns and I'm once more capable of action.

At two o'clock this morning I tuned a signal from W.N.E.W., and a few hours later experienced another blood-quickening sunrise, the forerunner of yet another scorching day.

The breeze has drifted sou'easterly, making it impossible to hold a second boomed out jib, so up goes the mainsail to keep the genoa company.

We're reaching now, as close to a westerly course as Mike can hold her. It's just too hot on deck, so I have to be content with his performance.

This morning, when filling the kettle from the daily-use can, I discovered that I'd used three quarters of a gallon of fresh water during the previous twenty-four hours. Much above my normal rate, and it was all used for drinking purposes, nothing else.

I also drank a can of beer, so, with the soup at midday, this means a total liquid intake of something approaching a gallon in the 24 hours.

And the answer to that mate, is.

'… stay out of the sun.'

The only place completely so is the cabin, and to make that tenable I must re-open the for'ard hatch.

'… an easy task?'

How I wish that it was so.

My mind is warped beyond the plane of reason. I argue to myself (if I unlash the hatch, it would only be creating unnecessary work) because I'm sure beyond even the hesitancy of doubt that the weather is deteriorating, that the not-forgotten hurricane is on its way.

'… how daft can you become ?'

But the hatch remains shut during the forenoon, and with the sun at its zenith, even though the blanket awning remains rigged, the cabin becomes unbearable.

Butter is oozing out of its greaseproof paper packets.

The drinking water is more than lukewarm.

Lying on my bunk, the sweat runs off in rivulets, soaking my sleeping bag. Thirst puckers my tongue and lips, so that at last, I'm driven to the hatch, with the cockpit knife in my hand.

'… how foolish can you get ?'

I feel, that as soon as I've cut the lashings, the weather will break. I tap the barometer (steady as a rock). I retreat to the main hatch, the better to judge the weather - the sun still shines from an almost cloudless sky.

The breeze is moderate, little more than air. The sea is calm, with only a slight sou'westerly swell, but . . .

'. . . can I risk it ?'

It requires a mental effort to even nod my head. Below I go, crawling to the for'ard hatch, placing the razor-sharp blade over the codline lashings (about to cut the throat of a pet lamb). All those turns of twine, put on with such labour - it will take me an hour to re-lash the wretched thing.

Shall I ?

'. . . I can't.'

Don't be such a bloody fool - cut it !

'. . . you do it.'

Give me the blasted knife.

Before I know it, the lashings are adrift. The clasp holding the hatch to the coamings is released. I'm pushing it open, head and shoulders following it upwards, to ease myself, running with sweat, out the hatch.

I can hardly believe it.

'. . . the weather remains set fair.'

I climb out on deck, and walk aft to the cockpit, where I sit, admiring my regained composure. Wondering how I ever came to suffer, and then escape from, such a stupid mental block. It seems incredible, something unbelievable; but it's a real experience, and not without a touch of the macabre.

As the day draws on, the breeze eases, making the atmosphere even more oppressive. I feel exhausted, enervated, my body tacky, my hair matted and sticking damply to my head.

I check the water - the best part of another gallon has been used.

I curse myself and my extravagance - impossible now to afford an evening bath.

A thousand miles from land, very little wind, the barometer high and steady; with only fifteen gallons of water, and we could be several more weeks on passage.

Much as I need a bath, it would be foolhardy to use the water and I resolutely put it out of my mind. Then, as dusk approaches, there's a darkening of the sky to the south'ard, barely noticeable, yet full of promise.

A squall, with the possibility of rain.

The breeze, what there is of it, still shapes easterly, but the cloud, with a mind of its own, is beginning to dominate the night, dropping the breeze to a zephyr, soon giving way to a calm.

A calm - but not a flat calm.

There's a dark patch approaching the boat, obscuring the stars of the southern horizon, offering the first faint tickle of a breeze.

The boomed out sails are taken aback, so I must go on deck and hand the genoa. Having finished that small chore, pull down two reefs in the mainsail, then attend to the main boom preventor in order to harden-in the sheet - now it can blow if it wants to.

And it does, coming quietly across the water, as a leopard, hunting in the night.

A puff of wind from the south'ard, with a darkening overhead.

Another puff, strong enough to heel the boat. Nothing that Mike can't handle, allowing me to go below, wriggle out of my jockstrap, find a cake of soap, then back on deck, hoping for what I'm expecting to arrive.

I can *hear* it.

A curtain of rain, hissing as it sweeps over the surface of the sea. The breeze is cool, yet I'm taken by surprise when the squall does reach the boat. Delivers a deluge of ice-cold rain that has me spluttering for breath.

The boat's smoking along.

Entering a roaring tunnel, while I'm standing in the cockpit, trying to lather my body and do the same with beard and hair.

The cake of soap has slipped from my hand and it takes several seconds to find it.

The cockpit sole is slimy, I can hardly keep my feet.

Bollock naked, and soaped all over, I sit slippery-arsed on the seat. Gasping for breath under the deluge that's lashing out of the night.

Hardly bearable - but immensely invigorating.

I stand and face it, cupping hands about my dick and balls to protect the family jewels, until the squall eases and I can take advantage of the downpour's lashing end; use it to rinse my hair as it (the rain) sweeps away to the nor'ard.

I'm clean, but shivering uncontrollably.

Down below for the last dry towel; marvellously rough on the skin.

On with the stove.

A cup of scalding tea, a buttered biscuit and honey.

A drop, not small, of brandy, then stick my head out of the hatch, just to make sure.

There's a vessel down to the south'ard, about five miles off.

Bugger-all to worry about.

Snuggle into the sleeping bag.

Plenty of body heat.

Clear headed.

Calm, nervous tension relaxing.

Close the eyes - no wind now, mainsail still up, sheeted hard in, must remember in the morning to . . .

Sleep, deep, refreshing, dreamlessly re-stitching the corners of a mind worn threadbare by the passage of the numberless days and endless nights; now aware of an altered perspective, foreshortening the task.

Bermuda only eight hundred and fifteen miles distant, with two thousand, five hundred, and forty-four miles already reeled on the log, lowered sights, and a second wind.

The barometer's still high, has even climbed during the night, and now stands at one thousand and forty-eight millibars; betrayed by its own extravagance - but another fine day.

Sou'easterly comes the breeze, with varying enthusiasm, requiring frequent adjustments to sails and self-steering gear - no matter, because we're making progress.

Passing great clumps of weed, occasionally clearing the log.

It's cooler now, with the breeze for'ard of the beam, refreshing the boat and myself - being surprised by the sudden appearance of more flying fish, which quit the startled ocean as a flutter of starlings leave a quiet wood.

A fish has flown aboard, perhaps when I was below.

It's dead.

Lying on the port side deck, robbed of life by incalculable chance.

It's small. Barely three inches in length. Its body shrivelled by the sun. Impossible large eyes for such a diminutive creature. Winged as a dragonfly. Transparently veined. Crisp as toast - before it has been smothered in thick-cut English marmalade.

A tragic little corpse which, when I return it to the sea, is snapped up by the quickest member of our convoy in a swirl of water paddled by a predatory tail.

Another minor tragedy - I've lost my plastic bucket.

It cuts me as the passing of a friend, the more so because it's entirely my own fault - who else?

'... don't answer that.'

I was leaning outboard, dipping up the bright blue water, which changes amazingly when it's encompassed by the yellow pail. As the lip of the bucket caught the 'oggin, its weight increased so rapidly that it was snatched from my grasp.

I can see it, just below the surface, as it rises for an instant inside a swell before it settles on its compressing journey to the ocean floor.

I was fond of that bucket, without murmur it accepted its necessary tasks.

Jack the cook spewed his guts up into it.

And so had I.

What contorted faces had peered over its lip.

I had bathed in it.

Washed the crocks in it.

Swilled the decks with it.

Sluiced away sulphuric acid with it.

It had been a purposeful bucket.

And now.

It's gone, all that remains is its red-coloured partner. The item that previously supplied the specially designated, shit into service as the vessel's one and only loo, which will now have to be used for every bucket needing task.

A disturbing thought.

Another good day's run - only seven hundred and twenty-five miles to Bermuda.

During the afternoon a dark object appears ahead.

No need to alter course, we merely pass close to it, twenty yards to the south'ard.

It's rusty, trails long weed, is three feet in diameter and stands similarly out of the sea - almost certainly a mine.

'... I have to laugh.'

'... there he goes again, vainly trying to rationalise - 'almost certainly a mine'.'

'... I ask you ?'

'... how can he possibly tell ?'

'... of course, he 'thinks' it's a mine.'

He saw it when it was three miles distant.

It stood out well on the top of a swell as a small black pimple.

He's very proud of his eyesight, you know - that's another of those little things I find so irritating - his boastful attitude, to what is, after all, little more than average performance.

I was watching him when he first saw this object (he stiffened as a pointer in a bog) now he's worrying about the number of similar objects we've passed during the night.

I can tell him - dozens; all sorts, shapes, and conditions of flotsam.

From where we are right now, I can see a large baulk of timber a few miles to the nor'ard.

And the night before last, we sailed within a few feet of a waterlogged lifeboat that's been drifting around for years, impossible to see the gunwhale as it was barely awash at the time.

I just sit and wait for the crash.

What fun it will be to see him scramble madly out of the cabin (he'll have been sleeping, of course). I keep telling him he's getting much too blasé about this lack of a lookout.

There'll be a splintering crash as she strikes (say the log we passed the other day) he'll only have a few seconds to get up on deck, barking his shins on the companionway steps, howling like a dog in his despair.

If he's lucky, he'll be able to cut away the liferaft before the boat sinks, then follow the raft over the side into the ink-black water.

He won't be able to find the lanyard to inflate it - he's not even sure it'll float, he's always thought it very heavy for its size.

If he does manage to get the thing blown up he'll scramble in, and sit, Buddha-like, week after week while he drifts helplessly about this part of the ocean.

I don't mind telling you, I don't fancy going with him on that job; would as soon take leave of him before it started.

Day after day in his little rubber life raft; just think of it, he believes he's badly done by now, but just you wait. As of now, he's got half a gallon of sweet water every day - in the raft he'll be reduced to less than a pint.

I've warned him about it, told him he mustn't drink anything for the first twenty-four hours, to let his kidneys get the message.

What a joke; just to let them know that after a few days of sweated sips, they'll gradually shrivel as he dehydrates beneath the canopy.

He knows I'll leave him.

I've told him, he'll be damned lucky to get us both into the raft.

About half a mile to the south'ard there are several sharks, big ones; poor Howells, they'll soon know there's something amiss and they'll be along to join the fun.

I've seen it happen so many times - people swimming in the water, dangling legs waving attractively in the sea.

The scent of fear (they can smell it a mile away those sharks) they'll be there, before he can say a round of prayers to that funny little God of his.

It just goes to show what I've been saying - you can't trust the bugger.

I've found that out.

But all his prayers won't do him any good; oh no, the sharks come in just the same. He knows what it'll be like; only yesterday I explained it to him in excruciating detail.

They cruise around for a while, just to make sure there's no danger to themselves.

There may be a dozen or more; then one of them, hungrier than the rest will come determinately in. He can thrash about as madly as he likes, that first attack will do for him (a leg perhaps, or an arm ?) not cleanly off.

Have you ever seen a shark's mouth ?

Built for tearing it is, not cutting.

A great bleeding hunk out of a thigh. The muscle off one of his calves stripped cleanly from the bone. The water reddening with blood.

And his screams, it'll be more than I can bear.

I can't stand the sight or sound of suffering.

Once they start, there's no stopping them. In they'll come, driven to a frenzy by blood and bits of tissue in the water. When they attack, they hit hard, punching at his belly, tearing away at his guts which unwind as a ribbon in the sea.

Maybe one of them will fancy the tasty morsel from his groin.

So many times I've told him, that pride always comes before a fall.

There's a lot in these old sayings y'know.

As I watch the menacing object drop astern, I wonder, vaguely, how long it's been wandering the ocean.

Later in the afternoon, I have a visitor, a large bird that flies around the boat. He seems to be nervously examining the newcomer to his hitherto unblemished home.

For a while he's flown astern, not disturbing the petrels that are busy in the wake; with each swoop he comes a little closer, his head cocking, first one side, then the other - a real inquisition.

He seems ideally suited to his environment. As large as the average gull back home, mostly white, with a trailing tail that offers real distinction.

His feet are black, his beak distinctly red. The tips of his wings are also black, as are the stripes across the upper side of his body.

He doesn't flap his wings, but soars over the waves with the twitch of an occasional feather - the petrels are transposed as nervous mice, scurrying about under the aggressive eye of a predatory hawk.

At last he's satisfied with his inspection, and then, the silly ass, he tries to sit on the top of the mast. An inverted example of the old banana-skin joke, as a distinguished gentleman, walking with some purpose down a busy street, steps on the offending fruit and up he goes, base over apex, arse over pavement-thumping head, providing merriment for the passing crowd.

This foolish bird is not content with his natural advantage, but hopes to thumb a lift.

Approaching the boat, soaring over the masthead in order to appraise its swaying movement.

Confident; he attempts a three-point landing (two legs and the long black tail), but his reflexes are awful.

The masthead hangs, steady for a second, so in he comes, all air brakes fluttering down.

But at the crucial moment, the boat moves on and he misses his perch by an embarrassing margin.

After several poor attempts, accompanied by plaintive squeaks, he starts a more determined effort.

Makes it, slips web-footed off the aluminium cap, falls two feet down the mast with what is obviously a raucous curse, one wing tip foul of the burgee halyard.

I sit in the cockpit, having my first real laugh for days.

This guy's a born comedian.

Perhaps his long tail, which suggests dignity, has added a pompous side to character? And because he preens, his mishap seems the more outrageous?

After a few more unsuccessful attempts, he gives up the struggle and retires to his station astern.

I give him a good round of applause, which unfortunately scares the petrels, but they soon forget their fright and return, dancing on the surface of the sea.

I wonder if our bum's a bosun bird?

While filling in the evening journal, I notice that the log has stopped once more, and while I'm clearing it of weed, slip on the afterdeck and cut the sole of my foot on one of the brass wing nuts that holds the cover on the locker.

It doesn't seem serious, so I just clean it with a little disinfectant and stick an Elastoplast over the wound.

'... *that's a laugh; it illustrates what I mean when I say you can't trust the bugger.*

This is the very subject he keeps constantly bothering me about.

His ugly great body.

He's always on about it, looking at it, feeling it, relating its present to its previous performance.

It's all perfectly revolting, and makes me feel quite sick.

It's obvious to me, that he's afraid something will happen to it.

As if I cared.

I keep telling him, it's no concern of mine, but he will persist that it is.

That's another thing about him that I find so irritating.

He will keep coming back to points I've previously dealt with, like a blasted homing pigeon.

It doesn't matter where you send him, back he comes, picking away at the same old problem (his fear) that's now hanging round him like a mantle.

Sometimes, perhaps the next time I go back, I'll have a job to regain my place, there could be such an impenetrable wall which will have to be circumvented before I can even talk to him.

I find it most annoying.

If I'm only away for a few minutes, I sometimes come back to the most dreadful goings-on.

Once, when he'd fallen, while doing some silly job up on the foredeck, he thought he'd broken his leg (the left one, I think it was), you should have heard the fuss.

A perfectly disgraceful cacophony.

I told him, there's not the slightest need for of that sort of behaviour. If he's broken his leg, he's broken his leg, and that's the end of that. And furthermore, he had to find his own way below.

You should have heard the language.

Perfectly disgraceful.

He did manage to crawl aft and heave himself into the cockpit.

It must have been agonising for him as he tried to negotiate the companionway steps. I even felt a twinge of pity for the brute.

He'd fallen awkwardly and his leg was broken just above the knee, which must be even more painful than a break below the joint.

By the time he'd managed to ease himself into the cabin, he was crying like a baby. He fell down the last two steps and the jagged end of the bone stuck through the skin. It gave me quite a turn to see it.

And then he couldn't reach the first aid box.

As a matter of fact, he fainted there for a while.

I was tempted to help him: but what could I do under the circumstances ?

He made it eventually, and then almost passed out again when he found there wasn't any morphine (the fool's forgotten being told it's illegal to carry the stuff).

Anyway, he used some of the alternative tablets that had been given him, then complained they weren't much good.

He lay below for several days.

I kept telling him he'd be better off on deck. (it's probably the thought of climbing the companionway steps that's keeping him below).

The wound soon turned septic, as I told him it would.

There you are, I said, everything I told you would happen, has happened. Straight up I told him.

And all he did was heap abuse on my head.

I ask you; how can you help a man like that ?

After a few days he became delirious.

I found it impossible to stay with him; that's why I'm up here now, waiting for him to get back to somewhere near normality.

It's such a bore.

As for me, I'm glad to see the dawn - it hasn't been an easy night.

With a freshening breeze, the sea has risen and is now running from broad on the port quarter with a similarly approaching swell.

Mike, at the tiller, is making heavy weather of it, so I spend most of the forenoon looking after the boat myself.

Though the sea's rough, the decks remain dry.

The sun's as hot as ever, but I feel I'm making a valuable contribution by holding the boat steady before the following lump of a swell.

At noon the log reads 2775, and sights put her only 605 miles off Bermuda, which is now beginning to come into the realm of what should be attainable.

For hour after hour I'm steering the boat; glancing over my shoulder at the log, cursing, when it's once again fouled with weed, delighted when another ten miles have been recorded, all the time keeping an eye lifted for shipping.

I feel more normal than I have for days.

During the forenoon we pass cork floats of the type used by commercial fisherman. A message from another world - an organised society that's purposeful, decisive, governed strictly by time (might as well forget the motion).

Time that means money, but for me, time has become elasticised.

It seems incredible that I have only been sitting in the cockpit for thirty-six minutes.

Since last I looked at my watch, I would have been prepared to stake my life that over an hour had elapsed. The whole rhythm of my existence seems to be grinding to a halt, and I wonder if this has anything to do with the easier movement of the vessel's hull?

It's possible - anything's possible.

but if the days seem endless
what of the nights ?
a week ago
I thought the nights impossibly long
now
they offer a separate existence

I can grow in them
live, struggle and die in them
I can orchestrate an effort
quite separate from that required by the sailing of the vessel
join the school of porpoise which lately visited the boat
and they would immediately accept me as another of the group

the water's green
the hull of the boat is blue
but there's little impression of movement
with my companions I swim, effortlessly
and when looking up at the surface of the sea
appreciate how easily we traverse this broad expanse of ocean

the rudder trails astern of the boat
as a thinly cut segment of lemon
followed by the trim tab, working this way and that
forcing the rudder out of line with the hull
the whole snaking its way forward
as the side-winding progress of an endlessly wriggling eel

my companions and I leave the boat
strike to the nor'ard at an astonishing rate
slicing through the 'oggin on our exhilarating course
breaking surface, with just the flip of a tail and an expressive grunt
lowering eyelids 'gainst the sun's bright rays
snatching a quick lungful of air, then down again to arse around once more

Then it's Thursday, the twenty-first of July, another hundred and twenty miles reeled up, the best day's run of the passage, with the dream-like quality of the day disturbed by the appearance of what first appear to be

small but purposeful whales
humped backs rise to scimitar blades
must alter course to give them a berth
though not large, they are menacing
the ruffians of the deep, with that ridiculous fin
the pencil-thin 'tash on the sneering upper lip of a ruthless contract killer

Then it's Friday, the breeze favouring southerly, broad reaching, which Mike takes in his stride, resulting in another one hundred and twenty-five miles made good (now only five hundred and ten to Bermuda).

This is the day I can put aside the ocean chart and transfer the vessel's position to

Admiralty Chart
3272
Newfoundland to Bermuda
Including the Gulf of St. Lawrence
&
a portion of the
East Coast of the United States

If it does nothing else, this informative, one page nautical encyclopaedia, helps bring the distance involved into better perspective.

I spend hours poring over details of the coast.

The more frequent indications of the depths of the ocean, three thousand fathoms hereabouts, feeling, as I look at the chart, that the Old World has been well and truly left astern.

Previously, I've been aware that we are travelling from one side of the pond to the other - the long line of daily noon positions has marched across the passage chart, recording progress made over the last few months and more.

But now that I no longer have to jog my memory, I seem never to have sailed *from* a place, only that I'm sailing *towards* another shore, as if my life's been held pause for an endless age of time.

Nevertheless, there's now the prospect of resuming normal activity, still no more than a hope - and one that's subject to violent fluctuations.

This afternoon, the breeze falls away and during the early part of the evening we're becalmed once more.

It seems strange to be motionless, after so many days of progress.

For over two weeks we've had the benefit of some sort of a breeze, but now it's calm, and the noise of the wind in the rigging, almost the sound of the sea itself has been silenced - puts me in mind of a large room, disturbed by the *stopping* of a loudly ticking clock.

The fish that have followed the boat for more than a hundred miles, seem not in the least put out by this loss of progress. Those that prefer the shade, stay there, while others depart, as people disembarking from a broken down intercontinental bus.

But there is one cheerful fact, in an otherwise endless drift of encircling depression - there's now no need to pump the bilge with such alarming frequency.

While we've been close-hauled, slogging our way to windward, the old tub's been making just a little more each day. The extra half-stroke night and morning that has nudged the conscience by its persistent, seemingly inevitable increase.

But when the breeze turned favourable, and she's no longer hard on the wind, she eased up - still making water, but not as fast as before.

For the last twenty-four hours, particularly the last twelve, and now during the period she's been stationary, it amounts to very little.

It should be one worry less, but it isn't as easy as that.

There's no relief from the anxiety, or a halt to the plunging depression that's been eroding my confidence ever since the passage started.

I look longingly to the western horizon - only five hundred miles distant lies the island of Bermuda.

My impatience nags me.

Stuck here, waiting for a breeze, wondering what's been the longest time, during this passage, that we've experienced a flat calm (the log book informs me it's thirty-six hours).

God forbid that we should be forced to endure another period of purgatory.

What about the hurricane?

No doubt it's dealing out death and destruction to untold numbers of poor devils in the Caribbean.

And in which direction will it be moving?

I'm afraid to contemplate the answer.

Here we are, becalmed, within four day's sail of a harbour, yet my wrinkled mind is too creased to wrap around that fact, too parched to feed the milk of reason to an emotion wrung dry by over-long experience.

I've not seen a ship for a week.

I feel listless, without energy, hardly bothering to do the necessary tasks about the boat.

She's rolling to a southerly swell, and the sails are thrashing about in a destructive manner.

Let them slat - to hell with the chafing they'll suffer.

I don't have enough spirit to get out on deck and let go a halyard, merely ninety seconds work.

Just a few paces along the coachroof, unhitch the cleat, and down will come the canvas - to hell with it again.

She can roll her guts up for all I care.

Tear the sails to ribbons.

Spill the teapot.

Waste the water.

Stay in this God-forsaken spot for ever.

And another bloody day if need be.

When I look at the sea, it seems to match my mood.

The swell's become heavier.

The cloud's increased.

It's growing dark.

I've never felt the sea so hostile.

Uncaring?

Of course.

Of such size, extent, and timelessness that the passage of a fleet merely begs a trivial entry.

But I now have the odd feeling, that I'm no longer an unknown speck.

Something has changed.

I pray for a breeze.

And at midnight, that longed for article returns.

Once more we're making progress.

Sailing into the blessed daylight of Saturday morning, as a train emerging from an over-long tunnel, which has deafened the ears and rendered useless the eyes, while choking the mouth and nostrils

with a grit-filled cloud of doubt

11

a change of view

This Saturday morning, I feel like a man halfway through a marathon, caught with a stitch, who struggles on, gasping for breath, until he's found a second wind; still running, perhaps not with his previous speed but with greater determination.

'… and about time too, I thought you were going a bit odd back there.'

I took care over the noon sight, and after the log was written, lunch disposed of, and the boat made shipshape, I got the last remaining can of beer out of the locker and put it carefully on top of the stove.

The last can.

The very last can, out of the two cases of beer that had been put aboard the boat while she was lying in Plymouth, before the commencement of the passage.

It looks somewhat the worse for wear, has started to show signs of rust, and is badly dented. Yet it remains a can of beer, the container embellished with a rampant dragon, designated Strong Welsh Ale - I hardly feel up to it.

But there's a reason for this small celebration.

The log is spinning with varying speed, because the breeze is fitful, but every revolution brings the hands of the dial more nearly upright, and when they are, and that shouldn't take long, we will have sailed three thousand miles from Plymouth Breakwater.

Three thousand miles.

I think, ruefully, that if I had taken the northern route, that would have been sufficient to see us in New York. It's no good bemoaning that mistake now, the Big Apple is over one thousand miles distant, and that's the end of that.

I have decided, instead, to concentrate on the simple pleasure at hand.

After searching, I've found the very special opener that punches a three-cornered hole in a can, and put it, the happy spanner, carefully alongside the Strong Welsh Ale, with the feeling that this is beginning to grow into some sort of ritual. However, I'm determined to wait for the arrival of the magic number - the 'three thousand miles' on the log.

Up on deck, it's a fine afternoon, but the breeze is falling away.

There's nothing I can do to improve the performance of the boat; she's already under full mainsail and the big genoa.

The staysail is hanked on the forestay, bundled up on deck and not worth hoisting; nevertheless, I take the tiller, determined to make good use of every puff that's available.

It's a blisteringly hot afternoon, my mouth is as dry as a cork.

I really do need that beer.

The log reads 2,999 (one more mile to make good) but the breeze has failed completely, the boat merely carrying-way through the water.

The spinner of the log has ceased turning.

The boat's no longer under control, swinging slowly to the south'ard, even with the helm hard up.

My mouth is cracking.

I contemplate unlashing the sweep and sculling the boat along, but that seems to be cheating.

A fitful puff comes, and we make good another fifty yards to the west'ard, another similar puff, and we can make good a little more. The Clerk of the Weather seems intent on keeping me dangling on this intensely irritating hook.

… still no wind.

I unlash the sweep, giving in to the impulse, and carry it to the after end of the boat. The logline hangs limply from the taffrail, the brass rotator is clearly visible a hundred feet below, although the surface movement of the sea is creating some distortion.

Before starting to scull, I haul a few fathoms of the line aboard and notice, with some amusement, that small barnacles have attached themselves to the rope (just *have* to be related to Rotarians?). I feel that I have someone sharing my dizzy existence, so ease them back into the water, then get to work with the oar, consoling myself by remembering that I only have to scull her for less than a mile.

I've just got the boat moving, when a zephyr cools the scene, giving me a helping hand. Instead of sculling, I merely steer with the oar, very restful, very Rider Haggard'ish, so I sing.

> *aye-yee-aye-Yo; aye-yick-ah-Dee*
> *aye-yee-aye-Yo; aye-yick-ah-Dee*
> *Sandy the Great; Sandy the Strong*
> *Maker of Kings; Righter of Wrongs*

the remnants of my shorts could grace an aborigine
my body is burnt brown by the sun
my hair is down to my shoulders
my beard's approaching my navel

(I feel very well cast)

With the log reading two thousand, nine hundred, and ninety-nine miles, *and a half* - it comes to me that all I have to do, to regain my self respect, is merely do the best I can, no matter what the circumstances.

Looking back on the previous week, I felt I had hit rock bottom.

Now, there was only one way to go, and that way is,

... *aye-yee-aye-Yo; aye-Dick-ah-Dee*

Another wandering puff approaches the boat, and she's gathering way, the log begins to rotate in earnest - perhaps it's held a few revolutions up its nautical sleeve?

Most of the time it's trailed half-heartedly astern and stubbornly refused to spin, now she's making the best part of a knot and a half in the right direction.

... 2,999, point seven.

Dash below for beer, while the breeze still holds.

... 2,999, point eight.

... 2,999, point nine.

Three thousand miles!

Three thousand miles !

As the crawling hand on the log face reaches vertical, I pierce the can of beer with a shout of joy, but there's no answering *hiss*, as from a normal can of ale, bursting with enthusiasm.

I put the can to my lips and try an experimental mouthful
hell's bells and buckets of blood
as flat as a tit on a witch
and not only is it flat
it's sour

187

(I try again, but it's just like drinking vinegar)

hell and damnation

I throw the thing over the side, as another good reason for getting to Bermuda as quickly as possible

The breeze, thank God, is holding up, and we can sail towards the evening, somewhat solemnly, but not without enjoyment.

Profitable night time sailing, reaching under all plain sail across a caressing southerly breeze.

Every mile made good now seems *one less* to negotiate.

Previously, it had just been one more to *add*, to those already reeled-up on the log (subtle, but absolutely true).

I sleep very little, try the radio, find that the batteries have at last begun to fade, the gadget only performing for ten minutes before giving up the ghost. After being switched off for an hour, it comes to life once more, for an even shorter period, so I reluctantly put it aside and wish the night away.

During the forenoon (now the following day) the wind has increased in strength and by nine o'clock is fresh and strengthening still further, so in comes the genoa.

The sea begins to rise, and by noon we're down to a double-reefed mainsail and sailing close-hauled to the familiar sou'westerly, which is working up to a moderate gale.

She's started labouring to the task set by the short steep sea, and also has me pumping - forty strokes before lunch - and thirty more during the afternoon.

I look at the barometer - it's fallen half-a-dozen millibars, and my morale's inclined to follow it.

During the evening, even though the breeze moderates, the weather retains its threatening look, the swell begins to mount, and when night comes all my old fears return.

Although there's not a great deal of weight in the wind, to be close-hauled again, after two weeks of more or less pleasant running and reaching has a depressing effect.

The sky overhead is not threatening, but the stars are obscured, particularly down to the southern horizon.

As I stand in the companionway hatch, I catch the flash of distant lightning.

Another look at the barometer, an hour later, tells me it's moved very little, yet I can't rid my mind of the dismal feeling - that we're sailing towards some sort of trouble.

Another night with very little sleep, some significant jumping up and down during the hours of darkness (in more ways than one) and at dawn, another thirty strokes to clear the bilge.

It's become overcast, with rain squalls sweeping over the boat.

I feel myself shrinking again, wanting to scuttle away to a corner (tough tit) there's nowhere to bloody well go.

I curse the vanity that's landed me in this predicament, and though I try to control these perverse emotions, my unreliable morale slips through sweaty fingers, which can do little more than twitch and twitch again at its passing.

I'm into the second jar of Live Long (the first has long been empty).

In the bottom of the carboy swills a dirty yellow sludge, all that remains of the eggs, sugar, lemons, and three-quarters of a gallon of sherry. It has never been a patch on the rum, has always been better than nothing.

I pour what there is into the handle-less mug.

It barely covers the bottom of the receptacle and what there is, seems full of dark spots which, when tasted, grit the teeth. The stuff is close to being rancid, it revolts me, so I throw the lot over the side, mug and all.

It rains out of the overcast sky, making A.M. sights impossible.

The clouds seem lower than they've ever been, although around noon I'm fortunate to have the sun pop out for an instant, giving me an altitude, even if it is of doubtful value.

As the afternoon drags on, the clouds shut in completely and recommence the downpour - with the rain comes wind, to do justice to the falling glass.

By five in the afternoon it's blowing up to a sou'westerly gale, we're down to a fully-reefed mainsail and the spitfire jib. It's far too much for her, she's being overwhelmed in the heavier squalls, shivering on recovery, as would my Labrador bitch, clearing her coat after a swim in the sea-sided tide, throwing spray everywhere - the motion's nothing less than appalling.

I struggle out of the cabin, to a crazily moving deck.

Hand the jib, easier said than done, the wind piling sea upon sea, on top of what's become a heavy swell.

As I struggle to lash the flapping canvas, she gets under a big one and I find myself kneeling, bum-deep, in a froth of water that tears the sail from my grasp.

Looking aft, for a fear-frozen second, the mast and boom gallows (prophetically described?) are sticking out of an engulfing ocean. She clears herself (thank God I secured the main companionway), then remember I haven't re-lashed the for'ard hatch, cursing myself for a fool as I hurry to get the canvas under control and secured with extra gaskets.

Below once more, I work on the for'ard hatch, but up in the bow of the boat, the motion's so severe that I have to abandon the task, and hold on as best I can.

Though the swell is large, the seas are not all that big, but they're incredibly steep, and when she falls off a crest it seems she's been dropped from a second-storey window.

Maybe only (only?) ten feet, but the interval of time, from the poised crest, to the thundering crash in the trough is more than enough to heighten the sea in my mind.

The cabin's a shambles - tins of biscuits, knocked from their shelves, are scattering contents with philanthropic joy.

The empty jar of Live Long is rolling lazily about - I boot it for'ard as it passes conveniently by.

The sails, bundled up just for'ard of the mast, are putting on a show of their own.

As she plunges in the trough, they crouch, as a cat preparing to spring; then, as she shoots to the top of a crest, they leave the deck and when the boat drops - they remain temporarily airborne - as pancakes being tossed, but not always being caught in an inexpertly wielded pan.

The stove is swinging madly in its gimbals, failing to keep pace with the boat - well out of kilter with sudden accelerations and decelerations which rarely coincide with the movement of the hull.

This pride and joy of the galley is crashing noisily against stops that would normally only come into play (?) at ninety degrees of heel.

Both the hatches are leaking, worse than ever.

The main companionway is pouring a stream of water on a previously dry sleeping bag and pillow.

When I'm for'ard, the badly split coaming piddles, either on my left, or my right shoulder, depending on how she lurches.

To complete the joyless picture, from beneath the cabin sole there comes the solemn swish of water which, judging by the way it's squirting up between the floorboards, is deeper than ever before.

It takes half-an-hour to clear the bilge; when it's empty, I lift some boards, and while picking up the odd matchstick and sodden bits of paper, have the opportunity of watching the 'oggin oozing from the lands of the lapstrake planking, making its way to the already slopping strum box, which has only just been pumped dry.

Although I know there's no immediate danger, it's not a pleasant sight - the trouble is, there's nothing I can do about it.

It's impossible to heat anything on the stove, so I dig out a tin of self-heating soup and, after searching for a dry match, light the fuse. Once again murmuring my thanks to Mr. Heinz - the hot broth and a ship's biscuit does the inner man a world of good (that might be a slight exaggeration).

It's been blowing hard for several hours and the weight in the wind has started to build a respectable sea. They're still not huge, as seas go, but they're awkward for the old tub to negotiate.

The rudder is banging about in an alarming manner. The rain has stopped, so I can venture into the cockpit, thankful it's still not too cold to do so without a stitch of clothing, and this, at least, is a blessing.

It's blowing harder than ever, scudding low clouds.

When I look towards the weather horizon, they seem to be growing out of the sea.

Nearer at hand, the wind is plucking madcaps of water from rearing crests, then driving them leeward as a blur of eye lashing spray.

She's lying athwart the seas, with the helm lashed down.

Mike's vane is trembling in the fiercer gusts.

The pressure of wind on the bare mast is sufficient to give her a 20° angle of heel.

She's not attempting to forereach, fortunately - is content to stay snugged down, as a bird with its head tucked under her wing; being blown to leeward at more than a knot, leaving a slick to windward which does much to prevent the threatening crests from breaking aboard; out of the slick, for'ard and aft, the seas are tumbling dangerously.

As I stand in the companionway, ducking to the flying spray, which stings with the lash of a whip, I feel some of my confidence return.

She's doing extremely well - not taking heavy water on deck, the odd awkward crest maybe, nothing of any great weight.

She's moving buoyantly and noticeably quicker than previously in the passage. All those gallons of fresh water, tins of beans, carboys of Live Long, dry and wet goods of one delectable sort or another - all these stores have been consumed, and the reduction in weight is proving beneficial.

Provided I keep the bilge clear, carry on putting old Nep back where he belongs, it seems she's more capable of looking after me, than I am at looking after her - but there is, of course, another side to that sort of coin.

A heavier gust has swept the boat, torn the staysail out of its hastily-cast ties and I'm forcibly reminded there's still plenty to do.

It seems like safety harness weather (the under-statement of the day so far) and I dash below to buckle it on. It's been unused for weeks and the patent catch has rusted, so I'm cursing and fumbling with the damned thing, while the flogging canvas is setting up a rigging-shaking din.

When I work my way cautiously out of the hatch, then shut and secure it, I'm faced with an awe inspiring seascape.

As the seas rear, so does the boat, doing her utmost to get over the heightened role (and roll) of the swell.

The sky is black, with low clouds scudding - it seems just over the top of the mast.

As I shelter at the for'ard end of the cockpit, crouching out of the worst of the blow, the sidedecks appear wet and slippery, with the bow of the boat seemingly much further away than mere measurement would make it.

The madly flogging staysail has burst free from the one remaining gasket and the wind is blowing it up the stay, exposing a greater area of canvas with each rear and plunge of the boat. This increased windage is causing her to payoff, and she's now fore-reaching out of her protective slick, running the risk of getting under a tumbling crest (plenty about right now).

What must be done, has got to be done quickly, there's no beating-about this particular bush.

I'm out of the cockpit, working my way for'ard, along the sidedeck, turning my back to the blast. She's unbalanced, lurching, with water swilling up to my knees. Arrived at the mast, clinging to it with one hand and hooking my safety harness to the weather-shroud with the other, feeling thankful that even if I do get swept overboard, with any luck ...

The staysail's been blown halfway up the inner forestay and is in danger of shaking the mast out of the boat. I hug the foredeck, get one hand on the tack of the sail, begin to haul the thing down. It's trying to leave the ship, streaming out to leeward; when I have it all but smothered, she dips, quickly, and for an instant, one fraction of a second, all seems quiet, apart from a threatening hiss - although I can't see it, I know what's coming.

She's lurching away from it, as a cur will cower from a stick, but there's no avoiding the outcome.

Down it comes, with an engulfing roar, striking my back, smothering the boat in a crushing weight of water.

The sail's torn from my grasp (I barely heed it).

I'm groping for something to hold on to, get hurled to leeward, to be brought up, partly by the stanchions and partly by my safety harness.

Gasping for breath, but free from the weight of water, I open my eyes, amazed to see everything's just about as it should be.

It seems incredible that the boat has survived the blow without suffering structural damage.

She's back to her work, mast leaning away from the wind, rising to the advancing waves, while I'm struggling to regain my feet. The staysail's flapping over my head and the clew cringle delivers a stinging blow, prompting me to keep my head down.

It seems easier to roll over on my back, bracing my feet against the rigging and the coachroof, both hands gripping the slapping canvas, hauling away like mad, as if my life depended on it (perhaps it does). I get it down, make certain of it by passing an extra gasket, and then scramble upright, holding on to the mast.

Relieved of the unbalancing weight for'ard, she's once again lying hove-to, under a bare pole, rising and falling as demanded by the passing seas.

They're bigger now, not mountainous, just the sort of conditions that occur when increasing wind speeds coincide with a heavy swell, with old Neptune taking great delight in laughingly curling the tops.

I'm upright, clinging to the mast, 'sheltering' behind its narrow but welcoming shield.

The wind is whistling about the rigging, rising to a higher pitched shriek as she lurches off the top of a crest and whips the stick to wind'ard.

I look aloft, wondering if the Saundersfoot Sailing Club burgee is still there. It's been partly torn from its stiffening wire, the trailing edge of the bunting flapping so rapidly that it's impossible to distinguish the individual flicks - reminiscent of giant hands tearing an endless bolt of calico.

The good old Welsh Dragon is still there, but he's in danger of disappearing up his own backside. A large part of his frayed tail has already disappeared - from where I stand (crouch) he seems 'relatively' undisturbed.

A quick look around the horizon.

Down to the sou'east'ard there's a ray of hope, a lightening strip 'twixt sea and clouds, a long way off, nevertheless offering the promise of an easing in the weather.

With another gasket passed around the mainsail, as an extra precaution, and an apprehensive glance at the encircling ocean, I unhook my safety harness and make my way to the cockpit, where I don't linger, slide back the hatch and make my way below.

She needs pumping again.

Thirty strokes that do nothing to lighten my mind as I work away at the handle. The bilge sucks dry, a gratifying, even a musical sound, that perhaps only a person afloat, by himself, on an unfrequented part of the ocean, and more than two hundred miles from land can appreciate.

With all snug on deck, and the cabin reasonably tidy, there's little I can do beside turn in.

It may seem an odd decision (apparently abandoning the boat to its own devices) yet the welcome fact is, in bad weather, you're better off in your bunk than any place else. With the overriding consideration being, that as every task is more difficult, sometimes impossibly so due to the movement of the boat, you think twice before attempting anything.

On a common or garden level - I want a bar of fudge, to chew while towelling dry.

I hadn't felt cold on deck, now I'm below, I notice my hands and feet are well on the way to being blue.

As I sit on the edge of the lower berth, drying myself as best I can, after five minutes bruising search through disarrayed lockers, I find the fudge.

I can now throw the towel for'ard and work my way into my sleeping bag. It's still blowing fit to bust, and the hatch is still leaking, yet I feel I can put up with it, because - I'm chewing the fudge (and ain't that well on the way to being an amusing situation?).

Now that it *is* blowing a gale, at least some of my previous fears have been blown to leeward, along with the whiplash of spray.

Conventional wisdom suggests that a prolonged calm is more wearing on the nerves than anything a single-handed seaman may encounter, with the exception, of course, of a major disaster.

Now, my immediate and ongoing experience is adding weight to previous knowledge. During the present contretemps (if that's the way to describe it) there's been plenty to do, and what has to be done takes twice as long as usual - a happy combination? (depends where you're standing).

I listen to the wind in the rigging.

Is it as high as ever?

Or does it sound a slightly lower note?

It seems hardly worth straining the ears to establish the difference. The barometer is no longer falling, and that's a blessing.

As that encouraging thought slips into my mind, she trips over another crest, and for her awkwardness, receives a ton of water, mostly over the after deck.

It fills the cockpit.

I can feel her down by the stern while the drains do their best to gurgle it away.

I'm surprised by the time it takes (make a mental note to have *much* larger bore pipes in the future).

Even though sticky with salt, I'm beginning to get warm and reflect, yet again, that a sleeping bag is the best place in world to endure bad weather; up to Force 8 and then - even further along good old Admiral Beaufort's ultimately *terrifying* scale.

I must have been more tired than usual because I've slept through several hours of rapidly changing conditions. This in itself is an indication that I've left behind some of the mental difficulties previously experienced. I've been refreshed by a good solid sleep, and during that time the gale has moderated and it's now nearly dark.

I listen for the wind. There's hardly a sound. An uncanny sensation after the shriek of wind in the rigging.

I know it's still rough, because I can feel the boat plunging and rearing, with her movement being even wilder now, because there's very little pressure of wind on the mast.

It takes time to orientate myself to these new conditions, so I lie a few minutes, slipping back to reality from what had been a dreamless sleep.

My left leg is stiff and the skin above the knee is painful to touch (that's odd, I hadn't noticed anything before I turned in).

My right shoulder gives a twinge as I heave myself up on an elbow.

One thing is certainly the same. The water in the bilge is making its unwelcome presence felt. I can hear it slopping about, as threatening as ever, so pumping her out will be the first job to tackle.

I do it, even before sticking my head out of the hatch.

It needed doing.

Then back with the flap of the hatch, and a good look round.

Damned near a flat calm, and getting dark.

The skies are clear and most of the stars are visible.

The sea is still hurling wetting great lumps of 'oggin about. Instead of marching in overwhelming ranks nor'eastward, they tumble aimlessly this way and that, without apparent serious intent (ho, ho).

It's hard to believe that such a short time since they had been well-drilled echelons of striding giants whose roaring crests gave threatening support to the urge of the tempestuous gale.

The boat is finding this disjointed kingdom an awkward place to inhabit - lurching hesitantly in and out of step, as she endeavours to match the disordered conduct of the ocean.

I reset the mainsail and the staysail. The lack of wind and the violent motion of the boat combine to make it an almost profitless task.

It's coming up dark, and with the darkness arrives a westerly breeze, and with the increase in wind speed comes more cloud (or perhaps that should be the other way about).

The first indication of this yet another deterioration in the weather is the loss of stars to the west'ard. Then those overhead are shut away and only those over the eastern horizon remain, and soon, they too are obscured.

Although the cloud base is invisible, it weighs heavily on the boat, a low and menacing presence.

Now comes the rain - passing squalls that *hiss* their animosity into the sea as they rattle contemptuously over the vessel.

I can't sleep.

During the early part of the night, the varying weight of the wind keeps me actively reefing and then resetting the mainsail, until I weary of the task and don't bother to reset the canvas in the infrequent spells of sailable weather.

While on deck I notice, ahead and a little to the south'ard, the flash of lightning.

For some time, I watch, fascinated by the eerie glow, which is too far away to add to its frightening charm by delivering an accompanying roll of thunder. It's coming closer, and above the noise of the sea on the hull and the wind in the rigging, the flash is now being accompanied by a stomach-knotting roar.

I'm frightened.

Caught in a situation that I would give anything to avoid, but escape is impossible.

From north through west, to the equally dark southerly horizon, the black belly of the sky hangs in blisters to the flash of occasional lightning, which is now approaching the boat, stabbing white-hot fingers into the broth of a sizzling ocean; when it's a mile or more away, the accompanying thunder reaches a heightened crescendo. Intimidates the ear. Prompts the hands to give succour to the head.

To no avail.

It comes closer, dazzling the shielded eye and stupefying the mind by its powerful display.

I sit below and shake with fright.

During the heavier gusts, the boat heels smartly, then resumes her natural gait. It seems more than chance circumstance that these manoeuvres coincide with peals of thunder, interspersed with the fork and flash of lighting.

I just *can't* remain below - spring to the hatch and stick my head out, in the only possible gesture of defiance.

An electrical disturbance surrounds the vessel.

The thunder rolls about, varying in intensity from a distant peal to an overhead ear-splitting crash that forces me to duck, involuntarily, below the cockpit coaming.

The sea and sky are joined in shattering intercourse, devoid of moderation.

In the midst of this holocaust crouches the boat, its metal mast pointing skyward, as the admonishing finger of a pious missionary - raised to what possible effect?

Dominated by this colossal display, I can imagine nothing in the world more out of context.

The metal spar seems a hideously inviting finger - and there's little I can do.

Pray?

As an immediate convert to an omnipotent deity?

> *I pump, to satisfy another need*
> *each stroke of the pump gives spurt to my spirit*
> *each murmuring prayer gives strength to my arm*

And still I pump, each measure of water moved five feet by a stroke that's dramatically (laughably?) aligned to the peals of thunder and the regular flash of lightning - but at least I'm joining the band.

Eventually, the bilge sucks dry, while the storm still rages overhead.

I sit in a funk, which swaths from head to foot, does nothing to secure me from the odour of my fear.

After a cold-sweated age, the storm moves on, passing to the eastward, leaving the Folkboat carrying its cowed crew into the prevailing westerly breeze.

During the night, the swell has grown to monstrous billows, and greets the red-eyed morning with unbelievable energy of movement.

The sea shimmers - black under an overcast sky.

A rain squall passes over the boat, releasing a cascade that can only be compared to the deluge that must have preceded the flood of Biblical proportions

To the south'ard, another curtain of rain, moving faster than the rest, seems to indicate a sight more wind. After a careful look, I conclude its spitefulness will pass astern of the boat.

I go below, to make a cup of tea.

The kettle hisses its approval to the warming roar of the primus.

The boat, moderately canvassed to the fresh westerly, is still labouring to windward.

It's five o'clock in the morning, and I wait, anxiously, for the kettle to come to the boil, while I sit, hunched, hugging my knees to my chest.

The hatch is closed.

I'm contemplating, either a ship's biscuit or a tin of sardines for breakfast (possibly both) when I feel the boat wobble, much as the rider of a bicycle might, for a second, lose his equilibrium.

After the recovery from this unusual quiver, comes the noise of an approaching express train.

Without further warning the boat receives a blow that throws the vessel on her beam ends.

It's quick, the movement of a clawed paw, but decisive as that of a descending club.

I find myself inverted, legs in the air, head and neck crushed against the side of the boat, the kettle follows me and crashes against the coachroof in a spray of scalding water and a clattering of lid.

In an instant, the boat has been knocked down, mast and sails pushed by a giant hand beneath the surface of the sea.

I struggle to get to my feet.

For what seems an age, I grope for handhold.

After a split second I find it, and heave myself upwards, to stand in the companionway, tearing at the hatch, which seems to be irretrievably jammed.

She's recovered slightly.

I slide back the hatch to be greeted by a scream of wind that, for an instant, robs me of breath and movement.

The boat still lies on her beam ends, with the cockpit full of water, which is lapping at the coaming of the hatch.

She is showing some signs of buoyancy, as a dazed boxer will attempt to rise from a blow. No sooner does she stagger a little more upright, than she's forced again to leeward by the weight of wind in the rigging.

She's lost all way through the water, and wallows before the onslaught of the squall that raises its impossible note to an even more piercing screech.

What length of time elapsed, from the initial knockdown to my scrambled appearance at the main hatch?

I just don't know, such an experience can't be measured by time, only by intensity, and as such - it's white hot.

My safety harness is down below, but if I don't get the canvas off her, she's going to be dismasted.

It's a miracle the stick still stands.

I wriggle out of the crazily leaning hatch and start to work my way for'ard, as if moving across the steeply sloping roof of a house (holding on to the ridge) which in this case is the gunwale of the boat; at the same time struggling to free my feet from an entanglement of the bungled-about ends of sheets and halyards. The noise is still deafening, assails my ears as a cauterising pain.

I get a hand to the mast, another to the halyards and, amid a welter of spray and foam, cast them off.

Nothing alters.

Heeled as she is, it seems I'm pulling the sail along, and *into* the blast, not down and *away* from it.

But I struggle on, claw some of the canvas from the grasp of the wind, heedless that what I recover is falling into the sea.

The end of the main boom disappears below the surface of the water.

I heave again on the luff of the mainsail (the slides must be stuck).

I heave again, still no progress.

Although I'm frightened, I'm still able to think of the next move (or what should be the next move).

I find the halyard, which has caught on some obstruction and hasten to free it. Both hands are needed, and as I grope for the rope, she lurches and dumps me into the sea.

Sobbing with fear, I scramble madly back on deck, but with the beginning of life-saving anger. I find and cut the halyard, with the damned half hitch which has cast itself over the end of the boathook (now ain't that just par for the course).

Return to the mainsail, which has to be fought every inch of the way along the mast. Using the first piece of line that comes to hand, I cast a bight over the head of the sail, to keep it under control, and then struggle to get the jib down on deck.

She's relieved now from the overpowering press of sail and comes a little more upright. I work at stowing the thrashing canvas, exposed to rain that falls on my body with the flail and lash of a whip. It pricks my skin with a host of darting needles, spurs me on to make a rapid, yet hopefully secure stow of the sails.

Then back to the cockpit to lash the helm hard down.

A quick look at the self-steering gear, which seems little the worse for wear, and then, through the still-sloshing cockpit, dive below, wanting to get to hell and gone out of this dramatic scene.

The cabin's a shambles.

Two dozen other things have joined the kettle on the cabin sole.

The place is a piggish mess.

I find myself shivering uncontrollably, search for a towel, find they're all wet. I pick the driest and attempt to rub a little warmth into my limbs, wondering, as I do so, how long I've been out on deck - it could have been five minutes, or an hour-and-a-half.

I look at my wristlet chronometer (at least, at the wrist, that should have held the timepiece) - it's missing.

I can't believe the evidence of my own eyes.

The imprint of the watch remains, lightly etched where my skin has been shielded from the sun's rays.

I have a quick look round the cabin sole, then amongst the gear that's ended up in a mess on the starboard bunk.

No watch.

As I kneel awkwardly to my task, I realise that I'm having difficulty bending my right leg. The knee is swelling and painful to touch, nevertheless, I open the hatch and have a quick look in the cockpit, which has now drained away the previously swilling water - there's nothing there.

I look for'ard - the still-leaning deck couldn't harbour an unlashed item for ten seconds.

It's blowing as hard as ever, and I'm glad to get my head out of the skin-blasting rain and slam the hatch - still can't accept the fact that the watch has gone.

I search the boat again, moving all the gear from each spot in turn. Shaking every item of clothing. Turning the bedding inside-out, searching the bilge, the lockers. Working my way further from likely places of concealment until I'm reduced to crawling amongst the sail bags and wet gear for'ard, in a vain hope that the watch will turn up there.

It's a hopeless task, but I'm reluctant to give in.

I hope against all reasonable hope that the timepiece has fallen from my wrist when I was still in the cabin, while all the time, a conviction grows, that it's been torn off while I've been wrestling with the sails on deck. At length, I give up, prompted more by the pain from my leg than any lessening of doubt. Yet still cling to the unreasonable hope that another more rigorous search, if that were possible, would reveal the missing item.

At last, I leave the cabin in its shambled state, and with some difficulty crawl into my sleeping bag, utterly exhausted.

My bedding is wet, but just to rest, without weight on my leg, is a sufficient blessing in itself.

I try to remember what's happened during the past hour.

Although I can't be absolutely sure the watch was on my wrist before I left the cabin, I'm convinced that it had been there.

The last entry in the log is timed at 4 am and I remember glancing at my watch. The only possible explanation can be, that when I was hurled leeward at the height of the struggle, the watch strap had caught in some part of the rigging and carried away under the strain.

I also have no recollection of damaging my knee.

It's a bad twist, and has all the symptoms of my old cartilage trouble. Though these are occurrences to be deplored, they seem barely significant in the wider context.

The immediate worry is the water that is once again slopping about in the bilge. I can reach the handle of one of the pumps from my bunk (useful pre-planning) and it takes ninety strokes to clear the bilge, which must have been damn near up to the cabin sole again.

It's still blowing like hell outside, but the movement of the boat is a little more regular.

Within an hour, the wind has moderated and once again is no more that a substantial breeze.

During this interval, I manage to snatch some cat-napped sleep and now struggle with the business of cleaning up the mess, with as much enthusiasm as I can muster. Recover the badly dented kettle and set it on the stove, hoping, as I do so, that we will have better fortune about our tea-making on this occasion.

I limp on deck to survey the scene.

There's a large sea running over the top of a colossal swell. The combination is not all that dangerous, yet. She's merely throwing the odd dollop about accompanied with considerable spray.

The mast still stands, and the working canvas is still lashed on deck.

Before going for'ard I unlash the tiller and have a quick look at Mike.

He's a little the worse for wear, the balance weight is bent and the stops that limit the movement of the trim tab are showing signs of strain. The gadget's still workable and should improve under the attention of a well-directed hammer.

Then I proceed to the coachroof and start sorting out the mainsail.

My knee is stiff and painful, so I take extra care about the task.

Several of the stainless steel slides that hold the luff of the sail to the mast track have parted and will have to be renewed. The sail itself, though it has lost some stitching, is still serviceable.

I check the sail battens and find them all broken.

Those that were made of ash have snapped into many small pieces, none of which are more than four inches long.

I assume that I will soon have these splintered remains out of the batten pockets, but never was a job so deceptive.

For twenty minutes I work away at just one of the battens. And then I'm forced, by a combination of short-tempered irritation and an aching knee, to seek an easier seat below.

Removing the slides from the mast track, I pull most of the mainsail into the cabin.

The extraction of the broken bits of batten from their tightly-sewn pockets proves an appalling job. The splintered ends of every piece persist in catching every snag (mostly the stitching) and have to be worked along, a fraction of an inch at a time. The job takes, unbelievably, over six hours, and that's not including an interlude for tea and several other relieving 'spells' made necessary by the tedious nature of the task. At length, new plastic battens have been rove, the main and staysail re-hoisted, and I breath a sigh of relief, that we're making progress to the west'ard once more.

It's still heavily overcast, sights are impossible and this day, Tuesday, the 26th of July the noon D.R. puts her at 32° 54′ North, 62° 05′ West, which means we're just over a hundred and twenty miles from Bermuda.

We're also some distance to the nor'ard of the island, so I must sit down, and have a quiet think about the best course of action.

There's no chronometer, so I will be unable to fix our longitude, and feel that the D.R. position might well be in error ten miles or more.

That means we should get down to the south'ard, until we're smack on the latitude of the island, and then 'run our westing down', in the manner of the old days of sail, before the advent of accurate timepieces, or, in our day and age, radio provided time signals.

Throughout the day, the wind holds mainly from the west, rain squalls are frequent, and there's a confused sea running under an overcast sky. The radio, during the receptive five minutes before the batteries run completely out, gives forth little more than an alarming succession of crackles and clicks, disturbing evidence that there are other electrical storms in the offing.

As we work our way gradually to the south'ard, I pump at regular intervals.

Fifty strokes.

Forty strokes.

More than fifty - she's making too much water for comfort.

During the early hours of Wednesday morning the breeze falls light and variable and I curse the necessity of having to tend the boat more carefully. My knee is extremely painful, and I begin to realise how much the small-boat sailor depends on his agility, for even the simplest task.

While getting the latitude at noon, I'm caught out by the weather, which drew an unexpected cloud over the sun before he'd reached his zenith. Without a chronometer, this leaves me with only an approximate position, little more than an inspired guess, say 32° North and ninety miles to the eastward of the island.

As we now seem to be a little too far to the south'ard, I alter course to accommodate the possibility.

The next twenty-four hours are a nerve racking vigil.

We've sailed three thousand five hundred miles from Plymouth, and are now almost within sight of land - not New York, it's true; but land, any land, surely has an attractive ring to it.

Now that the conditions have moderated, she's not making so much water, nevertheless the problem remains in the back of my mind, while in the forefront lies the imminent thrill of a landfall.

The isles of Bermuda are comparatively low, barely fifteen miles long, not five miles wide, surrounding on three sides by extensive coral reefs. The chart also mentions local magnetic anomalies.

I've lost my chronometer. Both radio sets are useless. The weather offers a threatening look.

The conditions are peculiar.

Although the breeze is moderate, the sky is full of ink-black clouds which toil about each other in the fearsome manner of celestial intestines. Some hang as blisters from the mass, others coil like snakes to unexpected places; around it all, sheet lightning flashes and occasionally crackles.

Although it's mid-afternoon, the ocean's 'shielded' from the sun. It seems more like a temperate dusk or dawn than the middle of a tropic day.

The swell heaves black and heavy - gigantic rolls of oily fat whose navel marks the boat and me.

The atmosphere is oppressive and I find myself panting, watching the sky, trying to identify the low pitched drone that comes from somewhere up aloft.

An aircraft circles, quartering the massive banks of cloud in a plotted search, then, much to my relief, comes below the cloud base and circles overhead.

A four-engined machine, with patches of high visibility orange paint on its fuselage and tail. I recall a barely decipherable sentence coming over the radio the previous day, *'planes of the hurricane hunter group have been despatched.'*

I no longer bother to look at the plane, which soon resumes its inquisitive vigil; but this machine, or some other, drones about the area for the rest of the worrying day.

It's amazing that the breeze remains little more than fresh below this terrifying sky, where clouds whirl about the threat of fatal treatment.

Colossal forces are involved. Thunder rolls. Lightning flashes. Towering cumuli are sucked thousands of feet into the air before my astonished eye - while beneath this awe inspiring display our small boat sneaks about the ocean.

As a precaution, I double reef the mainsail and set the spitfire jib, not wishing to be caught in a recurrence of the previous day's debacle.

So we creep, as a fearful mouse, to the west'ard, under the shadow of the encircling storm.

During the evening, the breeze falls away to such an extent that, against my nervous judgement, I increase the area of canvas in order to keep the boat best-footing to the west'ard.

All night long, throughout this endless period, our progress is illuminated by the flash of lighting, accompanied by peals of thunder, sometimes distant, at others, much too close for comfort. A fearful night, quite without sleep, yet not devoid of hope (Bermuda's drawing closer).

This morning, Thursday, the 28th of July, brought similar atmospheric conditions and the return of the circling plane, identified, through binoculars, as a four-engined Constellation.

At noon, a snap sight put her on the same latitude (32° North) so I set a nor'westerly course, to edge her up to the nor'ard. An estimated forty miles distant from the island, with three thousand, four hundred and thirty-five miles established on the log.

Although I haven't slept for more than forty-eight hours, my mounting excitement is driving any suspicion of tiredness from my body.

During the spells of lighter breeze, I coax the boat along, and when it freshens, still 'tend the tiller, standing in the cockpit, my body invigorated by passing rain squalls while I keep her footing west'ard.

I'm suffering from my usual attack of navigationitis (if it's not a real word, it is, by God, a stomach-knotting condition).

We've been seven weeks at sea. My sextant has suffered many a bump - supposing there's an undiscovered fault?

Can the compass be relied on?

When did I last calculate its error?

Yet sooner, rather than later, I float above these doubts.

I know damned well where we are.

I have that feeling in my water.

I also draw comfort from the fact that I've always checked my sextant before taking a sight, and have *never* let the opportunity of a compass-checking amplitude go by.

The voyage seems to have taken on some of the attributes of a pregnancy, in that its termination can be confidently expected, even if anxiously awaited. So I feel - I damned well *know* - it's only a matter of a time before we'll be making a landfall.

During the late afternoon, a further darkening of the sky to the south'ard prompts me to strip the boat of all sail, make a good stow below and lash everything that's moveable on deck.

The threatening squall marches towards the boat, so I set Mike the task of steering before it.

The wind comes first, freshening quickly to a moderate gale. As the sea respond to its angry shout, a wall of water, not to be described as rain, falls out of the lowest and blackest cloud yet seen. A downpour sweeps the boat. Ironing the surface of the sea. Cascading off the coachroof. Swamping the cockpit - the deluge of creation.

I remain below.

The boat runs before the wind, is overtaken by another bursting cloud that sweeps across my line of sight as a curtained wall of water.

In twenty minutes, it's all over. Everything back to near-normality; only a bank of leaden cloud to the nor'ard recalls the squall's intensity.

we beat west'ard
within thirty nautical miles of a landfall
make four

so six and twenty remain
seven more
and there's nineteen to score

as we're playing darts with the Neptune himself
we'll aim for one
because that leaves

just
double-nine
and she's mine

I'm standing on the coachroof, keeping an anxious lookout. I glance at the log; we should be eight miles from the island. The light on Gibb's Hill is charted as 335 feet above mean low water springs, so it should be visible twenty-six nautical miles - that's at night.

'... you won't see it much more than ten miles off today.'

I know, these rain squalls may bring it down to less than that.

'... are you sure of your position ?'

Shut up.

'... seems to me, you're a sight more nervous than you should be.'

What the hell do you know about it?

'... true, I'm only your....'

Never mind who you are. Can you see anything to starboard?

'... no, but there's a bit of a loom ahead.'

What's the time?

'... seven o'clock by the alarm, who knows how much adrift it is.'

I can see a faint shadow, a point on the starboard bow.

'... and about time too, it's been there at least ten minutes.'

Land-oh. Land-Oh !

'... no need of a song and dance, let's go below and make a cup of tea.'

Not a bad idea.

'... get the TEA.'

Yes, sir - yes Sir.

By the time we've closed the island, it's dark; all that remains of the shadow which caused so much excitement by its appearance on the horizon is the flashing light on Gibb's Hill, pricking the forgetful darkness into memory.

I think it's much too dangerous to try and come to an anchorage during the night.

Although the island itself is well-lit, the off-lying shoals are so numerous that a small sailboat, without an auxiliary motor and, more particularly, any local knowledge, would be better off waiting the dawn.

Although this is the third night without any real sleep, I can't turn-in - merely to lie on my bunk would be a hopeless exercise.

My blood seems to be circulating quicker.

My knee more flexible.

My eyes not sore.

My lips not cracked. My mind free from anxiety (and those insistent voices).

I feel five years younger.

Then I wash.

Splashing water into the plastic bucket as a miser runs amok amongst a hoard of bright doubloons.

I drink, until my belly's distended, and that on only a few pints.

I pour water over my head, long after it's required to remove the last traces of soap.

I clean my teeth, gargle and spit, throw the dirty water away and start again.

Standing in the cockpit, pouring gallons of fresh water over my head, around my shoulders, running down my body to gurgle happily out of the cockpit drains into the receptive sea.

An orgy of cleanliness, including even the masthead burgee, and the rampant Welsh Dragon, who condescends to have a quick dip in order to put on a bright appearance for tomorrow's celebrations.

Then.

It's dawn.

A bright sunny day with a moderate breeze. The island bearing west nor'west, eight miles distant.

All my previous anxiety seems to be pouring, and being pumped into a fountain of excitement.

I'm still nervous, but now, it's a nervous energy.

The tight feeling around my chest has gone. My aches and pains have disappeared. My knee is better. The soreness of my mouth is forgotten.

Up goes the mainsail, let-draw the staysail and we're reaching easily towards the coast.

The land, that for the past seven weeks we've been striving for.

The fact that it's Bermuda, when it should be New York doesn't matter a damn.

It's land.

People.

The opportunity of sending a message home.

We're closer now. The loom of the island has lost its undistinguished look and shows a tinge of green.

A lighthouse stands above a cliff and from this distance, through the binoculars, looks black against the sun-bright sky.

We're sailing on an azure sea. As we near the shore I can see the edge of the reef; take note of the white breaking crests, and when I stand on the coachroof, make out the feathering line that marks the top of the subterranean shelf.

> *houses are visible, squatting on the slate grey cliffs*
> *they are white*
> *dotted about as butterflies*
>
> *livened by the slope and colour of the red tiled roofs*
> *supported by swathe upon swathe of shaded pastel walls*
> *and the grass*
>
> *what little I can see is green*
> *greener than grass was ever green before*
> *it looks succulent*
>
> *if I were a cow, I would bellow*
> *as a mere man*
> *I can only feast my eyes*

Closer now, almost up to the harbour entrance. Still in deep water, while on our starboard hand, a ledge of coral is barely covered by the surge and suck of the sea.

We're accepted by the ocean; within a short stone's throw, old Neptune's swells are rearing crests that curl and topple as they deliver the foam and thunder of an ocean-swept reef.

There's also a deeper growl. From over the land appears a four-engined aircraft.

This machine has the familiar splashes of orange paint on the wings and fuselage (a hurricane hunter?). I wave to the crew (do they wave back?).

I don't care - I just want to wave to people.

Proceeding to the nor'ard, there's a buoy ahead, probably the channel marker.

So much bigger when we're alongside it.

Harden-in the sheets; beating close-hauled up the channel which narrows as it leads to the harbour.

We're close to the shore
I wish we could stop, right here, so I could admire the view
The breeze is blowing directly out the narrow butted entrance
Both sides of the channel offer low, but steep-to cliffs
Carefully at the tiller now
Keep her in the middle of the channel, closing the southern shore
Hold on to the last moment
Deep water right up to the rock
Another few feet
Now, helm hard up
Rattle into the wind
Pull like mad on the jib sheet
Don't bother to make fast
Hold it
Watch the heading
A stronger puff dips the rail
We don't seem to be making much progress
The tide must be running out
Mid-channel again, closing the shore, hold it
Ready about ?
Lee-Oh
Round she comes, ten feet from that large rock, (a bit too close)
Beat across again, tack back to the other shore
Making progress
Channel getting a little wider
Time to look around
The place is prettier than ever
There's a fellow fishing
Must give him a wave, now we're tacking past his rock
Good morning, I hope I'm not disturbing your fish

Not at all
That's what he said ... not ... at ... all
Not-at-all
Notatall
Fish on
Friend
We're safe in the bay

The town of St. George's lies on the starboard hand.
Buildings, blinding white 'gainst a lush green background.
Further away, on the port bow, storage tanks that seem to have some connection with the airfield. They're painted in red and yellow squares, as tidy heaps of children's gaily-coloured playing blocks.
Where shall we go?
Fine on the starboard bow, past the town, I can see a group of tall masts - that's the place for us.
As we get closer, I note two vessels, one alongside the quay, the other moored outboard of her partner.
Both American, the nearer a beautiful yawl.
She has her name in gilt letters plashed across her counter.

GRACE

A beautiful name for a handsome vessel
Several lads about the deck
Hold her off
Spill a little wind out of the mainsail
Do you mind if I come alongside?
Not at all *(notatall)*, have you any fenders?
Yes, but they're rather small
O.K. we'll rig a few
Let-draw the main, sail a distance off, get the fenders out
(should have thought of those before)
And the mooring lines
Bring her round, well down to leeward
Sidling her in
Up on the coachroof, down with the mainsail
Just enough way to come alongside, hardly brushing the fenders
Throw them a line
Somebody jumps aboard with their own rope
All fast in thirty seconds

Thanks

There's half-a-dozen of them, all looking at me. I can't complain, I'm looking at them with equal intensity. They're young, in their twenties, tall, crewcut, wearing white shorts and blue deck shoes. The nearest has fair hair, beads of sweat on his forehead, candid blue eyes.

He's chewing gum and the muscles of his throat are sending ripples down his neck.

His arms are folded across his chest, brown-skinned over a faintly-downed belly - one of his shoelaces is undone.

Next in line is looking at me with an amused expression on his face.

'Nice little boat you've got there.'

' ... yes.'

Then it comes to me that I'm looking a little too intently at them. After all, you don't normally greet a stranger with the sort of scrutiny you would receive from a suspicious Custom Official.

Why the devil *are* they looking so hard at me?

I haven't developed web feet - to make sure, I take a quick look down. Must be something else (but what a daft thing to do).

'What's that flag, flying from the starboard crosstrees?'

' ... that's the Red Dragon of Wales.'

'Wales - where's Wales?'

It's just like walking down a busy street, in a strange town, and everyone you meet, particularly when you enquire the way, is a stranger there himself; but here, the whole thing's been inverted. I'm tempted to ask them (where am I ?) but they get their retaliation in first.

'You mean England, Ireland, Scotland and Wales?'

That's not what I mean, but I nod.

That's right, and singing, Sospan Fach, Rugby Football, David Lloyd George, Owen Glendower, The Fair Ness, the Tudor Kings of England, the ancestors of Frank Lloyd Wright, the poems of Dylan Thomas, I don't know what in heaven or hell I'm saying the words are tripping over ideas in my mind possibly because I haven't conversed with anyone

for two long months

211

are there fairies at the bottom of your garden ?
or
are the sands of time always this abrasive ?

We stay at Bermuda seven days, the boat and I (makes three of us, if you count my erstwhile sailing companion?), everyone's having a rest; of the group, I feel my need is the greater.

She lies moored quietly to the quay
I roam the island
She takes no water aboard
I soak liquids inside and out
She's exposed to the scorching subtropical sun
I lounge on shaded balconies and nibble at sweet cakes
She hears the raucous laughter of sailors
I go to church
She's piqued
So, I scrub her bottom
And have all her canvas overhauled

I soon get over my rather odd response to the Yankee crews of the boat we're berthed alongside. They ask me aboard, and give me a cool beer, then press another on me, which I fail to finish. I think they're faintly disappointed that I have a need less than that of a camel, but find my capacity is limited and feel full, perhaps too excited to drink any more.

They take me to the signal station and I send a message home, making acquaintance while there of a young chap who has digs in the town; he later took me to meet his hosts.

I hire a room, and sit to lunch.

Ice cold milk, thumbs into the crisp shell of a warm bread roll, its wheatened smell watering the mouth on its buttered passage to the lips.

A salad, fresh lettuce, green as any grass, blooming with sliced tomatoes whose succulent pips escape my mouth and hide away in my beard.

A plate of cold beef, emblazoned with golden fat, its tender brown tissue circling-about the pink melt in the mouth heart.

Salt, that I can leave on the side of my plate.

Pickles, that are not required, because they would spoil the budding taste of fresh food, after seven weeks living out of tins.

Strawberries, nipples wrinkled with desire and blushing scarlet as they're smothered in spooned-up quantities of freshly clotted cream.

A peach, its soft skin clinging to my fingertips as it appeals in vain to be spared the knife - cut to the stone, which is curiously dry in its succulent pod of chin dribbling juice.

Coffee, on the terrace, in the shade, feet up on a stool.

A carefully-lit cigar.

'Brandy?'

'No thanks, I feel marvellous - anything else would spoil it.'

The magnificent view over St. George's harbour, fringed by coral strands, with fleecy white clouds moving serenely across the bluest of bright blue tropic skies, quite foreign to yesterday's harbinger of gales and life-threatening squalls.

Was it yesterday?

Last week, perhaps?

Last year?

An age ago?

Just another - soon to be forgotten experience?

The drive to Hamilton, fascinated by the passing countryside.

Neatly laid out houses, made of white, sawn coral blocks.

An overwhelming impression of prosperity.

A self-conscious walk around the town.

A beer in a club, and then back to St. Georges's, which I prefer, because it's quieter, has less traffic and much more charm.

I feel a little odd. The things that interest me, I wish to spend time over, not wanting to rush.

People (not only the women) hold a fascination.

Somebody's blonde moustache, flowering under a bulbous nose that could have held its own in Barnum & Bailey's hard drinking circus.

Another person's over-large ears.

The way they talk, and particularly the way they laugh compels attention - they're all forever laughing, not at me, but at what they see as *circumstances*.

I also find it amusing.

'… what would you like for dinner?'

'You're not contemplating another meal? We've only just eaten.'

'… that was hours ago, time to eat again.'

It seems somewhat indecent (force-feeding a goose before slaughter). Just as meekly I'm led to the table. It groans under the weight of food, enough to last a frugal man a week, while my metabolism seems to be in neutral, compared with that of my companions, who eat enough to satisfy the calorific requirements of a hard working Irish navvy. Yet they all have sedentary jobs and wield nothing heavier than a pen.

'… Jack had a mild heart attack last year.' (says Dot, his wife).

I say nothing, amazed he's lasted so long, quite forgetful that a few months ago I also ate like a horse, swilled beer with the best of them, enjoyed a randy night out on the tiles (that was farther back still). I don't seem able to control my self-righteous attitude, which must be one of the unexpected by-products of spending perhaps rather too long in a boat.

It's the same with the women - all I want to do is *look,* not seeking further intimacy.

Are there any chances?

I think there could be, but I keep myself to myself (and this *is* a strange feeling).

After dinner, I book a phone call to New York, a gross extravagance, but feel that I must find out how everyone got on.

Bruce Robinson, of the Slocum Society, is soon on the line.

'… where the devil are you, Val?'

'Bermuda.'

'… good God. What are you doing there?'

I sigh (I can't afford to tell him, at two dollars and fifty cents a minute).

'… when will you to get to New York? But hold on, I have a surprise for you.'

'… hello, Val; had a good trip? (the voice is unmistakeable).

'Hello, Blondie; yes, thanks. And you?'

'… pretty good. I got in last week. David's not here, but expected daily.'

'Who won? Jean Lacombe?' (although he's seven hundred miles away, I can see him smile).

'… Francis took forty-two days. Is there anything you need?'

'

'Yes; a chronometer if there's one knocking about, and a battery for the radio, but that's not vital.'

'… OK. We'll see what we can do; if we can help, we'll cable you.'

'Thanks Blondie, goodbye. Say cheerio to Bruce for me.'

'… goodbye.'

Time for bed.

The room is high, cool, and, quiet.

The bed low, wide, and amazingly stable.

As I lie on it, half under the crisp white sheets, with my head cradled on a perfumed pillow, I'm fascinated by the escalation from a small wet boat to a large dry house - I fall asleep counting the steps.

Although I stay in Bermuda a week, exploring the island, doing the necessary repairs to the boat, meeting scores of people and enjoying every minute of it; not once have I shaken off the feeling that this is merely an interlude, in some way divorced from reality, suspended above the friendliness of the island and its charming people.

After a few days, a spare chronometer and a lightweight battery arrive from the 'States, thanks to Bruce Robinson and Blondie, so I haven't the slightest excuse to remain another day. But Roger, who has given so much help about the boat, lets me know, in no uncertain terms, that he expects me to accompany him on an escapade, with the argument being, 'you can't go, without having at least one night out on the town.'

He's twenty-five, single, has been on the island a year or two and knows the ropes. It requires an effort of will on my part to agree to the evening out. After weeks of solitude I find too many people (in the pluralist, not the individual sense) overpowering.

The busy streets of Hamilton don't attract me.

I'm happier wandering around the quiet backwaters of St. George's, and happiest of all strolling the deserted island roads. Taking one thing with another, Roger is asking an adoptive monk to a randy night out on the town.

But what am I to do?

'I suppose a few drinks would be nice, where shall we go?'

He's delighted, offers elaborate plans, going on about this cabaret and that.

' Hold on a minute, I only have one suit and that's badly creased, and my only shirt is grubby.'

'… don't worry about that. Dot will fix it in no time at all - won't you, Dot?'

She smiles, the resigned reaction of a woman who not only holds down a demanding secretarial post, but at the same time runs a large house with only part-time help.

'Why don't you come along as well?'

'… good lord no; you two young lads will be chasing the girls. You don't want me getting in the way.'

Nothing could be further from the truth.

I'm thirty-four, happily married, with three children, and feeling far from being a 'young lad'.

I don't know what in hell's the matter - I've just 'gone off' women. This is such a basic readjustment (some sort of a subconscious blip?) that I'm surprised to find myself viewing the gals from a changed aspect. Everyone I meet seems to possess the remoteness of a figurine. I can no more imagine myself becoming intimate with them, than I would contemplate seducing my grandmother.

'… come on Val, let's get cracking, we haven't much time.'

Before we pile into his wagon, for the drive to Hamilton, he pours a few stiff gins, determined that we should start on the right foot.

'… do you know this island is loaded with good-looking American gals, of all ages, every one of them determinedly out on the spree?'

I have to admit that I didn't.

'… the chicks keep saving their pennies, 'til they've enough to blow on a cruise. The *Monarch* brings them over in thousands. They outnumber the men three to one.'

I'm beginning to get the gist of it. However, he still doesn't know that he's attempting to cajole a recently admitted ecclesiastical novice into a conducted tour of what he might see as a brothel. Nevertheless, we make it to Hamilton, abandoning the peaceful seclusion of the vehicle for streets crowed with hurrying people, all of whom seem to be shouting.

There are two cruise liners in port, and the place gives the impression of a pasture, descended on by a host of gaily coloured butterflies, fluttering from shop to shop, flitting over the streets, to the alarm of cautious traffic, swarming around some unusual sight - then coming to rest, on row upon row of tall bar stools.

'… two gin and lime please.'

We could be in the Middle West, seem to be the only foreigners around (Roger's correct, the women do outnumber the men) and they are all, without exception, intent on whooping it up.

'… what about those two over there?'

They're presentable enough, one of them is downright pretty, but to my out-of-focus eye they seem blooms in an attractive bed of flowers, meant to be viewed, not plucked (close, but that'll have to do). They have already glanced in our direction, and it's obviously up to us.

'… come on, let's strike while the iron's hot.'

I'm glued to the stool. An adolescent at his first party. I know that if I do walk over, I'll be struck dumb, would merely stand there gaping like a fish.

'… come on, what the hell's the matter with you?'

'You go over and ask them to join us for a drink. I'll get another round in meanwhile.'

'… coward!'

And he's right. At this moment, I would rather face a gale of wind, in a leaking boat, with the pump part blocked - as he walks towards them I have high hopes they'll refuse.

I see him ask, watch the back of his neck and his ears twitch, as he smiles and pops the question. The tall brunette flicks a glance in my direction, then turns and says something laughingly to her companion.

I know I've had it. Feel a ridiculous urge to cut and run before getting involved - stuck like a fly to a paper.

It's too late, here they come, bearing down as a troop of cavalry, flashing teeth, bold chested (in more ways than one) a hellbent echelon with cocktail glasses poised as cutlasses eager for the fray.

'… Hi-there: well Hello ! I'm Mary and this is Joan. My, you *are* tall.'

I wish to God I was four-foot six, instead of being six-feet three, but even then I doubt if I would have been allowed to escape.

'… I've always been interested in men with beards.'

Liar (I thought), if I'd been possessed of a domed head, innocent of a single hair, only the opening gambit would have varied, she would still have wanted to play it out to mate.

'… what are you doing in Bermuda?'

My heart sinks even further. God forbid I should have to explain my presence on this blasted island. Roger starts the yarn that I've just arrived on a yacht, but I cut him short before he can develop the story - give him a warning glance.

'What would you girls like to drink?'

'… Scotch on the rocks for me, please.'

'… and for me.'

I put a pound on the counter, and don't get any change.

They're both nice types, Middle Westerners, roommates, working for the same corporation. Roger's doing marvellously well, it's my fault I'm failing to follow suit.

My date (if that's the right word) is above average height, dark-haired, vivacious, an attractive lady with whom any sensible person, let alone a hairy-arsed seaman, would be only too glad of the opportunity of spending a flirtatious half-hour with, at perhaps a more convenient occasion. Yet I'm stumbling.

'Another drink?'

'... I haven't finished this one.'

'Never mind. Barman, four more Scotch on the rocks.'

That's another two quid down the drain.

Roger is leaning towards me, obviously pleased with the way things are going, the age-old light of the halfway-there male lighting up his eyes.

'What about going dancing, Val?'

I would have preferred being asked to a public execution, have the horrible thought growing within me that I'm being led towards my own, but I can't see a reasonable avenue of escape.

What am I to say?

Can't just up sticks and leave Roger stuck with two dames. The unwritten rules of the game don't allow that sort of - 'up your's Jack, walk quickly away from it all.'

Persuade Roger to leave?

Not the faintest hope of carrying that off. He's a hound who has just found, and is now following an irresistible scent (the other's the perfume they're wearing); nothing short of a whip would be required to re-box him.

Should I fall down in a faint?

I think, ruefully, this is a dodge that has been successfully used on occasions, by one sex, but not unfortunately my own.

'... what about dancing, Val?'

'Yes, it's a marvellous idea - where shall we go?'

Of course he knows just the right place, only a short distance from where we are now (and my God, isn't he doing well).

On the way to the nightclub he's enjoying high jinx in the front of his automobile, hands straying all over the place, while I point out places of interest to a tall, vivacious, and equally cuddlesome - somewhat bored female, in the back of the same vehicle.

We arrive at the smart hotel that offers food, dancing and, as a cabaret, a well-publicised troupe from Polynesia. There's a hefty cover-charge, Roger and I pay.

The Maître d'Hôtel escorts us to an advantageous table.

The girls are hungry.

We discuss the enormous menu. The prices are scandalously high. Roger rattles through what's available, encouraging his partner to pick just what she fancies.

'Try the fresh salmon, they have it flown in specially from the Highlands (these 'highlands' are the highlands of Scotland, which is a long haul, not to say a very expensive trip from Bermuda).'

Both the girls are undecided, so Roger keeps at it, as a gastronomic tub-thumper, drumming up support. At length, the ladies decide to give the salmon a try, while I order melon.

Roger then suggests, as the main course, lobster thermidor - in its fanciful arrangement, by far the most expensive item on the menu.

I protest they're opting for fish-after-fish - to no avail.

I choose the modestly-priced chicken.

Now comes the wine waiter.

I make a determined effort to deflect the inevitable by positively grabbing the offered list; but with an engaging smile, Roger casually orders the best champagne in the house - for his gay abandon he receives a deferential bow from the waiter, and a look that could (indeed, *should*, kill him) from me.

'Let's make a night of it.' he declares, rubbing his hands together, while paying extravagant compliments to the girls, who are now entering into the spirit of the thing, brightening by the minute. They positively bloom when the gold wrapped champagne pops its cork to the ceiling, and another bottle is ordered.

'... we never dreamed, when we left home, that we'd be dining at the best hotel on the island, and drinking vintage champagne - did we, Joan?'

I'm damned certain they hadn't.

I also think Roger's taken leave of his senses.

I started out with about thirty-eight pounds sterling, which is all the cash I have after paying for my digs, the services of an expensive sailmaker and a present for my family, which I've already airmailed home. It should have been a more than adequate sum for an evening out on the town, but the way things are going there will be precious little left.

Yet I must admit that it is a damn good meal, they eat.

Beautifully cooked, well served and more than helped down by the second bottle of bubbly.

After coffee, we dance; Roger and Mary, rhythmically and well. Joan and myself, leastways myself, as a stiff-legged nothing less than embarrassing automaton.

Normally, I'm willing to give it a go, particularly if my partner is attractive, moves well, and is taller than average (when you're that way yourself, it always gives things a lift). Right now it's useless. I try, God knows, I try, and so does she, but I'm apparently musclebound.

She's wearing a smart dress, which bares her back. I can hardly bear to look, let alone savour the feel of her skin.

Wherever I put my hands, I seem to encounter her silky smoothness.

When I withdraw, she assumes my trouble is shyness and grips my elbow, guiding my hand once more to the muscles that are rippling, seductively on either side of her spine.

She moves closer, brushing my face with her hair which, though it's soft, clean, and faintly perfumed, has about as much attraction for me as the hairy legs of a tarantula (I think I'm going to scream), then the dance ends, and I find myself sweating.

'It's hot in here, isn't it?'

She says she finds it cool enough.

Back at the table, Roger has called for brandy (I feel I need mine) but the more I drink, the more sombre I become. We dance once more, changing partners this time, while I feel obliged to make some sort of an excuse for my poor showing.

'... don't you like dancing, Val ?'

I stammer that I do. So she also puts my difficulty down to shyness, and moves in towards me as an enthusiastic lock-forward packing down at a Rugby Union scrum. Her pelvis rubbing against my thigh (I'm not sure if it's the block, or the axe) as we pass close to bum-hugging Roger and Joan, who is obviously enjoying the trip.

'... hey, come on Val, change partners. Remember me? I'm your friend.'

Back to the back.

She's getting warm, starting to perspire, my fingertips stick intimately to her skin. She's dancing with her eyes closed (I realise, quite suddenly, she's probably a little drunk) while I'm as sober as a solemnly-robed judge.

The music stops. A drum roll announces the cabaret.

During the opening number, we drink more brandy.

Then follows a singer, a heftily proportioned lady in a flowing dress, she's excellent. Then, with the dimming of lights and an insistent tapping of drums, the main act of the evening leaps on to the stage.

I know, without looking, what sort of performance it will be.

The couple are Pacific Islanders, gorgeous chocolate bodies, oiled and glistening, scanty strips of clothing accentuating what's supposedly concealed. A spotlight plays on them as they stand facing one another, motionless, but for the heave of her breasts and the movement of his chest. Hairy, with rivulets of sweat trickling past his navel. If you were that way inclined, you could hear a bra strap slip off the slink of a sloping shoulder and go on to wonder if she's got anything on under the grass of that sexy little skirt.

The audience are being prompted into thinking they're joining halfway through a private act. The stage, which supports these vibrant statues, is surrounded by a hundred fascinated people.

Roger is perched on the edge of his seat.

There comes the insistent throb of a finger-tapped drum, softly, as if from a distance. The protagonists stand firm. The girl with her legs slightly apart, knees thrust out, legs bent; the muscles of her thighs quivering, at first barely noticeably, then picking up the rhythm of the drum.

As the beat grows louder, another force comes into play, promoted by another drum that prompts a separate rhythm, which the dancers weave to, as fronds respond to the hot blooded fanning of a passing tropic breeze.

The girl's arms rise and wave, as silken scarves held in this seductive zephyr. Her partner clasps his hands behind his neck, pumps-up his quivering biceps and follows the insistent tap.

Another drum joins in. A deeper note that prompts the girl to swing her hips.

His eyes are rolling on her navel.

As she dances, he responds, in subtle ways that accentuate the flavour of the scene.

Another drum joins in with yet another rhythm. It seems impossible to accommodate it, but they do. Her belly opposing her hips, writhing in a mouth-drying offering of sensuous display.

Yet another drum joins what has become a blood-pounding crescendo, as male and female circle one another. Oblivious of the audience, whose drinks remained untouched, cigars and cigarettes un-puffed.

As they circle, they draw closer; the girl's eyes having a glazed look, body overcoming mind with animal requirement.

She entices him.

His eyes rake hers, pupils flashing in the gleaming spotlight.

They're closer yet, every quivering muscle she displays finds an answering rhythm in his form.

While she previously made the pace, the madly pounding drum now gives him the lead. It seems impossible to intensify the scene, but his hand snakes out, whips away the flowered cotton strip that had contained her breasts.

There's an answering hiss from the crowd.

The rhythms becomes more pronounced, rising and falling in a pulsating cauldron of emotion that has her gasping for breath, breasts and belly heaving.

He's moving ecstatically about her.

The drums roll to a thundering climax.

She writhes.

He leaps - higher with each ear-splitting crash.

She falls to her knees, buttocks on heels, arched backward, prostrate before the bow that's drawn to initiate the arrow's penetrating flight; yet she has her eyes wide open as the rhythm swells to an overpowering crescendo.

I steal a glance around the room.

The audience seems paralysed. The sexual appetite of those present has been so much more than merely titivated by this passionate display.

The girls at our table are leaning forward, breathing quickly, eyes bright, hands tight-clenched.

Roger's mouth is partly open, the red tip of his tongue moistly peeping out, then slithering over his drying upper lip.

While our collective ears recoil, all eyes are focussed now on that palpitating form.

The drums cut off; shearing the razor-sharp edge of sexual display.

The spotlight fades, it seems reluctantly. Dim lights alone illuminate the room, which remains shrouded in silence.

He stands above her, quite triumphant.

She moans, still arched backwards, dark hair pooling about her head in glistening strands.

For a second they remain so. Then attendants appear, lift her to a silk-covered stretcher, and while the audience is still recovering, carry her ceremoniously off the stage.

'Good God.' says Roger, making a valiant effort to recover himself (seems too embarrassed to look at the girls) 'I could do with a drink.'

'Make mine a large one.' says Joan, examining her face critically in the mirror of her compact, which is shaking slightly.

'What did you think of that?'

A reply seems hardly necessary. It had been a shattering performance. We look at each other for a moment, brought to a halt by the intimate nature of the dance.

'Do you think they're lovers?'

I damn near choke on my drink.

'... Lovers? Hells bells woman, he's screwing the arse off her twice nightly.'

Then I realise she's pulling my leg, and with our laughter the tension eases.

While they chatter on about him and her, her and him, I try to analyse my feelings.

I have of course been captivated by the performance, the sort of compulsive viewing it's impossible to ignore. Yet I feel that I hadn't been drawn into the thing as comprehensively as the others. I had been able to take that quick look around the room which had been so revealing - my companions hadn't been so detached.

It's nothing to boast about, just one more indication that right now I'm far from normal. Even at the climatic height of the show I had found myself floundering amongst a certain revulsion - for me, it was too close to the bone. A little voice persisted that it was not the sort of cabaret to which I would take my maiden aunt, and yet I was annoyed with my own prudery.

After all, was it any more than a commercial display of down to basics Polynesian art ?

But it has left me with a strange, odd man out feeling.

We have another round of drinks and then pay the bill which, with the tip, comes to thirty-four pounds sterling. As we pay, Roger declares it's worth every penny, while I fork-up with what grace I can muster.

We walk away from the cabaret, enveloped by the warm night air. It's well after midnight and the island is quiet, surrounded by the murmur of the ocean as it breaks on the nearby reef, only a few hundred yards from where we're standing. For a moment, we pause, delighted, as birds escaped from the hotel cage - it's Roger who breaks the spell.

'What about a swim? I know a quiet beach only a few minutes from here.'

'We haven't got our swimsuits.'

'For heaven's sake. Who wants a costume after seeing that?'

It seems reasonable enough.

We run around the headland, climb carefully over the rocks and reach a deserted bay. The sea, behind a sheltering reef, laps gently at the receptive coral strand.

'You boys turn your backs, while we slip out of our things.'

Again that feeling of revulsion. I don't give a damn if there are ten thousand women naked on the island - the dance failed to stimulate me to that extent. I feel they are all people, just people. I'm experiencing a feeling of detachment which keeps at bay what intimacy might be offered. As far as I'm concerned she can stand on her head, bare arsed, legs apart, while she whistles a specially orchestrated version of the Star Spangled Banner.

I undress, and walk towards the water - the others are already splashing about.

'Come on, Val. Don't be shy.'

Shy? I don't feel a damn bit shy. I could walk naked down Bond Street without turning a hair (might even turn a few heads), it's they who are persisting in pushing this to what seems needless intimacy.

We swim and fool around.

After the drinks and cigars, it's good to feel the refreshing slap of the sea. I look towards the reef - beyond it lies the restless ocean, and I experience the odd feeling that I should be sailing on it, alone once more.

I look back over the previous seven weeks, quite forgetful of the nerve-racking ordeal, remembering only the beauty of the sea, the silently swimming fish, the friendly birds; even the previously horrendous nights fall into place as my mind conjures up a romantic vision of what seems to be the voyage.

During this reverie, the play is getting more intimate.

Roger swims underwater and grasps Mary's legs. She hardly bothers to go through the routine exclamation, and the horseplay becomes unfettered as they move away, making for the seclusion of the sandy beach.

That leaves me with Joan.

We swim a little longer.

I feel an utter mug.

She's attractive, floating on her back, pale body supported by the lapping sea, she's beautiful - but I make no move.

She comes towards me, pushes me under, hove down by a smothering of breasts, flat belly and firm thighs. As we surface, she plants a smacking kiss on my lips, then drags me by the hand, leading me ashore, on to the sand, throwing herself headlong, pulling me down beside her.

It's obviously my move, but I feel paralysed.

'Oh, Val, it's been a wonderful evening, so far.'

She snuggles up to me, wet bodies touching intimately in a way that makes her shudder, as she puts arms around my neck, tightening her breasts, proud nipples rubbing hard against my chest.

I'm still paralysed, incapable of any constructive thought or action.

'Make love to me, darling.'

Dear God. I think it's a superfluous request, made redundant because her hands are straying over my body.

'What's the matter with you?'

How I wish I could tell her (it would mean that I know myself).

She feels around a little more, then brushes aside whatever inhibitions she has (if any) and really tries to rouse me.

Without success.

After a minute, she stops, raises herself up on an elbow, and speaks directly to me.

'Come on Buster, what's the matter?'

'... I'm afraid, I won't be able to make the grade.'

For one second, she's speechless.

'You won't be able to make the grade? I don't believe it. You're just trying to be funny.'

' ... no, honestly I'm not. I'm afraid I can't explain it, it's a long story.'

For a minute, or so it seems, she looks at me, then the fact (if nothing else) sinks in. At first, she's refusing to believe it, but now, as the reality of the situation crowds about her she's becoming annoyed.

'I thought there might be something queer about you.'

She moves away, kneels on the beach, hands on her thighs, still breathing hard, breasts thrust out - she looks better than ever; it just doesn't seem to be the right time to tell her.

'Do you mean you're impotent? I don't believe it !'

I don't believe it either (and I know it isn't true) but what am I to say?

'I come all the goddamned way from the 'States, and get stuck on the beach with a *fairy* ?'

Her voice is rising now, becoming outraged.

I try to make a convincing explanation, but my mind remains a total blank.

'... no, you've got it all wrong, Joan. It's not like that at all.'

'Got it wrong' she says, getting to her feet. 'I know there's one thing I haven't got wrong buster. It's sticking out a mile.'

I think that may be a less than appropriate remark, but things seem to be going from bad to worse and I can't see any way out. She's kicking at the sand with her foot, growing madder by the minute. We stand, looking at each other (naked, but for my inhibitions) which now seemed to be affecting her, as she's drawing them about herself.

A few minutes previously she'd been eager for every intimacy, now she feels her nakedness and wants to cover up.

I begin to feel sorry for her, start to stumble to my feet, protesting my innocence, while she marches off towards her clothes, throwing a remark over her shoulder as she goes.

'Save it for the birds.'

I assume she's referring to my faltered explanation, so follow her across the beach, recover my clothes, and when we've both dressed, try again.

'... I'm terribly sorry, Joan. Please don't take it this way. It's not in the slightest degree your fault.'

'You're goddamned right it isn't.'

It seems hopeless trying to approach her, as she shouts 'Mary, I'm going home. Mary, where are you?'

'Over here.'

The voice sounds distant, distraught even.

'Come on Mary, it's time to go home.'

There's no answer.

She starts walking to the corner of the beach indicated by the strained reply.

I think it hardly fair on the other couple.

'... come on, Joan - don't spoil their fun. I really am sorry for what's happened.'

She takes no notice, walks away, bends and snatches a handful of fine dry sand, quickening her pace as she does so.

She's out of sight, and for an intervening second I wonder what she's going to do, then hear a surprised male voice, having suffered some indignity.

'Hey, what in hell are you doing,' followed by an outraged female voice 'for heaven's sake, what was that?'

There's a momentary silence, followed by a giggle, then a bolder laugh, while from out of the night Joan runs, laughing, and it's my turn to smile.

'Come on Val, let's go back to the car.'

While we wait for the others, I try to explain my actions, or the lack of them. She listens well, becoming quite forgiving, maternal even.

'Why didn't you tell me before?'

'... I never had the chance. Then it was too late.'

As we talk, we sit close together, her resentment fading. She moves closer, looking at me with interest.

I'm no longer repelled. She seems a desirable woman. It's as if we've turned the page in a book, found ourselves faced with a new, onward-leading chapter.

I put my hand on her shoulder and pull the lobe of her ear.

She smiles at me, moving her head sideways, rubbing my hand against the side of her cheek, I'm just leaning forward to kiss her when the car door opens.

'That was a lousy trick to play on a friend!'

We all laugh.

'Why did you do it?'

I hold my breath, hoping against hope she's going to withhold the explanation.

She does.

'It's a long story; it'll keep.'

As we drive towards the town, I look back at the beach - somewhat to my discomfort, I'm hankering about going the other way.

Ain't life amusing?

Ain't life a challenge?

Ain't life a gamble?

Ain't life, sometimes, nothing less than perverse?

The next day, we (that is, the boat, complete with her skipper) intend to sail for New York.

I had met scores of likeable and interesting people, and many of them come down to the quay to see us off.

During the earlier part of the morning, I visit a training vessel, the *Albatross*, and have a long chat with Bill Sheldon, her owner-skipper, and his wife. They make a living taking parties and paying guests up and down the American eastern seaboard, at the same time continuing the education of the younger members of the crew - a sort of floating classroom. After I've been shown over the ship, and while we're in the chartroom, I remember that I don't have an American 'Light List' aboard my boat, so take the opportunity of copying out the details of the lights around Cape Hatteras, just in case we make a landfall further to the south'ard than intended. I have all the necessary details of New York and the coast to the nor'ard, including Nova Scotia and Newfoundland.

While I'm scribbling away, the skipper asks me about my own vessel, seems unimpressed by her size and the fact that she's without an auxiliary motor. We discuss the trip to New York, which is not much more than six hundred miles distant.

'The hurricane season's well under way, Val. It's not the best time of the year to make the passage in a small boat.'

He's preaching to the converted. I'm well aware that the portion of the voyage yet to be completed could prove to be something of an ordeal.

He goes on to explain the difficulties that might be encountered. The bitter squalls. The electrical disturbances. The big seas that build up quickly off Cape Hatteras, particularly if there's a weather-going tide. I begin to wonder what subject he teaches in the classroom, thinking it might as well be scripture - he seems to be doing his best to daunt me, perhaps not deliberately - or could it be that he's voicing some of his own repressed anxiety?

As I walk towards my boat, I'm glad the day will see me afloat once more. That the voyage is incomplete stubbornly refuses to leave my mind, everything I do seems to be influenced by the fact that I'm still at half-cock (the over-the-shoulder glance at the beach-induced double entendre is certainly intended).

While listening to the conversation of a friend, I find my attention wandering, my mind jumping ahead, probing the problems that might be expected on the forthcoming passage, making a score of anticipatory sallies, only to be brought back with a bump to the necessary present.

The boat herself is in much better shape than when we arrived a week ago. She has all but stopped leaking, partly because while lying alongside the quay, I've nipped-up the keel bolts, some of which I had been surprised to find quite slack.

The rigging has been set up. The sails extensively re-stitched.

I've scrubbed the hull, brushing away the long-stemmed goose barnacles which must have done a great deal to retard the vessel's progress.

I feel quite fit. The sore condition of the soft tissue surrounding my eyes and my mouth has gone, diagnosed as an indication of a vitamin deficiency. My diet, lately, of fresh vegetables, milk and eggs has routed that condition.

My knee is better. And I've had the benefit of a free beard trim and haircut.

What more can a man ask?

The girls are here to say goodbye.

I had obviously been discussed amongst themselves, and now they want to know a lot more. I dodge the issue, reflecting that the ladies are the most forgiving creatures (she's left me in no doubt that she's more than ever interested).

My only real regret, at leaving the island, is the feeling that I should stay one more night and tidy up that particular loose end. It's very tempting. But the sobering light of day helps keep these emotions well in check, my anxiety to get to New York overrules all others. Yet another sign that, even now, I'm still a long way from normal?

By early evening, everything's complete.

I have a new stock of food aboard, plenty of oranges and other fruit. The water cans have been refilled, nothing remains, but to let go the warps and leave the shelter of the harbour for the lure of the encircling ocean.

Perhaps a small island, to which you have recently sailed, is easier to leave than a familiar continent that, as it recedes astern, holds so much previous endeavour?

As the sun is setting, we sail out of the narrow harbour entrance, running before a light nor'westerly air.

Halfway along the narrow channel, a man sits, fishing.

I give him a wave, wondering, vaguely, if he's the same person who was fishing there when we entered the harbour.

Over the quiet, now darkening water, floats his voice.

'Good luck, *bon voyage.*'

He waves.

I answer (he seems to know what we're about).

This isn't surprising, the boat's arrival at the island has caused a minor stir in circles of concentric interest, and I've done the familiar radio, press, and rotary lectures.

Some time later, I hear over the radio of a maritime disaster.

A school ship, cruising the American coast, has been caught in a squall, the vessel overwhelmed by the blast, some of her crew drowned, the rest shocked by the fury of the ocean.

And the name of the ship?

Albatross

photo: **author**

location: **Bermuda**

folkboat: **Eira**

(lying alongside the quay)

topsail schooner: **Albatross**

(in the background)

13

so near
and not so far

As we drop the island astern, I'm surprised to find that I can leave a place of such varied attraction with such little real regret.

Now I'm alone, I enjoy slipping back to the old routine - what once seemed irksome, becomes a pleasure thankfully restored.

The warm oak of the tiller welcomes my hand.

As the boat responds to the resurgence of the ocean swell, Mike resumes his squeaking conversation.

The Welsh Dragon flutters his fraying tail, in a gesture vulgar enough to be in keeping with the two-fingered accolade sometimes used by rudely departing seamen.

Clear of the buoyed channel, we alter course, and sail nor'easterly into the gathering gloom.

I feel relaxed.

So many other nights, spent afloat, have been nerve-racking emotion wringing rolls of time, moving slowly, as they set about my personality with flattening intent - now I'm free of fear, I enjoy the surrounding blackness of the sea, the unseen slaps and splashes spread an indulgent tale, of intimacy, not only with the boat, but also with the ocean.

I meet her as an old affair, having time to sit and talk.

I know her, and she knows me, so well, that I know just what she's thinking.

I know her body's not constrained by her dress.

The endless, wind-induced movement on the surface of the ocean, offering an awesome display; actually revealing little more than window dressing - so much more below the seascape than ever meets the seaman's eye.

And she knows me.

We have both, occasionally, indulged in a posturing façade, but meet now on a different level.

Eye to eye.

Shoulder to shoulder.

Elbow to elbow, fingertips touching, as my hand trails a caressing wake that marks the sensual passage of an ocean.

The wind holds westerly.

Ahead, flashing its seafaring message, is the buoy that marks the nor'eastern extremity of the dangerous coral reef.

We waft before the breeze.

Below, the swinging kettle, hot-bottomed on the roaring primus, makes a deal more noise than the chuckle of the bow wave.

We weather the buoy, haul away to the nor'ard, making a bare two knots over the heave of the welcoming swell.

I stream the log, set Mike to his night's task, and go below.

The kettle's just come to the boil.

Having to some extent refitted the vessel, I now have a light in the cabin, which illuminates my attempt at a seamanlike stow.

Everything is, once again, where and as it should be.

The crocks are clean, the pans are shining, the stove swings in its gimbals.

I make a few strokes on the pump.

The bilge is dry.

After a careful look around the horizon, and having made sure the steamboat scarer is full of oil and burning brightly, I turn in, leaving Mike to get on with it. Warning him not to make anything to the south'ard where, for several uncomfortable miles, there runs the treacherous shoal.

I'm convinced the breeze will hold 'til we're well clear, and even if it did unexpectedly back four points (which Mike would foolishly follow, regardless of the fact that we'd be sailing directly towards the reef) I'm sure the change in motion, the altered rhythm of the boat, in response to the surge of the sea and the heave of the swell, will prompt me to wake in time to rectify the error.

In short.

I feel at home.

Up at dawn's light, breakfasting on fruit juice and a cup of coffee, even at this distance, maybe subconsciously making a cultural allowance for our expected landfall off New York.

If the weather's reasonable, the six hundred and fifty mile passage shouldn't take much more than six days. The fact that my average daily mileage, during the previous seven weeks at sea, has been little more than half this figure doesn't disturb me in the slightest.

How can confidence so shape reality?

We sail on, beckoned by the sinking sun's reflected ray into the restful second night. The moon rises on the peaceful sea, brings to mind that little bay where, not long since, I had watched a woman sporting, supported by the inky pond and her lewd enough intention.

I smile
to myself
to 'fence-about' an embarrassed chuckle

now, if
yes
if only

but it's no good if'ing
I must tell no one
of the night I ate my humble pie

Dawn comes soon enough, and at the appointed time I make a radio signal.

'... this is the yacht *Eira, Eira, Eira,* calling the US Coastguard, Bermuda.' (go through the procedure several times) then sit back and listen, to nothing but a succession of crackles and squeaks from the loudspeaker, so I try again.

'... calling the US Coastguard, Bermuda.' (right through the rigmarole, from beginning to end) with the same depressing result.

Not a sausage.

But cause for a smile.

All those weeks of tortuous regret, that the radio had been rendered useless by the damage to the battery, and now, perhaps due to faulty aerial installation, it's effective range is demonstrated to be something less than had previously been supposed, which was, in any case, never much more than thirty nautical miles.

At noon on this particular Saturday, the sixth of August, she's at 34° 05' North, 36° 46' West, approximately five hundred miles from the city of New York, still close-hauled to the westerly breeze which has remained moderate since clearing the island.

We've made good ninety miles during the previous twenty-four hours. A satisfactory performance that's only been obtained by easing both the main and the genoa sheets, allowing her to close-reach, footing so much faster than if pinned hard in.

She's started to make a little water as we cleared Bermuda and was put to her work - nothing like the frightening amount that plagued us during the few weeks prior to our arrival at the island.

Throughout the night, and during the forenoon, she's been kept hard at it, reeling up another ninety-two miles, which gives the crew cause for rejoicing.

The only difficulty, apart from the usual incontinence of a small, clinker-built boat being driven to windward, is the heat and humidity that during the day becomes oppressive. The cabin, even with all the hatches and ventilators open, becomes untenable, and I'm back to my old habit of sitting out on deck.

While thus engaged, I notice, to the west'ard, the upperworks of a liner, seemingly on a parallel course to our own, which I take to be either the *Ocean Monarch* or the *Queen of Bermuda*.

I've been aboard the former, taking a noggin with the Master and the Staff Captain, so seeing a similar vessel, almost hull-down, seems to be a good opportunity to try out the transmitter again.

I can hear them working the radio telephone, and know they keep a continuous listening watch on the 'marine distress' and 'general call' frequencies, so spend an excited fifteen minutes trying to raise them - not to send a message, which hardly seemed necessary, merely to have a chat with the senior radio officer whom I've also met.

I fail to make contact.

They are steaming at something in excess of twenty knots, while we're plugging along at not more than four, so they soon draw ahead and pass out of sight. As they do so, they leave a twinge of the old feeling, that little tweak of loneliness which, somehow, seems inescapable.

Although I've been glad enough to embark on the last leg of the voyage, just two days of solitude have been enough to whet the appetite for a little conversation. To add to the slightly deprived, but *not* feeling sorry for myself reaction, the breeze is freshening, kicking up a short steep sea, so we're back to the old condition of a labouring boat with her lee rail awash and throwing plenty of deck wetting spray.

Just before midnight, it deteriorates still further - driving rain squalls, with a frightening accompaniment of thunder, together with a hell of a lot of lightning.

It's interesting to compare my reaction now, to the cowed state a fortnight previously.

My physical and mental condition is undeniably better, and I can no longer plead a prolonged period of solitude as an eroding influence on my morale. I'm now comparatively fresh in mind and body, and yet, to my annoyance, find myself still scared.

It's the blasted lightning that gets under my skin - while the thunder crashes out another intimidating drumroll, my nerves are fraying at the edges.

Having passed through a series of emotional disturbances, and achieved a measure of tranquillity, it's now exasperating to find myself still susceptible to the complaint that dogged the earlier part of the voyage.

As the lightning forks its way into the water, at times not far from the boat, my stomach tightens and my mouth becomes dry.

I'm standing at the hatch, gripping the coaming, blinking protectively at the flashes of lightning, while ducking involuntarily, trying to dodge the roar of the thunder as it crashes overhead.

We are passing under a giant belfry, with an overwhelming peal of bells, prompted by the manic attention of an illuminating hand.

It seems a careless display of unbridled power - during the lightning flash, the metal mast seems stark and naked as it points at the cause of my fear.

Throughout the night, the weather conditions scare the bejeebers out of me. When I try to analyse the feelings, which are at the root of my irritable state, I come to the partly relieved opinion that, if I *am* a coward, it's because I have no desire to be fried to a smoking crisp, by a heedless bolt of lightning, which I wish to God would move on to the east'ard, where it has three thousand miles of ocean to spit on while old Neptune rubs his trident-toying hands with anticipatory glee.

As the night passes, the seas become steeper and Sheldon's warning, delivered while I'd been aboard *Albatross*, trickles its way to my mind.

The old tub's also making more water, requires pumping every hour, if I want to keep the bilges reasonably dry.

To cheer myself up, I look at the chart, which displays the amazing extent of the North Atlantic ocean.

My present position, measured in nautical miles to the city of New York, seems a relatively short leg in comparison to the distance already sailed. A reassuring fact that does indeed relieve some of my anxiety.

By noon, although the observation is difficult to get, because the vessel's pounding heavily to the still steeper sea, the reducing distance to our objective keeps me cheerful enough. Another ninety-seven miles have been made good, and we're still slamming away nor'westerly.

Noon the following day, Tuesday, and another ninety-four miles have been wiped off the slate, so only two hundred and eighty remain.

During the early part of the afternoon, a dragonfly comes aboard, alighting on the starboard cockpit seat, I think perhaps with gratitude.

She's some way from likely pasture, and now stands, motionless, except for the quick but irregular flick of her indeterminate tail.

Blue, bright and hard as a sapphire - seems crystallised, would shatter if touched.

Her crisp wings remind me of the long-gone flying fish, with eyes, large, black, bright, but serious, as she contemplates her newly-found predicament. Evidently solves the problem, because after half an hour's rest, she takes wing, sou'easterly, towards Bermuda.

I wish her luck.

The breeze falls light, and what there is, offers little more than variable puffs. I sit for hour after hour at the helm, trimming sheets to passing zephyrs, keeping her ghosting along, jealously adding to the precious miles made good.

Throughout the night, the moon shines.

The humbling electrical display has moved away to the east'ard. The visibility's excellent, with the lights of passing steamers much more frequent.

When the breeze fails to move the boat, it seems we're stationary, yet nothing could be further from the truth, or more misleading.

We're in the Gulf Stream - that immense river, flowing about an ocean, so while we appear motionless, we're actually moving smartly to the nor'ard. A constant reminder that this is not the best of places to be becalmed, being carried away from our destination by the current.

During a flat spell, it's pointless to fool around with the tiller, so in order to satisfy a long felt need, I write a note on the back of a section of an unused chart (good strong paper), roll it into a neat cylinder, then pop it into a tightly corked bottle.

'Will the finder please write to, giving details of … '

As I throw it into the sea, I wonder what are its chances of survival.

> on what unvisited seaboard may it lodge ?
> dashed to pieces on a rock-bound shore?
> deposited on a well-walked strand ?
> at the feet of a sharp-eyed stroller?
>
> but the bottle hangs about the boat
> as if reluctant to start on it's speculative journey
> then a light air enables us to sail quietly away
> leaving it to be carried on the ocean's further whim

What had previously been tedious, now becomes frustrating. To be stuck here, so tantalisingly near the journey's end, sends me off on a burst of nervous energy. I tidy the cabin, scrub the decks, rearrange the charts (for the sixteenth time), polish the binoculars, getting ready for the great event.

When the breeze does eventually come, it blows fresh enough, sweeping low clouds over the boat. Within an hour the wind is piping up, but I maintain the press of canvas until she's smoking along, the freeing element in the wind pattern allowing her to reach under eased sheets, bounding along at her very best speed.

Although there are squalls about, I hold to the full mainsail until she's straining as an over-eager dog on a leash.

And yet I hold, the wind whistling in the rigging, the belly of the mainsail bulging, pregnant to the mast's erection.

She foams along.

I have the thrill of a man astride a runaway mare - make no effort to rein her in.

The wake now curls above the counter, lapping over the afterdeck. A sure indication that she's pressed beyond the reasonable care of seamanship.

I have the tiller - it requires all my strength to keep her somewhere near the course.

The twisting moment of the mainsail is intent on driving her to the south'ard - but I hold her to it.

The weather runner is quivering - as a thread line, salmon fast.

She's creaming a quarter wave to leeward as an extended roll of foam; to wind'ard the wind whipped spray is driven over the boat, then passes out of sight before its hissing return to the sea.

New York, **New York !** (after that delightful musical).

Here we jolly well come !

A tremendous thrill. A flat out gallop, mane (the billowing main?), and her tail (the seafarer's tale?) streaming to the screech and fury of the squall.

Now comes the rain, sweeping up astern, ice cold needles lashing at my bare-backed ride - but the worst (or the best ?) is over.

The wind speed dropping. Relieving the pressure on the canvas. Allowing the boat to resume a more respectful gait, before what's now little more than a moderate breeze.

The rigging ceases singing.

She no longer shoulders aside the ocean.

Settles to canter.

Eases to a trot.

The rain has cooled her ardour.
Left me, with a memorable thrill.

At noon the following day, we're at 38° 31' North, 71° 25' West, with only one hundred and sixty miles remaining to be notched up on the log.

At four o'clock in the afternoon, the sea changes.

At a minute wanting the hour, we move from a blue expanse of ocean, to a sea with shades of grey (the characteristic 'edge' of the Gulf Stream), while the puff ball clouds still dapple the lighter blue of the sky.

Throughout the night, we run on, and at noon on Friday, the twelfth of August, at 39° 33' North, 73° 21' West, we've logged another one hundred and eight miles, leaving a bare sixty to the Ambrose Light Ship.

Less than a day's run.

I enter our position on the American coastal chart, and plot the last leg of the voyage - allowing for leeway and drift, we should steer 340° by compass to be sure of making the course we need.

A great feeling.

Of all the hundreds of positions I have ever marked on a chart, this one gives me, without a doubt, the deepest satisfaction.

We have sailed over four thousand miles from Plymouth, England, maybe by a devious route; nevertheless, four thousand nautical miles is a long way in anybody's boat.

And we're about to make the landfall.

I'm certain of our position.

The conditions have been favourable for a sight and I've taken a succession of observations, then plotted the results on a graph. I'm absolutely sure of the chronometer, having checked the timepiece and found it keeping an excellent rate, and yet.

And yet.

Although I'm certain of the boat's position, I suffer another attack of navigationitis.

Hell and damnation, if we were approaching the pearly gates, I'd be forced to enquire of Peter, if this really is the place we're bound for (so it seems all the old apprehensions are only just under the skin).

Or is it unbridled excitement?

Maybe a little of both. The former as a mixture of doubt, found in the intoxicating draft offered by the landfall, which remains in suspension until we can actually see the shore.

And then, of all the infuriating circumstances, we're becalmed for ten maddening hours, until five a.m. on Saturday morning, the thirteenth day of August.

Ten hours without making progress, at what seems only a stone's-throw from the American coast, with commercial shipping streaming past, bound north and south.

Tankers, inward laden, outward light.

Coastal traffic, of all sorts of shapes, conditions and sizes.

A host of hurrying shipping, unhindered by the lack of wind.

But I'm glad we've no auxiliary.

The temptation might (would) be irresistible.

And then, after a nail-biting age, here comes the breeze.

Easterly.

A mere zephyr, so everything's up and drawing. The mainsail, masthead genoa, staysail, even the ragged old awning raised on the spinnaker pole. The whole madly flapping bag of tricks giving her barely one measly knot, yet she's slipping persistently through the 'oggin, which turns from grey to muddy brown as we enter shallower water.

There's a group of small boats, right ahead, perhaps five miles distant, at the extreme range of visibility, which is tending to grow hazy with the extension of the day.

The breeze remains fitful, while I'm near enough fit to be tied.

The small vessels ahead appear stationary, so there's plenty of time to scrutinise them through the binoculars.

They seem to be 'sports fisherman', some drifting with the tide, others trolling, perhaps tempting larger fish. As they pass close to our old tub, they raise a hand in greeting (I wave back).

One of them, more curious than the rest, comes alongside.

'… Hi there.'

'Hello.'

'… I see you're flying the Red Duster. What's that flag at your *starboard* yardarm?'

'I can afford to smile (because I'm ready for him). That's the Red Dragon of Wales; some people would say it's the hilly part of England.'

'… well, fancy that. My great-grandfather came from Swansea, over a hundred years ago. Where have you come from now ?'

I'm not even tempted to say Bermuda, the lie is too attractive.

'I've come from Plymouth, England.'

'… is that so?'

It's obvious he views me with suspicion.

It just goes to show.

Give a dog a bad name.

And you end up with

Taffy was a Welshman
Taffy was a thief
Taffy came to my house and stole a piece of beef

'... how long has it taken you ?'
'Fifty-six days.'
(he now seems more inclined to accept the previous statement)
'... is there anything you need?'
'An ice-cold beer if you've got one.'
'... coming over.'
He pitches an accurate, but curving ball, which bends back the top of my middle-finger as I field the can. I offer to exchange one of my warm beers, but he waves it away - his is soon open.
'Cheers.'
'... good luck.'
We toast each other across ten yards of water.
It seems they're out for a good time. The boat is stuffed with booze. There are four in the crew, a mixed party, two men and two attractive women, dressed in Bermuda shorts set off with gaily-coloured, undeniably sexy, boob-displaying, halter necking sun tops.
'... where are you bound?'
'New York. How's the fishing ?'
'... poor, so far.'
'Best of luck. And thanks for the beer.'
They motor slowly away, trailing lines from expensive-looking rods and reels.

The sea is calm, without even the suspicion of an ocean swell, and I rack my brains, trying to think back to the moment it ceased to affect the boat. It seems old Nep has dropped surreptitiously away, left no indication, or declared intention of his return to ocean-going duty.

Yesterday, we rose to the heave and surge of the swell.

Today, we sail on what is little more than a pond, even if it is protected by a continent.

The heat haze thickens. The breeze, what there is of it, is light but favourable, so we're making progress; after looking at the chart, I put her, as a guess-estimate, about ten miles from the lightship, which bears due north.

The sea is changing as we close the coast, which comes to my straining eye as a brown smudge, smeared between the haze of blurred horizon and a doubt of joining sky.

Hardly an inspiring sight?

To me, it's more exciting than any view of the Statue of Liberty, seen from the deck of a steamer.

Also, it's so - quiet.

Drifting as we are before the breeze.

Now I can hear the buzz of motorboats as they troll the foreshore for fish, then the low murmur of the land itself.

Barely a mile away, an automobile (what we know back home as a 'car') sounds its horn.

It comes over the water as a protesting squeak, prompted by, and representative of, the host of environmental indignities imposed by Man's mechanical age.

The breeze sighs a tired gasp, and we're becalmed once more. I can afford to smile, as I pump the small amount of water that's collected in the bilge.

If she sank now, I could swim ashore.

I'm also certain the old tub wouldn't play a trick like that.

She's had plenty of opportunities to ditch me in the past - has put up with my failings, as I've put up with hers.

We're as a long-married couple, for whom the thrill of physical attachment may have diminished, yet left something of greater purpose, as we lie together on the surface of the sea, waiting for the lazy wind to make its tantalizing presence felt.

We hardly need it.

The tide is setting to the nor'ard and although we're apparently stationary, we're moving towards the harbour.

The logline trails from the instrument, hangs directly beneath the boat, its duty done; I pull it aboard, make a neat coil of the water-laid rope, and hitch it in the rigging.

And then, indistinctly out of the haze, a vessel with outstanding upperworks.

I recognise it immediately - have a good look through the binoculars, not without a feeling of satisfaction, because the end of the race, and the completion of the passage is in sight - marked by the red hulled Ambrose Light Ship.

we're at the entrance to New York

14

why must you do it ?

When the Ambrose Light Vessel bears due east, the race is over as far as *Eira* and myself are concerned.

As we sail quietly up to the unpretentious red vessel which, when we're alongside, towers over the little Folkboat, it seems the curtain is about to fall on the last act of an over-long play.

For two months I have lived in a confined space - for a man over six feet tall, a very confined space.

During that period, I've got to know the boat in the way that a person in solitary confinement would get to know the confines of his prison cell. However, my little yacht hasn't been in any way confining. To the contrary, she has more in common with the lifestyle of a turtle, because it is *she,* who has carried *me,* across the Western Ocean, and I'm proud of her.

As we drift quietly towards the finishing line, I note that the Welsh Dragon is as tidy as can be expected, after he's spent most of the preceding two months fluttering from the starboard yardarm, perhaps worrying that the fraying bunting was not going to enable him to arrive in the New World in a respectable condition.

Some of the crew of the lightship are leaning over the rail and I ask them, as casually as I know how, if they would please report my arrival to the New York Coastguard.

'You another of those crazy bums who have just raced across from Plymouth, England?'

I have to admit that I am.

'You just keep on sailing that way, buddy,' says the welcoming American gob, indicating the New York skyline, 'the cutter will be out soon to take you to the quarantine berth.'

I'm absolutely delighted with this throwaway approach, and wonder how I can bat the ball back at him. Fail to think of a bright remark, being reduced to enquiring, sheepishly, how many of the OSTAR competitors had crossed the line.

'Jeez, I don't know. I guess you're the fourth. There was a guy called Shychester passed this way some time back.'

This is a little too much, so I give him the old up you too Jack sign, which he accepts with a broad grin.

The entrance to the harbour is easy enough made, and we join the hundreds of craft that are littered as far as the eye can see.

Several large liners, dozens of smaller coastal vessels, tugs, barges, ferries, sightseeing pleasure boats of one sort or another and, of course, plenty of private launches and yachts.

As we close the shore, we make our number with flat bottomed punts, most of which are occupied by smiling Afro-Americans out for a day's fishing.

It's a sunny afternoon and the towering skyscrapers of Manhattan have their silhouettes softened by the heat haze that has gathered over the river. As I look at these extraordinary buildings, I experience a slight feeling of apprehension.

I've been living a simple life for some time, so I'm impressed by the complexity, the stridency, the go-getting, hell for leather American philosophy the skyline represents. But this twinge of country bumpkin anxiety doesn't last long; it's going by the time the Coastguard Cutter comes alongside and throws me a line, and the yokel quickly assumes his other persona as they tow *Eira,* at boat breaking speed, so that I have to shout at them, in a roughly phrased nautical manner, in order to slow the cavalcade down.

The quarantine island is a friendly place, which belies its name, and I'm introduced to the senior Port Medical Officer by Blondie Hasler, who describes Dr and Mrs Dresher as 'one of God's sweet gifts to the single-handed voyager.' They certainly start out on the right foot, as far as I'm concerned, by giving me an armful of mail, and then keep people away while I settle down to read it.

I think that some of those present have put me down as pretty tame stuff (behaving in what could be seen as a withdrawn manner, after sailing three thousand miles from Plymouth, England). However, I don't want to dash madly ashore; would much prefer to settle down to the news from home, with my wife and family uppermost in my thoughts.

It seems that the Health and Customs formalities are easily dealt with, because before I can finish my mail, arrangements have been made to tow *Eira* to Sheep's Head Bay where a mooring is available.

It's not until I have the buoy aboard, the sails neatly stowed and everything shipshape below that I truly feel that we (the boat and I) have arrived in America, and the long slog of the past two months really is over.

Jester and *Cardinal Vertue* lie swinging at their moorings, only a few boat lengths away, and they have an air, as well they might, of being ocean-worn and slightly down at heel among the smart paint and chromium of the American yachts that are gathered about the Yacht Club.

These vessels (those owned by members of the yacht club) represent the type of person for whom I'm unable, sometimes, to avoid a twinge of envy. The sort of lucky individual who can so organise his life that he has a secure, even satisfying job, a good house, a large family filling it, a couple of cars, and then, last and probably least, a yacht.

I feel envious, because I've never managed to elevate myself to this nautical Nirvana. I have, from time to time, possessed the necessary ingredients, but somehow the pot will persist in coming to the boil, perhaps held too close to the dancing flame of my enthusiasm for old Nep and the extent of his magnificent briny.

The rational man can organise his year with precision, save for a holiday and take it, slow and easy, with his family - enjoy his boating and fishing at weekends, and so regulate these normal appetites that everything fits in and shapes up to a satisfactory whole.

I think, for myself, it's the boats that bugger it up. Although it has been, on occasion, the wife, booze, fishing, farming, horses, even just a view of the sea. Sometimes a soft sweet voice will whisper, that it really is time to settle down, arguing, that being the proud possessor of a boat is not sufficient in itself to give cause for the planning of a circumnavigation.

But I've never been convinced.

> *wives are built to love and cherish*
> *and take to your bed*
> *with varying emphasis*
> *as the years roll by*

> *but boats are built to sail the seas*
> *and that's the end of that*

As I sit in the cockpit, looking at the attractive clubhouse and the comings and goings of the dinghies to the jetty, I realise I've done it again; that my enthusiasm for ships and the sea has demolished my striven-after, orderly existence. I certainly do not feel, as so many have enquired or assumed, that sailing across the Western Ocean is an achievement, satisfying enough in itself, to enable the successful mariner to sit on his broad backside with a complacent smile spread large across his weather beaten features.

The truth is, the crossing of an ocean, in a small boat, creates as many desires as it satisfies.

> *and I can feel the stirring of some of them*
> *as I sit looking at the shore*

photo: **Jean Lacombe**   **Port O'call Marina**
Newport, Rhode Island
1960

Chichester & Howells

talking about the first single-handed transatlantic race
for
Canadian Broadcasting Corporation

15

New York
NEW YORK
it's a wonderful town

but doesn't Mammon cast a shadow ?
nothing
that Tin-Pan-Alley can't adequately handle

Anyone docking in New York, sailing his or her own boat, recently arrived from Europe, is enjoying an event which is far removed from journeying up the Hudson aboard a commercial steamship, arriving on an ocean-going liner, or even storming the place aboard an almighty nuclear battleship.

The key words here are *in your own boat*, because there's nothing quite like the feeling experienced when you're in the delectable position of being towered over by all those steeple-jacked skyscrapers. And you don't even have to *sail* up the Hudson; the skyline is quite capable of impressing from a distance. It is, after all, that powerful image - *Mammon*, in silhouette, not a softening contour anywhere in sight.

Then there's tying up at Newport, Rhode Island's, Port O'Call Marina, where the superintendent, Pete Dunning, turns out to be ideally cast for creating order out of chaos. Patient yet firm, dealing with all that comes along with absolute assurance; and that's just as well, because as far as at least one of the just-arrived seamen is concerned, this looks like a place where you would be well advised to keep a firm grip on your almost certainly about to depart hat.

There are so many *people* !

Not only friends, fellow competitors, and an army of well wishing visitors; there are also the gentlemen of the Press, who long ago learnt how to elbow their way to the front of whatever queue has assembled.

During the first few weeks I was moored at Port O'Call, I was taken to, or visited under my own steam, the *New York Yacht Club* (yes Sir! **The New York Yacht Club** !) had lunch with a bunch of the most delicately house trained Admirals you would ever be likely to meet; was shown *The Cup* (America's Cup) in its presumably bulletproof case.

Journeyed to *Mystic Seaport*, went aboard the whaler *Charles W Morgan,* saw the twelve-metre *Columbia*, took a look at a 'Sand-bagger', a Friendship sloop, a Noank smack, a Catboat, a Carry-away sloop, a Dragger, and then, a plain old-fashioned fishing vessel.

I perched on a stool, while visiting a supposed replica of The Grog Shop where Herman Melville might have sat (he wasn't a goody-two-shoes you know, eventually hob-knobbing with the likes of Nathaniel Hawthorne, Longfellow, and Franklin Pierce), he got thrown into gaol in Tahiti for being involved in a not very successful mutiny.

I became a recognizable dropper-in at a gin-mill known as 'Annie's Bar' (perhaps the least said about that the better).

Paid a return visit to Frank Lloyd Wright's *Guggenheim* museum. Looked again, and yet again at Picasso's *Guernica*; convinced myself I could see Benito Mussolini's bullet-shaped head - just one of the many intriguing images on display in that enormously complicated canvas.

Opposite *Guernica,* taking up the whole of another wall, was a painting which seemed eight feet long, by seven feet high; one half of which was painted red, the other half was painted blue.

The Village wags, who I met, said the hanging committee had ruled that it should be displayed, when there was an 'R' in the month, with the Blue half *up.* And then, when there wasn't an 'R' in the month, with the Blue half *down* (could it possibly be true?) anything's possible in New York.

I was taken to Fire Island, and when some of my rougher, but now amused waterfront friends heard of the trip, I was advised by one old reprobate that *'if you drop a coin Val, even if it's only a dime, you'd be well advised to kick it to the corner of the room, before you pick it up.'* Nevertheless, just for the hell of it, I went skinny-dipping with what turned out to be a very nice group of people.

Strolled along the strand to another beachside bar, and was only just sensible enough, after comparing too many Manhattans with Whisky Sours, to avoid being dragooned into a chorus line made up of professional dancers who were playing fast and loose with the Charleston.

I was driven around 'the mansions'. Some had been built, first by the really old money (wealthy southern planters) by others who had made their pile in the China Trade; and then, with ostentation heaped on ostentation, those paid for by the up and coming Yankees - the Widener's, the Vanderbilt's, the Astor's, all built places that had massive ballrooms, but very few bedrooms, as the guests were all expected to have their 'cottages' located handy-by.

I was taken up the Empire State building (my second visit, as I had rubber-necked the place during the war, when serving in the Merchant Service). Managed to get tickets for Radio City Music Hall (another second visit) where we had the usual eyeful of that amazingly well matched, leggy and precision-drilled chorus line. *The Rockettes*, the very best group of fanny-flashers you'll find anywhere in the world.

Visited a yacht that had been owned by Burl Ives. A nicely varnished, well planked mahogany hull, with the largest fridge-cum-freezer, almost a walk in job, that could possibly be fitted into a boat that was not much more than forty feet long. Strolled the waterfront, visiting the famous boatyards that had built so many beauties in the past - there were lovingly restored Herreshoffs, beautifully designed and built Sparkman & Stephens; craft like the rather narrow-gutted, but still marvellous *Dorade* and, of course, the even better *Stormy Weather*.

Then there were the power boats, the so-called gin palaces; but these vessels were providing just what their owners wanted, movable penthouses, where they could suitably impress and *then* entertain their equally wealthy friends. On and on it went, forever bolstering the silent but nevertheless flag-waving message - that America really is a step or two ahead of everybody else (?).

Got taken to a country club, with a whispered aside from my companion, *'this is where the **real** money is, Val.'* A long curved drive, beautifully tended lawns, dotted about with flower beds. Extensive stabling, paddocks, polo ponies, a polo field with a very smart grandstand - no plebeian rows of seating, just tables, chairs, and parasols, all within easy reach of the bar. A landing strip, where the members could park their not so light aircraft - there was no hangar, the unglamorous maintenance was all done further afield.

The spoon-doon free enclosures, if you're an Irishman (couldn't possibly be a horse dropping on this manicured greenery). These paddocks had white painted, post & rail fencing, of a size and robustness that was necessary to contain the bloodstock, some of which were entire. The white paint was well maintained, sparkling fresh, not a trace of mildew, even under the shaded lap of the bottom rail (I know, because I looked).

The Club Secretary - tall, military type, mid-Atlantic accent, very smart blazer, regimental badge - craggy features that were reminiscent of (Sir) C. Aubrey Smith, except his eyebrows weren't so bushy.

While I waited in the foyer, my companion, a distinguished attorney at law, carried the documents he was delivering to a very important client. When he returned, he was frowning slightly. I asked him if there was anything wrong, and he told me this was a segregated club: [1] no Jews, blacks were out of the question, none of the hoi polloi would ever enter this hallowed work of art.

[1] *refers to 1960, since that date things have moved honourably on.*

Shortly afterwards, that same week, that same man (his name happened to be Sol Lieberstein) flew me up to Block Island.

Sounds a simple excursion, but we first drove to a local airport, one of seemingly dozens nearby. My companion hired a float plane - he was a regular customer, so he knew, and got, exactly what he wanted. Off we went, made the island, circled once or twice, then landed and moored the kite off the beach where the party was in progress.

A week or so later, due to the generosity of my very good friend Jean Lacombe, I was happily ensconced with him in his 'brownstone', so was then living not far from the centre of the city, which turned out to be another significant step-change from what now seemed like sleepy Port O'Call.

From Jean's address, Times Square and Greenwich Village were both within journeying distance.

With him at my elbow, I got to know some of the clubs that were scattered about the place, many of them offered live music, and there were first-class musicians blowin' and tootin' away.

Traditional Jazz was one of the genres I was interested in; not, I must hasten to snobbishly add, to the exclusion of the classics.

In that neck of the woods there were Chopin nocturnes, Beethoven sonatas, played by, so it seemed, about-to-arrive talented concert pianists.

Moving along the street, there were restaurants that featured singing waiters, reputedly understudies at The Met, so you could enjoy the friendship duet from George Bizet's *Pearl Fishers* while fork and spooning about in your Moules marinière, to make sure, amongst other things, that all the beards had been removed.

Regarding the jazz: the top men may not have been present - Louis, Dizzy, Charlie, Fats, Joplin, Tatum, but there was a large and very friendly gent by the name of Peterson, who was more than capable of giving anyone a dizzying run for their money.

So the music was there, booming out of jukeboxes that were ensconced in every joint. Sinatra was crooning, Bing was groaning, Jo Stafford was wowing them in the aisles. Judy Garland was doing so much more than merely keep her end up. The sophisticated lyrics of Cole Porter made everybody smile. Fred Astaire and Irving Berlin were central to it all.

You could listen to the sometimes repetitively raucous, but still enticing Nelson Riddle arrangements, which provided the imperative summons of trumpets, the blare of the 'bones, right down to the brass tacks of cymbals. A musical delight that led to a seismic shift and a note by note tsunami that floods, yet delights those diverse people who inhabit vulnerable shores.

Delights, not threatens, because the walls don't come tumbling down. This is the stuff that's keeping the walls not only *up*, but beautifully embellished.

the

Great American Songbook

is in the course of talented construction

. All this is available - you would have to be a yokel not to do all you could to step aboard the whirling carousel.

Then something happened, which I'd been expecting.

Perceptive readers will be aware that not only was I experiencing a little emotional difficulty, but was also a member of a Masonic Lodge.

(you missed it?) turn to Chapter 6, the last line on page 78.

yet I feel safe enough
close-tiled
not a prying eye in three degrees
supported by a vessel that lists two thousand in its crafted title

one fathom more
and some will know the tight-knit feeling
that brothers-all can face the flood
an inner-guard 'gainst apprehension

The trigger words are there - close tiled, three degrees, inner guard, even the registered number of the Lodge I approached as a joining member.

Before I left my home port, I had been advised, when in New York, to get in touch with fellow Masons; there were lots of Lodges in the city, reputedly 29 independent organizations in New York State itself.

I had been given the telephone numbers, yet had always managed to postpone making the significant contact.

But I had at last done it, and was now waiting for the two people who, I'd been told, would meet me at this pre-arranged venue.

I knew exactly what to expect - successful city businessmen, plenty of well-oiled contacts, the people, I'd been told, who knew just the right sort of people to know. They were, of course, absolutely charming. One of them, who opened the conversation, gave me a shakedown on his yacht, which turned out to be a great deal bigger than mine. The other - it would be unfair to describe either of them as smooth talkers – but they were of the sort who were never short of a word, just as long as it sooner or later led to something they particularly wanted.

But then again, my dear old Granny used to say I'd been blessed (or was it cursed?) with that particular gift of the gab.

I made the usual excuses - didn't have my regalia, my only suit had been torn, was being repaired, would have to go to the cleaners.

In the end, I turned them down, so I never did find out what those gilded halls contained.

I
also
ultimately
let my subscription lapse
to
Narberth
2001

16

in praise of Captain Slocum

the Grand Fleet sails
ten thousand ships steam by
leave not a ripple on the broad face of the ocean

those that sank
in thousands
all sank without a trace

then a tough old Nova Scotian
built himself a boat
launched, and sailed it all alone

old Neptune laughed
a Spray-engulfing bellow
blew a topplin' crest, clean-off the face of another towerin' billow

then, having made his mark, he bestowed his regal favour
on one so foolish
but so bold

The person who shoulders the task of creating some sort of a record of - or, more correctly, setting down one man's necessarily narrowly focused impression of the first single-handed transatlantic race - had better be sure he includes an account of the part the Slocum Society played, in not only helping to organize, but particularly in supporting the event.

Not everyone was inclined to do so at the time.

There were lots of Jeremiah's about, who were not slow in coming forward with the view that the whole daft enterprise was inevitably bound for the rocky shore of disaster. However, the Society had a background that led it, without too much trouble, to adopt a supportive position.

It was founded in 1955, by Richard Gordon McClosky, with the expressed intention of fostering long-distance passage making in small boats. In pursuit of these goals it developed into an association of people with similar interests, specifically charged with keeping alive the memory of Captain Joshua Slocum (the tough old Nova Scotian) who was the first man to sail alone around the world.

His boat was called *Spray,* and when you look at the craft now, the

photo: **D. H. Clarke/PPL**

Captain Joshua Slocum

martinet

the Master and proud part-owner of the clipper

Northern Light

233 overall, 44 feet beam, 23 feet depth of hold

photo: **New Bedford Whaling Museum**

Josh

ocean vagabond

'thin as a reef point' aboard

Spray

the vessel he built himself
then sailed single-handed around the world

257

photo: **New Bedford Whaling Museum**

Spray

take note of the stuck-on bumpkin
the mizzen mast
mounted so far aft, it's almost without visible means of support
taking one thing with another
more of a work boat than a yacht

but none the worse for that

modern yachtsman would have to judge her (setting the romantic attachment well aside) as perhaps more of a work boat than a yacht

Take note of that roughly sawn off counter, the stuck on bumpkin, the mizzen mast, mounted so far aft that it's almost without visible means of support.

Then there's her windward ability.

The decent thing would be to draw a discreet veil over that aspect of the hooker. I have met up with a host of replica *Spray's*, some built of timber, some composite, some steel, one or two alloy - not one of them went to windward worth a damn. Several of the hulls were modified to include massive, hydraulically operated 'dagger-boards', 'centre-boards', 'drop-keels', call them what you will. It didn't make much difference. The sensible owners had all, without exception, installed a large diesel, so if they needed to get up wind they fired up the donk and motored where they had to.

Yet what this does, is highlight Slocum's astonishing achievement; puts it up in Broadway-flashing lights, because he sailed this tub around the world, by himself, no crew, no self-steering gear, no engine, no sat nav, no echo-sounder, no electronic aid at all.

No radio - weather forecasts were a tap on the ancient aneroid and a careful look to windward, to gauge what's on its way.

But Joshua Slocum was a very special kind of seaman.

He was born, the fifth of eleven children, on the farm that had come into his family when they were compensated with a 500 acre section, as recompense for the injury loyalists suffered because of their opposition to the American War for Independence.

However, he wasn't cut out to be a farmer. By the age of 14 he had left home and gone to sea, in commercial sail, starting at the very bottom, but applying himself so diligently that within measurable time he obtained the ticket that enabled him to serve as a captain on ocean-going vessels. He also saw the advantage in becoming a naturalized American citizen.

He sailed for thirteen years, in a variety of position, out of the port of San Francisco, shipping freight to China, Australia, the Far East generally, as far away as Japan.

During that time he was Master in eight vessels, four of which he commanded in the employ of others, but in four of which he either held shares, or outright owned.

He married Virginia Albertina Walker, an American whose east-coast family had migrated to California; she sailed with Slocum for thirteen years, bore him seven children, either at sea, or in foreign ports (some partner she).

He was a multi-talented individual - under a commission from a British naval architect, he organized the local, native labour, and built a 150-ton steamer, in a shipyard at Subic Bay (part of the Sea of Luzon, nor'west of Manilla Bay, in the Philippines). In partial payment for this work, he was given the ninety-ton schooner, *Pato*, the first vessel he could proudly call his own.

Unencumbered ownership of this craft offered Slocum the sort of freedom and scope he had never experienced before. Hiring crew, he contracted to deliver cargo – general freight along the west coast, and voyages from San Francisco to Hawaii. During this period, he also partially fulfilled a long-held ambition - to become a writer, obtaining a position as a correspondent for the *San Francisco Bee* (whenever did he find the time to file his handwritten copy?).

In the spring of 1878, he sold the *Pato*, in Honolulu; when returned to San Francisco, Mr & Mrs Slocum purchased the *Amethyst* and owned this ship until June, 1881.

The next improving move was a third share in a *Northern Light* (the second-named vessel in her class). This substantial clipper was 233 feet overall, 44 feet beam, and with 23 feet depth of hold. Big enough to carry 2,000 tons of freight; but mutinies and other, perhaps man-management problems, led to the sale of these shares in 1883.

The next ship was the 326 ton *Aquidneck* - she became mired in tragedy - his wife, Virginia, became ill while the vessel was in Buenos Aires, and ultimately died.

Slocum married again, his 24-year-old cousin, Henrietta Elliot. They took to sea, aboard the *Aquidneck* again, bound for Montevideo. But 'Hettie' wasn't really enamoured with seafaring life, which was not made easier to bear when her husband, perhaps for once in his life, failed to out-manoeuvre a storm, and they were lucky not to lose their lives and the vessel (the couple's only home).

There was worse to come: the crew contracted cholera, and the ship was quarantined for six months. Later, Slocum had to defend his vessel from pirates - he shot the ringleader - was hauled before the court on a charge of murder; found 'not-guilty' on the ground of self-defence.

The next awkward happenchance saw the *Aquidneck* infected with smallpox, which led to the death of three of the crew. Disinfecting the vessel placed a considerable financial burden on the owners (Hettie & Josh, who could barely sustain the enterprise). Shortly afterwards, the craft, through a series of unfortunate circumstances, was set ashore on the coast of southern Brazil and, after time on the beach, judged a total loss.

So there was Josh, on the bare bones of his arse, hardly a cent to his name, combing the beach for driftwood which he could use to construct some sort of a contrivance that would get his family home.

Scavenging material from the wreck of the *Aquidneck,* to supplement driftwood found on and about the beach, he built a vessel which he described as *'half Cape Ann dory, and half Japanese sampan.'*

Half of this and half of that she may have been, but Slocum sailed her, with his 15 year-old son as the working crew (by this time, it would be reasonable to assume that Hettie had had a bellyful of sailoring) 5,500 miles to Cape Roman, South Carolina - then via the inland waterway to Washington DC., finally reaching Boston by way of New York in 1889.

When Hettie stepped ashore, she didn't look back, never boarded a vessel again in the whole of her pastoral life (and who can blame her?). But Slocum, never one to miss an opportunity, published an account of these adventures in a book titled *Voyage of the Liberdade,* with the given Portuguese name commemorating the fact that the Cape Ann/sampan was launched on May 13th, 1888, the day slavery was abolished in Brazil.

So now what?

Slocum records the fact that *'times were hard,'* perhaps the understatement of his year. Nevertheless, by jocular circumstance (his friend, an old whaling captain, had said he had a 'ship' for him) which turned out to be a rotten hulk, roughly 45 feet overall, propped up in a field, some distance from the shore, it having been assumed that she'd never be up to, or even be capable of, ever braving the salt-laden wind again.

Undeterred, Josh put an edge on his axe, felled a pasture oak (no record of who it belonged to) then, after he'd trimmed and lopped it, hauled it to the local sawmill to have it sawn into planks.

The heartwood he shaped, using the natural curve of the grain, into the stem of his new vessel, which, by this time, was known as *Spray* - fit enough to *'shunt ice',* boasted the owner (tongue firmly in cheek), because he knew damned well that you didn't *'shunt ice'* - the floes were shunting you.

It went on from there. He built the vessel, a massive task, considering that the tools available were little more than rudimentary. A cross-cut saw, a panel saw, a bow saw. A mallet, with a decent selection of chisels. A wooden box-plane, another, longer, try-plane. A hammer, double-headed, for use with a caulking iron. A brace, with a selection of soft (file sharpened) bits.

There was more, but that's about it - plus 553 American dollars and

62 cents; the total material cost of the vessel.

As a new 'owner', Slocum spent a season long-lining on the coast, but soon came to the conclusion that baiting a hook and gutting fish wasn't the sort of lifestyle that would lead him to prosperity.

And he knew well enough what he really wanted to do - something that had never been done before – sail old *Spray* around the world, by himself.

He departed on the morning of April 24th 1895, bound for Gibraltar, where he found himself *'in excellent health, not overworked or cramped, but as well as ever in my life, though I was as thin as a reef point.'* (see the accompanying photograph).

So began this extraordinary adventure.

He sailed from Gibraltar: instead of heading east, changed his mind; gave up the idea of negotiating the Suez Canal, decided on the much more fearsome passage involved in the rounding of the Horn.

The list of places sailed past or visited reads as a roll call of the oceans, which indeed it is.

The Canary Islands, the Cape Verde Islands, Pernambuco, Rio de Janeiro - time spent on the sands of Uruguay (lucky to escape with only minor damage), on to Montevideo, with an excursion to Buenos Aires, where he shortened the mast and bowsprit in preparation for the Horn.

Submerged by a great wave off the mouth of the Plate, where he *'bore away for the Strait of Magellan.'*

Off Cape Froward, he was chased by *'Indians'* from Fortescue Bay.

On February 11th he rounded Cape Virgins and entered the Strait itself - passed through the narrows without mishap, cast anchor at Sandy Point (a Chilean coaling station) on February 14th 1896.

Found the *'natives'* both Patagonian and Fuegian a *'squalid lot'*, mostly as a result of alcohol abuse (the same old worldwide, waterfront problem).

While in this area, and going ashore for firewood and the like, he never once left *Spray* without his loaded shotgun, and from what we know of Josh was certainly prepared to use it.

In his own words, *'there is little to be said concerning the vessel's first passage through the strait.'* He found the sailing *'difficult'*, as well he might, had to anchor many times, and beat many days against the current, with only his superb seamanship and iron will making the passage possible.

Finally (and he doesn't actually record the number of days it took him) he gained the shelter of Port Tamar, with Cape Pillar in sight to the west'ard.

'here I felt the throb of the great ocean that lay before me (the South Pacific). I knew that I had put another world behind me, and that I was opening out another world ahead. I had passed the haunts of savages. Great piles of granite mountains of bleak and lifeless aspect were now astern; on some of them not even a speck of moss had ever grown. There was an unfinished 'newness' all about the land. On the hill back of Port Tamar a small beacon had been thrown up, showing that some man had been there. But could one tell but that he had died of loneliness and grief? A bleak land is not a place to enjoy solitude'.

'The few fur seals I saw were very shy, and of fishes next to none. Here in the Strait I found great abundance of mussels of excellent quality, and I fared sumptuously on them. There was a sort of swan, smaller that a Muscovy duck, which might have been brought down with my gun, but in the loneliness of life about that dreary country I found myself in no mood to make one life less, except in self-defence.

And Captain Joshua Slocum wanted to be a 'writer'?

Hadn't he already displayed some of those qualities that separate the good, from the merely competent?

There was a great deal more to come - he was 'driven by a tempest towards Cape Horn – his greatest sea adventure'.

He was 'cast into the Milky Way' - those tumultuous overfalls that reflect, on the surface of the sea, the cataclysmic fissures, cliffs, and canyons that form the fractured ocean bed - this being the sort of place that would threaten a substantial vessel, up to, and including, an ocean-going trawler.

From this point on, it's better to read the book old Josh wrote:

Sailing Alone Around the World

by

Captain Joshua Slocum

The original edition, with the Thomas Fogarty and George Varian illustrations being the best of quite a bunch.

So this was the man I had in mind when I was on my feet, thanking the members of the Slocum Society for the assistance they'd provided.

I kept it as brief as I could, within the remit of paying tribute where it was due, and compliments where they were needed.

But when I saw the print of the photograph that my friend Jean

Lacombe had taken, I did feel the urge to draw his attention to the very poor lighting.

'Jean.' says I, 'The background is in almost total darkness.'

' ... *Ah, mon ami, I thought it best to concentrate on getting the back of Ellen's neck well-lit, the rest didn't seem important.'*

So there you go - was Jean getting his priorities right?

following in Captain Slocum's footsteps ?

photo: **Jean Lacombe**   location: **New York**

OSTAR

1960

the author addressing the members of the Slocum Society
on behalf of the other competitors

thanking them for the effort they had made
the many kindnesses shown
the significant help provided

17

the Observer paid
but
Milner Gray, Guy Wellby, and George Friend
supplied rather more than just another artifact

The prize-giving ceremony for the first single-handed race, now known as OSTAR 1960 (the Observer single-handed transatlantic race) was held at the Arts Club, Dover Street, London, on the 22nd of March 1961. This was nine months after the event took place, but nobody thought it unusual. It was a relaxed affair, very well-organized. The guest list was impressive and the speeches reasonably short; nevertheless there were one or two things that deserve examination because, later, these seemingly inconsequential items became of some importance.

The prize, for the winner, was a very fine gold and silver salver, beautifully engraved, and presented by H.R.H. The Duke of Edinburgh; a suitable trophy for a man who had entered the event while facing the sort of adverse medical prognosis which, for most men, would have led to a less challenging way of passing what might have been assumed to be a few declining years.

But Francis Chichester was not that sort of submissive character, which his subsequent adventures (listed later) adequately prove.

The other four competitors received identical, but smaller salvers, which I'm sure gave the recipients an enormous amount of pleasure, mixed of course with pride, because of all the scores of people who had been invited to join the race, only five had actually made it to the start line. There was also the little matter of five starters and five finishers which was also something to be proud of (never since equalled).

It also gave me a tremendous amount of pleasure to see that Jean Lacombe had not only been invited, but efforts made to make sure he would be present. At the time, he was working in New York, and was perhaps not in a position to drop everything in order to spend an expensive weekend in London, even though he would be paid the tribute he deserved.

The next thing of note was that Blondie Hasler, who made a witty and well-informed speech (could have gone on longer) was credited with being 'the originator of the idea.'

This may seem a trifle obvious, but things happened later which eventually led to all sorts of difficulties, every one of which could have been avoided.

It was also nice to see that the Slocum Society was represented by Bruce Robinson. He had put a tremendous amount of work into the preliminary organization, and then made sure that the end-of-race reception was adequately arranged.

It was also important that David Astor, the editor of The Observer, who was an essential cog in the geartrain, had made sure the engraved prizes displayed the legend that they had been awarded by the Royal Western Yacht Club of England, - *in association with,* the Slocum Society of America; a fact that the Press, at the time, often overlooked.

It was a fine evening. The menu was perhaps not as carefully thought-out as that arranged by Chris Brasher for the eve-of-race dinner which had been held at Pedro's, not far from the waterfront at Plymouth (reference previous text). But the wine was good, the company congenial, and taking one thing with another, it provided a satisfactory conclusion to what turned out later to be a seminal affair.

The Royal Western Yacht Club of England
and The Observer

The Awards Dinner
for the First Singlehanded
Trans-Atlantic Race 1960

Presentation of The Observer Trophies
by
H.R.H. The Duke of Edinburgh

22nd March 1961 Arts Club Dover Street London

Speakers

Grace by the Revd. J. S. Clarke R.N.V.R.
Chaplain to the Royal Western Yacht Club of England

Mr. David Astor
Editor of The Observer

H.R.H. The Duke of Edinburgh

Lt. Col. A. J. Odling-Smee O.B.E.
Rear-Commodore of the Royal Western Yacht Club of England

Mr. Francis Chichester
Winner of the Singlehanded Trans-Atlantic Race, 1960

Lt. Col. H. G. Hasler D.S.O. O.B.E.
Second in the Race and originator of the idea

photo: **Planet News Ltd.**   courtesy: **The Observer**

location

The Arts Club, Dover Street, London

occasion

the presentation of awards

by

HRH
The Duke of Edinburgh

to those people who had taken part in

OSTAR

1960

photo: **author**

the silver salvers, with gold inlay, awarded by

Royal Western Yacht Club of England

in association with

Slocum Society of America

presented

by

The Observer

photo: **author**

reverse of the silver salvers

designed by

Milner Gray

made by

Guy Wellby

engraved by

George Friend

It's important to take note of the hands-on involvement displayed by David Astor at the time when single-handed ocean racing was being established.

The above telegram arrived before the start of the 2nd OSTAR (note the date, and the typographical error), but I also received a similar message before the first race in 1960.

These items were greatly appreciated - unfortunately the first has been mislaid.

And I have another regret - that I can't remember thanking the editor for his kind thought, and must also add that I can't recall writing to remark on the quality of the trophies, those beautiful salvers his organisation generously planned for and provided.

These are serious omissions, and the excuse isn't available, that at the time there was a certain amount of hurly-burly involved (could even be described as organized chaos).

Time *should* have been made.

But then, isn't there a saying, tucked away somewhere, that

it's never too late

18

OBITS

&

APPRECIATIONS

Lt Colonel H.G. 'Blondie' Hasler DSO, OBE, RM

The distinguished soldier, who was known throughout the international yachting community by his nickname, was born in Dublin on February 27th 1914, during the time his father, Lt (QM) A.T.Hasler, MC., RAMC, was temporarily stationed in Ireland. His mother's family also had a military background, so it was natural for her son to choose the profession.

After attending Wellington (English 'public' school), Hasler commenced his probationary period in the Royal Marines in September 1932, and obtained his regular commission three years later, having served afloat for a short training period in the ex-battleship HMS Iron Duke, and then an operational posting aboard HMS Queen Elizabeth, at that time the flagship of the Mediterranean fleet.

During these formative years he made significant progress, gravitating naturally to the small boat end of the service, being appointed Fleet Landing Officer to the then re-forming Mobile Naval Base Defence Organisation in 1937.

He was promoted Captain on May 23rd 1939, and so was well-trained and positioned to take part in the war with Germany, which was declared in the September of the same year.

Anyone interested in Colonel Hasler's career could do no better than read Ewan Southby-Tailyour's biography, entitled, *Blondie,* published in 1998 by Leo Cooper (Pen & Sword Imprint) designated ISBN 0 85052 516 0.

This well-researched book records the pre-war years.

Describes an engagement that took place during the first few months of the war, in the Norwegian theatre, where Blondie served alongside a detachment of the French Foreign Legion.

After recording this relatively minor skirmish, the author deploys the main thrust of the book, describing Hasler's involvement in the conception, planning, training, and courageous leadership of an amphibious assault team which, because of its clandestine nature and breathtaking audacity, not only earned an honoured place in British military history, but became the forerunner of the special undercover boat service (SBS) the companion arm of a similar organisation now known as the SAS.

After the war, in which he served with such distinction, Blondie decided to take up the challenge presented by the events organised by the Royal Ocean Racing Club, but in a vessel, *Tre Sang*, which most people at the time thought unsuitable for the task.

Even now, an argument could be made that a 30 square metre,

developed in Sweden for relatively sheltered Baltic conditions, was perhaps not an ideal craft to undertake passage racing, some of which takes place on and about the eastern seaboard of the North Atlantic Ocean. However, although her crew would occasionally describe the vessel's performance as something akin to 'driving to windward aboard a half-tide rock', under Blondie's expert guidance *Tre Sang* was entered for six of the seven races in the RORC's small boat section (winning three of them) and in 1946, won the Class 3 Championship and the Ortac Cup.

Having successfully explored this avenue, Blondie conceived and organised competitive single-handed ocean racing which was, at the time, perhaps a step too far for some of his contemporaries.

With the hardship imposed by *Tre Sang* no doubt in the forefront of his mind he decided on a different approach, vis-à-vis single-handed sailing, relinquishing the concept of a half-tide rock and altering a Scandinavian Folkboat so she could be sailed by one man, who stayed dry. The result was *Jester*, perhaps the most famous small ocean-going vessel since Noah embarked in the ark.

From the year of the first organised single-handed transatlantic race (1960) *Jester*, or her replica, has made eight Atlantic crossings, mostly sailed by Mike Richey, who was, for 40 years, the Director of the Royal Institute of Navigation.

Amongst Blondie's other gifts to yachting, the pendulum-servo steering gear remains high on the list.

Anyone interested in this device should consult *Self-Steering for Sailing Craft* by John S. Letcher, Jr., published by International Marine Publishing, Camden, Maine, in 1974.

The *Jester* saga, and Mike Richey's central position in it, is set out in *Classic Boat*, July and October editions 1992, while the Jester Challenge can be contacted through www.jesterinfo.org

Blondie married late, eventually meeting the right person, Bridget Fisher, the daughter of a distinguished Admiral, with the wedding taking place at Aberfoyle on October 30th 1965.

There were two children, Dinah and Tom, who were brought up on the Scottish farm Blondie retired to, towards the end of his, by any standards, quite extraordinary life.

He died on Tuesday, May 5th 1987, admired by all who had known him, mourned and undoubtedly missed by the select, and without doubt proud group of people who had served their country with him.

photo: **author**

Blondie Hasler

1959

outside his workshop
where he was fitting out

Jester

charming
unassuming

a force to be reckoned with

fascinating boat

Blondie Hasler

(appreciation)

My meeting with Blondie came about in what can be best described as a convoluted manner.

My wife and I were farming, a modest place, situated near the town of Narberth, in the County of Pembroke. We had a small herd of Ayrshires, a few sheep to keep the ragweed down, a loveable black labrador (a bitch) called Twinkle, and the very best neighbours it would be possible to meet. Some of them owned riparian rights on the Eastern Cleddau, so there was fly-fishing for trout, sewin and the occasional salmon.

There was also rough shooting, woodcock, pheasants, and the like. But there was also ferreting, augmented by snares and traps, which were absolutely essential in the attempt to control the rabbit population which, at that time (1949) had reached plague proportions.

Two children arrived, Rosemarie and a year later, Philip.

Not all that far away lay the seaside village of Saundersfoot, which not only boasted a small harbour, but also a sailing club, with a class of G.P. 14s (I built one in the barn); when things moved on a bit, we turned to the relatively high-performance *Osprey* - so there we were, scooting about Saundersfoot Bay, sometimes with two very small kids crammed into the forepeak (not enough room to swing one cat, let alone two) with my darling wife dangling on the end of a trapeze.

Then, one day, when I was browsing through the Yachting Press, I noticed a piece, signed by a gent called Hasler, a letter which asked *'if there was anyone interested in a single-handed small-boat race from Plymouth to New York ?'*

At that time, just about everyone in the country had heard of Lt Colonel H.G. Hasler. He was a recognizable wartime hero (the second World War was not a distant event) and not only that, a film had been made, first screened in 1955, entitled *'Cockleshell Heroes'* which had further enhanced the central character's profile (he later told me he hated it).

But here was this man, suggesting a race across the pond, from Plymouth to New York.

Now: there are only two ways to approach this proposition, either it's a madcap suggestion, or (and I'm afraid it was the 'or' that appealed to me).

So I persuaded my wife (how, I still don't know) that I should enter for this event.

There were one or two problems.

I didn't have a suitable boat, and not enough money to buy one. Nevertheless, we went ahead, sold the farm (sold the farm) [1] and entered into a contract with Kelpie Boat Services to build a Scandinavian Folkboat.

With the boat built – the contract had been signed late 1957, and the boat built and launched by the summer of '58 – we cruised the Pembrokeshire coast, getting used to the vessel.

During that winter, I beefed-up the rigging, made a few other improvements, and built a self-steering gear with single-handed sailing in mind, and although the gadget was far from perfect, it did at least offer reasonable control of the boat.

What's the next move?

Before you embark on a single-handed passage from Plymouth to New York?

If you've got any sense - and I had spent six years at sea, some of it during the later part of the war, in commercial shipping, so I knew a thing or two about it – if you have any sense, you had better make damn sure you are up to single-handed sailing, it's not everyone's cup of tea.

I sailed the folkboat *Eira* (named after my wife) down to Spain, spent a few days at La Coruña, and then cruised, with a great deal more confidence, back to Saundersfoot.

So much for that. However, unbeknownst to me, a yachting correspondent had taken note of the passage, and inserted a small piece in the magazine he was concerned with, to the effect that *'this farmer had sailed down to Spain, and back again, single-handed, in a Folkboat; and enjoyed the trip, principally because he had no need to steer as the self-steering gear had taken over that small chore.'*

The next happenchance was the arrival of a letter from none other than H.G. Hasler, asking if I was interested in the race he was promoting, but in any case, invited me to spend a weekend down at his place in Curdridge, Hampshire.

What would you do?

(1) *This may sound a monumentally selfish thing to do, but it wasn't as bad as it seems. True enough, the farm was sold, but the proceeds enabled a waterfront property to be purchased in Saundersfoot, with the modest amount left over enabling a clinker-built Folkboat to be ordered and built by Kelpie Boat Services, who charged £900: included a mainsail and jib.*

I drove down to Curdridge in our bit of a rattle-trap old Land Rover, met the man himself - perhaps the most unassuming, but nevertheless engaging person I have ever met in my life.

We got on well.

I had taken the precaution of carrying two bottles of quite good claret, and after dinner (my host cooked baked beans, bangers and mash) and the second bottle about to be opened, it somehow transpired that I mentioned to Blondie I had served aboard a depot ship during the WW2 allied invasion of Normandy, explaining we were certainly not 'first-wave', arrived soon after, yet played a significant, even if minor role in that tumultuous happening.

How 'things' change the course of events.

Aboard the steamship *Ascanious*, which was serving as a 'rest and recovery' vessel - but armed to the teeth with a 4" on the poop, four 20mm Oerlikons on the boat deck, and a 40mm Bofors on the forecastle head - were a detachment of Royal Marines (Blondie's regiment) who were crewing the landing craft that were very much part of the scene.

There was a very young 2nd Lieutenant, who must have been little older than I was (born in 1926, I still hadn't reached my 18th birthday).

Every morning this young, immaculately turned out officer addressed his detachment, issuing orders for the day – who would be crewing which craft, what they were carrying, and so on. It was quite an entertainment, watching this young buck, geeing-up his platoon of old sweats, leaving them in no doubt at all, that he expected them to '*press on, uphold the magnificent tradition of the Service.*' etc., etc.

Then, on one never to be forgotten morning, about ten days after D-day, there was a ear-shattering explosion. *Ascanious* had either been hit by a torpedo (most unlikely) or had struck a mine, which turned out to be the case; a nasty little magnetic gadget which had lain undisturbed until we swung to a particular tide and triggered it.

The old tub didn't sink, went badly down by the head, with the whole of the foredeck awash. The second watertight bulkhead held and some sort of order was eventually restored.

There were casualties, particularly amongst the Royal Marines, who were billeted in the for'ard part of the vessel.

The crew were ordered to abandon ship, but a small number were kept aboard, and we tended the vessel while she was towed back to Southampton.

So Blondie and I had plenty to talk about, at the Old Forge, Curdridge, where I slept on a rickety camp bed that was a foot too short to be comfortable, snugged down under one threadbare army blanket.

The next day, Blondie took me to his workshop, where he had '*Jester*' hauled out for a refit.

She was an amazing vessel, another Folkboat, but with a difference; she was fully-decked and sported a Chinese junk rig, shown to me as a drawing, but the mast and the fully-battened mainsail were there in the shed.

She was also fitted with a trim tab self-steering gear, which turned out to be a great deal more sophisticated than the kit I had aboard *Eira*, with the principle difference being, that Blondie knew all about positive and negative feedback, which, correctly applied, converted an agricultural implement into a gear which provided the sort of subtle nudge an experienced helmsman would apply to the tiller of a vessel being sailed close-hauled to wind'ard.

It's almost the end of the story.

I told Blondie I would be there when they fired the gun (at that stage, there was a certain amount of uncertainty about 'when' and even 'who' would fire the gun), but not the slightest doubt that the gun would certainly be fired.

Blondie also put me in touch with a Dr David Lewis, and a short while later my wife and I paid this gent a visit, at his London home/cum surgery, which also developed into another of those minor events that turn out to be of some personal significance.

DAVID HENRY LEWIS

(1917 – 2002)

He was born in the U.K. of a Welsh-Irish family, but brought up partly in New Zealand, and also in Rarotonga; one of the Cook Islands, proclaimed a British protectorate in 1888 and annexed by New Zealand in 1901.

He studied medicine in New Zealand, but left in 1938 to complete his degree in England. After the outbreak of the second World War, having qualified, he joined a British airborne regiment as a medical officer and saw extensive military service.

On being de-mobbed, he worked as a general practitioner in one of the poorer parts of London, and later became involved in the establishment of the United Kingdom National Health Service, a contribution to the land of his birth of which he was justifiably proud.

In the late 1950s he became aware, through the yachting press, that Lt Colonel H.G.Hasler was organising a single-handed sailing race, for small vessels, with the prospective course being from Plymouth (England) to New York. This fired his imagination as a 'first-ever' event, and fitted in with his adventurous background of rock climber, canoeist, military parachutist and general devil-may-care man about rather more than the town.

He competed in the first, 1960 single-handed transatlantic race, sailing a 25 foot Vertue, *Cardinal Vertue*, a class of vessel that was, at the time, being mostly used for coastal and estuary cruising, although one or two extensive passages had been successfully undertaken.

Lewis came third in the race, after suffering a major setback shortly after the start - barely departed from Plymouth Sound when the vessel was partially dismasted, which necessitated a return to harbour where the staff at Mashford's Boatyard worked overnight on the necessary repairs.

Returned to England, after the race, in which he came third, David Lewis wrote the first of his eleven published works, with the book '*The Ship Would Not Travel Due West*' enjoying a commercial success that went some way to financing his next seafaring adventure. This involved taking part in the second (1964) single-handed transatlantic race, sailing a catamaran, launched as *Rehu Moana,* in which he subsequently circumnavigated the globe - the first such passage in a multi-hulled vessel.

He returned to the Pacific in 1967 and with the aid of a grant from the Australian National University, undertook a study of the traditional navigational techniques used by the Pacific Island people, with this work being recorded in *'We, the Navigators'* and *'The Voyaging Stars'*, both books being recognised as making a significant contribution to the understanding of the ocean-voyaging achievements of the Polynesian and Melanesian peoples.

His next seafaring adventure had, as its major objective, a single-handed circumnavigation of the Antarctic continent. Short of funds, the vessel he purchased was launched as *'Ice Bird'*, a small steel yacht that could not, by any stretch of the imagination, be judged suitable for the task her skipper was engaged on. The vessel offered poor sea-keeping qualities, subsequently capsized, and Lewis was lucky to survive - eventually, after being missing for over 3 months, he managed to struggle into Palmer Base, on the Antarctic Peninsula, where he was nursed back to life by members of the scientific community who were serving there at the time. However, the book he wrote, published, sensibly enough, as *Ice Bird,* became a bestseller and was translated into many languages.

Returned to Australia, Lewis set up the Oceanic Research Foundation, financed largely by similarly inclined buccaneering types - the Australian adventuring entrepreneur, Dick Smith, was a major contributor.

This organisation initially sponsored private expeditions to the Antarctic, with Lewis undertaking the pioneering voyage in *'Solo'*; but the authorities concerned were not enamoured of this activity, and the enterprise never really flourished, although it did provide exciting sailing for the people who took part.

There were many other adventures, both personal and practical, before David Lewis retired to New Zealand to write his autobiography, published as *'Shapes on the Wind'*.

Towards the end of his adventurous life he meandered, in a variety of craft, up the Australian east coast, eventually ending up in Tin Can Bay, suffering from failing eyesight; but with the help of his friends he continued cruising, visiting Rockhampton and then the Keppel Isles before returning once more to Tin Can Bay.

He was awarded the well-deserved accolade of Distinguished Companion of the New Zealand Order of Merit.

He died in 2002, leaving three wives, four adult children and many, many friends, with his last wish being that his ashes be scattered over the broad, and surely smilingly receptive South Pacific ocean.

photo: **author**

David Lewis

outside his home/surgery
located in an unfashionable London suburb

complex
quietly spoken
a declared atheist
a card-carrying communist
a marvellous friend
not always as well-prepared as he should have been

David Lewis

(appreciation)

There were scores of people around and about during the week or so before the start of the first single-handed race in 1960.

The dockside at Millbay, Plymouth was crowded with newsmen, photographers, wives, and girlfriends, together with Flag Officers of the Royal Western Yacht Club. There were also representatives from The Observer, and some who were just plain rubber kickers, strolling the waterfront, and then casually enquiring, 'what's going on?'.

Of all those people present, it would be a fair bet to assume that not one of them presented the complexities of character that David Lewis, not ostensibly displayed, but more often than not didn't bother to conceal.

He was far from being reticent: when asked about his political views he would declare, with a disarming smile, that he was a card-carrying communist.

The same absolute directness was employed when he was asked about religion. 'I'm an atheist' was the stock response, which sometimes discomforted the overly righteous, who assumed their strongly held beliefs were somehow above debate (really a matter of 'faith', you know).

So when in David's company, it paid to listen carefully to what was being said, because, sometimes, the most penetrative remark would be spoken sotto voce.

Perhaps because we both had partial Welsh backgrounds (my maternal grandfather was a Gloucestershire man) we got on well from day one. After Blondie had paved the way, my wife and I took the train, and then an expensive taxi ride from Paddington to David's house/cum surgery which was located in one of the poorer eastern suburbs of the city. It wasn't a slum - and there were still some of that type of catastrophically dilapidated dwellings on display in London at the time - but the place where David had decided to hang his shingle housed what could be realistically described as disadvantaged families.

His political conviction had obviously influenced his decision to work where he thought he could do most good - he had, after all, been involved in the political process that resulted in the establishment of what became known as the National Health Service - although I'm still not absolutely sure how this came about.

Perhaps it was through his political friends and acquaintances.

It doesn't really matter, because the David we saw leaving his house, just as we were approaching it, was Doctor David Lewis, a physician who was well-groomed, collar & tied, dressed in a camel hair overcoat, and sporting an expensive pair of leather driving gloves.

We were given, generously enough, the run of the house while David was 'out on his rounds'. When he returned, two hours later, he was accompanied by a very attractive Maori lady, early twenties, gorgeous brown skin, flashing eyes, and the most infectious laugh you are ever likely to hear - this side of being safely brought-up, on a sandy bottom (good holding ground) in four fathoms, in the evocatively termed area of New Zealand most wandering seaman have tagged as the 'just must visit' Bay of Beautiful Islands.

All went well. We went out to supper, to a place that was not far removed from a 'greasy spoon'. It didn't matter, David's almost whispered conversation, interspersed with gales of Maori laughter galloped the time along.

When we returned to David's house, my wife and I had the use of a 'put-you-up' settee, in the sitting-room. This would be O.K. in normal circumstances, but it was just about a foot too short for me, and as it was wintertime, bitterly cold, with the only heating in the house apparently being a small (one bar broken) electric fan heater - the fact that my feet were hanging out over the end of the bed was hardly going to be conducive to a good night's rest.

However, as soon as Eira and I were accommodated, David and friend went upstairs to bed.

For about twenty minutes, everything was quiet, then came the sounds of what seemed to be a disagreement of one sort of other.

Whatever had been said before, was now being repeated in rather more forceful terms. As Eira and I listened, things were obviously deteriorating. The Maori gal was bellowing (couldn't exactly make out the words) but the gist of it was pretty obvious, and we weren't really surprised when the well-stacked Bay of Plenty stormed down the stairs, stark naked, having blown her top, the result of the tempestuous eruption that had begun a little earlier.

My wife, always a resourceful lady, offered her a dressing-gown (gratefully accepted), then there was somewhere to sleep – a hastily arranged collection of cushions provided something that was obviously better than the cold stone floor.

What a night: Eira and I, snuggled down on the put-you-up, were facing each other. She was smiling, then obviously doing her best to repress her desire to giggle, which she was afraid might deteriorate into the sort of laughter that would offend the Maori gal.

Time past, dawn broke. Bay of Plenty's clothes were upstairs – she didn't want to fetch them; both Eira and I were also somewhat reluctant to make the fatal ascent.

In the end, and it didn't take long, Eira had rigged the gal out in spare clothing she had carried from Wales. A pair of knickers, tight-fitting jeans, a blouse, a sweater, she could keep the dressing gown, had fortunately left her shoes at the bottom of the stairs, all of which were gratefully accepted by you know who. She did stay for a hastily brewed cup of coffee, then she was off, into a bitter winter East London morning with flakes of snow being driven down the still deserted streets.

David, when he appeared, after he was certain his fellow-citizen had departed, just didn't mention the affair. Cool as a just out of the fridge cucumber, clear-eyed, bushy-tailed; still so softly spoken that you had to sometimes lean in to hear him. We talked boats, self-steering gears, the sort of food he was planning to carry during the race he was obviously delighted to be involved with.

We became good friends. He asked me to be best man at one of his weddings. He came down to stay with us in Wales, but the Bay at Saundersfoot, he said, was not anything like North Wales, the *real* Wales, where he had enjoyed rock climbing in Snowdonia.

He once complained, in the middle of summer, that there wasn't any skiing, so (more fool me) I rigged up a powerful outboard, borrowed some water skis, and towed the bugger about.

The David Lewis my wife and I knew, was a charming man, to the point where it was almost too good to be true.

The ladies adored him; three wives and countless liaisons were ample proof of that.

He was under average height, but I never thought of him as being in any way small. The disparity in inches just didn't, in our friendly world, make any significant impact, mostly because, I would freely admit, that in almost every respect he towered over me.

Except in one regard:

I was married to the same lady for 57 years - wife, lover, business associate, co-conspirator - the person who tearfully shared the burden of mourning, when we buried two of our children. You could take your pick and never be disappointed.

I also knew how many children I'd fathered.

Just for the record, Bay of Plenty returned the clothing within a week. All freshly laundered and pressed. Also in the parcel was the bloom of a white lily, packed in the sort of hard cellophane box that florists use to protect their wares in the post.

photo: **Lifetime Associates**

courtesy: **Australian Television, Channel 7**

'This is your Life'

outlining some of David's astonishing achievements

the disparity in inches just didn't, in our friendly world, make any
significant impact, mostly because, I would freely admit, that in almost
every other respect he towered over me
except in one regard
I was married to the same lady for 57 years – wife, lover, business
associate, co-conspirator; the person who tearfully shared the burden of
mourning, when we buried two of our children.
you could take your pick and never be disappointed

SIR FRANCIS CHICHESTER

Born in Shirwell, North Devon, on the 17th of September 1901, he received his education at Marlborough College, a traditional English (public) school which normally advanced students for university entrance, but Chichester left to emigrate to New Zealand when he was 18 years of age.

Because he didn't possess much working capital, he took a variety of jobs, varying from coal miner to gold prospector, later becoming successful enough to enter the commercial world, initially in real estate, then the timber industry. In 1927, he and his partner established the Goodwin & Chichester Aviation Company which carried over 9,000 passengers 'without injury, or loss of life'.

While in New Zealand, Chichester married Muriel Blakiston, with the union (1923) producing a son, George, born in 1926, who spent most of his time in Australia/New Zealand, but died in 1967, having apparently been estranged from his father during the greater part of his life (his mother had died in 1929).

In the same year, Chichester returned to the U.K., learnt to fly, and in December of that year flew a small biplane, a Gypsy Moth, from Croydon, London, to Sydney, thus becoming the second man to fly, solo, from England to Australia.

This trail breaking spirit was again demonstrated when he made the first solo flight from New Zealand to Australia, across the Tasman sea, via Norfolk Island, having converted his biplane into a seaplane by fitting somewhat unconventional floats.

For this flight he received The Johnston Memorial Trophy (the first holder of this aviators 'Hall of Fame') which he subsequently embellished by flying solo from Australia to Japan, at the conclusion of which he unfortunately crashed and suffered serious injury.

Nothing daunted, he flew another small airplane, a 'Puss Moth', with one passenger, to England, where he met and later married (1937) Sheila Mary Craven, there being one son of this union, Giles, who was born in 1946.

During the years 1939-1945 Chichester became the Chief Navigation Instructor of the Central Flying School. Initially involved with teaching British fighter pilots to find their way back to base, using low level, seat of the pants procedures. And then adapting his 'island-finding technique', which he had used successfully in the Pacific, with this method becoming something akin to the standard practice used by Coastal Command in the latter part of the second World War.

The end of that conflict saw the establishment of Francis Chichester Ltd., a map publishing business that was concerned with London and its environs, later developing into a broaderscale enterprise whose products (information on hotels, restaurants, museums, and other places of interest) were sold throughout the world.

Chichester's sailing career dates from the early 1950s, when he purchased and campaigned his yacht *Gipsy Moth 2* (reminiscent of his record-breaking aircraft, but spelt slightly differently). He took part in 16 RORC organised races, winning the Southsea to Harwich race (the Stuart Cup) in 1956. However, despite this outdoor sporting activity, he was diagnosed as suffering from lung cancer, with the medical advice being that he should have one lung removed - the worst-case scenario being that he had little more than six months to live.

It was at about this time that Lt Colonel H.G. Hasler was promoting the idea of a single-handed transatlantic race, with the course being from Plymouth, England, to Sheepshead Bay, New York. A challenge that most people would surely have judged as being beyond the capabilities of an individual in Chichester's physical condition.

Nevertheless, supported by his family, he declined the surgical route, opting instead for his wife's belief in an altered lifestyle and what would later be described as a 'nature cure', with this holistic approach proving beneficial, to the extent that he was able to take delivery of the yacht, *Gipsy Moth 3*, which he had ordered prior to his alarming diagnosis.

Having competed in, and won, the first east/west single-handed transatlantic race (1960), he was voted Yachtsman of the Year, and awarded the Blue Water Medal by the Cruising Club of America.

In the following year, the President of the Institute of Navigators, when he was presenting Chichester with the institute's Gold Medal, described the recipient as 'the greatest single-handed navigator of the age', an accolade which pointed the way to the New Years Honours list and a C.B.E. (Commander of the British Empire) for 'services to yachting' in 1964.

In 1966, having competed in the second single-handed transatlantic race in 1964, coming second, to Eric Tabarly, he took delivery of another, larger yacht, launched as *Gipsy Moth 4* - he then declared his intention of attempting to sail, solo, from Plymouth to Sydney in one hundred days, spend no more than 30 days in Australia refitting the vessel, and then make the return journey to England - achieving an aggregate time of less than 230 days, thus bettering the average sea-going time that the Australian 'wool clippers' took in the commercial days of sail.

Later that year, during the award ceremony held at Greenwich, London, on the 7th of July, when the voyage had been successfully accomplished, Her Majesty Queen Elizabeth the second, used the sword that Queen Elizabeth the First had presented to Sir Francis Drake during the previous Elizabethan reign (1533-1603) with the popular consensus being, 'it can't get much better than that'.

There were other sea-going adventures, all well documented. But in 1971 he suffered a physical decline, being once again diagnosed as suffering from cancer, this time manifested as a tumour located near the base of his spine.

The setback would surely have been deemed sufficient to at least limit the scope of his ambition. Rather to the contrary, Chichester entered for another single-handed transatlantic race, which were now being held at four-yearly intervals.

He actually started, sailed from Plymouth, bound for America, in 1972, but was ultimately forced to abandon the endeavour - being taken ill, with the yacht *Gipsy Moth 5* sailed back to the U.K. by his son Giles, together with three volunteers from the aircraft carrier HMS Ark Royal.

Two months later (August 26th) Chichester died while a patient in the Royal Naval Hospital at Stonehouse, and was buried at Shirwell, in the County of Devon.

His published works include 3 books on flying, *Solo to Sydney*, 1930; *Alone over the Tasman Sea*, 1933; *Ride on the Wind*, 1936; followed by 11 navigational treatise, produced under the aegis of the Air Ministry from 1941-1945.

His sailing books include, *Alone Across the Atlantic*, 1961; *Atlantic Adventure*, 1962; *Along the Clipper Way*, 1966; *Gipsy Moth Circles the World*, 1967; *Romantic Challenge*, 1968.

In addition, he wrote *How to Keep Fit*, published in 1969, and his autobiography, *The Lonely Sea & The Sky*, the first edition of which appeared in 1964.

Other awards, decorations, distinctions and appointments include, Warden of the Court of the Guild of Air Pilots and Air Navigators.

Fellow and Member of Council of the Institute of Navigation.

The issue of a special postage stamp to commemorate the Voyage of Circumnavigation.

A 'Figurehead of Courage' award from the State of San Remo.

The Freedom of the Town of Barnstaple, Devon.

A second (unprecedented) award of the prestigious Blue Water

Medal by the Cruising Club of America.

The Australian Institute of Navigation Gold Medal.

Yacht Club de France Special Centenary Award.

Member D'Honneur of Yacht Club de France.

Royal Yacht Squadron, Special Bronze Medal (made from a bolt from the clipper ship *Cutty Sark*).

The Chichester Award from the Royal Yacht Squadron for the outstanding solo yachting achievement in 1967.

Royal Geographical Society, Gold Medal.

Honorary Master of the Bench of the Middle Temple.

Institute of Navigation Special Award.

Superior Achievement Award of the American Institute of Navigation.

Younger Brother of Trinity House.

Guild of Yachting Writers Gold Medal.

Marconi Memorial Gold Medal, awarded by the Veteran Wireless Operators Association, New York.

Royal Cruising Club, Medal for Seamanship.

photo: **author**

Francis Chichester

working aboard

Gipsy Moth 3

with the Folkboat
Eira
in the background

accomplished
determined
ambitious
wonderfully supported by his wife
deserved it

Francis Chichester

(appreciation)

As a pair, and it's difficult to think of them without pairing them together, because Francis and his wife Sheila offered support to that old adage - 'the sum was greater than the parts', but there's not one syllable in that statement which should be interpreted as being in any way derogatory.

They obviously adored each other.

And not only that, they complimented each other in so many unspoken ways, that when I was in their company I was aware of a 'forcefield' that was almost tangible. It was only later that I noticed the gate was sometimes left ajar, and this incautious act, as is so often the case, led to a certain amount of trouble later. Nevertheless, and without reservation, I liked them both.

Francis was in some ways a reticent character, as people are (can afford to be) who have accomplished so many different, attention-grabbing things they have no need to embellish their image.

Sheila was different; some talked of her as being formidable, and to those who were left bobbing about in her wake she could be reasonably described in those terms.

Was she an assertive character?

In this regard, everyone must speak as they find.

Would she take advantage of someone, when she knew she had the upper hand?

The same judgement applies.

I didn't find these idiosyncrasies in any way disturbing.

I had spent over six years earning my living at sea, some of the time in tough Chinese crewed ships, and another seven years farming on my own account. If I'd been provoked, I was quite capable, and I'm certain Sheila knew it, of tearing her off a strip using rough nautical language that she could have used to paper the walls.

It was good basis on which to conduct a relationship.

She was a business lady, who knew not only how many beans made five; knew how to thread them permanently on her abacus, and there's surely nothing wrong with that - I only wish I'd been able to do it.

This was all very well, but there were one or two shaded areas which we (the entrants, who were about to take part in the 1st single-handed transatlantic race) should have paid attention to.

There was the unspoken assumption, on Sheila's side, that Francis was somehow the 'senior' partner in the event about to be started.

That didn't stand examination.

Lt Colonel H. G. Hasler DSO OBE RM (but 'Blondie' to everyone around) outranked Francis by a very long country mile, in every conceivable direction.

Then there was Doctor David Henry Lewis, a well-qualified physician, who also had a military record, as a Medical Officer, with the rank of Major, who had seen action and jumped with the Parachute Regiment at Normandy, amongst other places.

Jean Lacombe?

His seafaring experience in small boats - *two* single-handed transatlantic voyages *already* accomplished - made the skipper of *Gipsy Moth 3* (experience confined, mostly, to the English Channel) seem rather a doubtful hook on which to hang an aspiring Admiral's hat.

Yet that was the direction in which things were incrementally moving.

There was sort of an assumed wisdom (being actively promoted) that Francis had been involved with the concept of the race – when he'd had absolutely nothing whatever to do with what was a well-documented decision, of several years standing. But, and it turned out to be quite a serious *but*, it was allowed to slip by, partly because it seemed so trivial.

However, there is something that needs correcting now:

At the end of Chapter 5, there occurs the remark that, *'when I visited Francis in London, he wanted to know all about my own and other people's preparations, but was not inclined to discuss his own. As a parting gift he gave me a map of Central London.'*

That is factually correct, as far as it goes, but gives a distorted picture of what actually took place.

When I visited Francis, at his invitation, he invited me in, and introduced me to Sheila.

Tea was served, conversation joined, the technical bits and pieces of single-handed sailing and self-steering gears were broadly discussed.

Came time to go; Francis gave me a map of Central London (he was a publisher of maps – earned his living doing so).

However, the map he gave me was displayed on the inside of both the front and back cover of a very nice leather-bound diary.

I kept this memento for years, treasured it as something closely associated with the first single-handed transatlantic race, and was very upset when, during one of many family 'moves', it disappeared – how, I've no idea.

For those interested in the Chichester saga, and it is quite a saga, Sheila's autobiography, published as

Two Lives – Two Worlds

Hodder & Stoughton Ltd

SBN 34010626

is a volume that makes for fascinating reading

She states, on the first line, of the first page, of the first chapter, that *'my father committed suicide, when I was three days old'*, which is quite a statement, well-followed by a fascinating insight of how financial difficulties, and what *she* saw (was perhaps haunted by) the loss of social status which, at the time, was perhaps more apparent than real.

It all came justifiedly right in the end.

doesn't

Sir Francis & Lady Chichester

have rather an accomplished ring to it ?

JEAN LACOMBE

1916 - 1995

The French sailor, painter, photographer, and traveller of note, came to the attention of the international sailing community when, in 1955, he made a passage from Toulon, France, to Puerto Rico, in 68 days, aboard a diminutive vessel, merely 18 feet overall, which he built himself and launched as *Hippocampe* (Sea Horse).

He then sailed to Atlantic City, with his final destination being New York, where he took a job in the catering industry.

Later, through various items that were appearing in the yachting press at the time, he became aware that a single-handed race was being proposed, with the course being from Plymouth, England, to Sheepshead Bay, which, as it happened, was only a few blocks from the hotel in which he was working as a chef.

Having scrimped and saved to accumulate the necessary capital, he purchased a timber sloop, now known as *Cap Horn*.

This boat, although slightly larger than the vessel in which he had completed his first North Atlantic passage, was still very much at the lower end of what was thought suitable for the type of ocean racing in prospect. Nevertheless, he contacted Lt Colonel Blondie Hasler, and convinced him, without too much trouble, that both skipper and boat were up to the job, and having paid his entry fee, made plans to arrive in England in time to take part in the race, scheduled to start on June 10th 1960.

Lacombe came fifth, out of five starters, after a delayed start; but that's a long way from saying that he came no better than last, because merely to compete in such a small vessel, against what was a well-campaigned ocean racing yacht (*Gipsy Moth 3*) was a display of guts and determination of which he could justifiably be proud.

The next single-handed transatlantic race took place in 1964, the decision having been taken to hold the event at four-yearly intervals.

Lacombe competed again, this time in a vessel, *Golif*, with slightly more waterline length, which allowed him to compete on perhaps not quite such disadvantaged terms. However, he was still up against much larger boats that had been specially designed for single-handed ocean racing, and he was once again well out of the frame.

Soon after his arrival in America, Jean had been attracted to, and had become a member of the Brotherhood of the Coast, later being voted to serve as Captain of the New York Chapter, a position he thoroughly enjoyed.

He continued to cruise extensively in the Caribbean, and died in Fort de France (Martinique) in 1995, at the age of 79.

His only known publication is *'moi l'Atlantique,'* but this volume has apparently not been translated into English.

The class of vessel known as *Cap Horn* was designed by the French naval architect J.J.Herbulot, specifically to meet the needs of the then active Midget Ocean Racing Club. The cold-moulded wooded hull was built by Joet & Company of Sartcuville, France, and offered with Dacron sails, a nylon spinnaker, and alloy spars.

The boats were imported into the United States during the late 1950's by the European Research & Supply Company at 724 Fifth Avenue, New York 19, New York, with the pier head price being $ 4850 US, complete with mainsail and working jib (the exchange rate then was about four American dollars to the pound sterling).

The Brotherhood of the Coast: the title of an association dating back to the heyday of Caribbean piracy (the middle 1600s) then based largely in Tortuga. Now typified by the present-day members of the brotherhood, almost exclusively yachtsmen, displaying a romantic attachment to the good old days, when the likes of Henry Morgan were afforded some protection from the gallows by being granted a commission from the monarch to act as 'privateers'.

These freebooters were a useful adjunct to the regular but sparse forces available to the states, mainly British, Dutch, and French, who were opposed to Spanish domination of the area.

Henry Morgan (1653-1688) the scion of a well-connected Welsh family who held title to a manor in the ancient Hundred of Newport, Monmouthshire.

As a professional soldier he was well versed in the art of war, and made his mark in the Caribbean through his ruthless command of men, which included those buccaneers who plied their trade afloat.

Dudley Pope's *'Harry Morgan's Way'* published by Secker and Warburg, London 1977, offers a fascinating account of a swashbuckling character who climbed an alarmingly precarious ladder sufficiently to gain a Royal Appointment as Governor of Jamaica.

Acknowledgement:

Ms Toni Austin, 200E. 24 st., New York City, NY

photo: **author**

Jean Lacombe

an experienced small-boat seaman
underrated
not an avaricious bone in his body
a romantic attachment to

'the sea'

JEAN LACOMBE

(appreciation)

After the 1960 single-handed race was over, and all the competitors had arrived safely in Newport, Rhode Island, it was perhaps natural that Jean and I, as tail-end-Charlie's, should get to know each other.

Our vessels were berthed, initially, only a few boat's length apart.

After the welcoming scrum had subsided, and I'd had time to read my mail, Jean invited me over for a cup of coffee.

We got on well.

There was a slight problem, in so far as my schoolboy French and his fractured Anglais sometimes led up a blind alley, but we soon retraced our steps, and didn't really have trouble communicating - it just took a little longer.

We had all the time in the world. You do, if you have just spent two wet months driving a small boat three thousand miles to windward, and have eventually tied up in a safe enough haven.

My new-found mate was someone you could talk to, an easy man to confide in.

I was short of money, would have to sell my boat before I could buy an airplane ticket home; but that significant little gem was not long out of the locker before Jean said *'don't worrie, mon ami, you can stay in my apartment.'*

This is good news, because, as Jean knew very well, when you put your pride and joy on the market, particularly one that has attracted a certain amount of attention, quite a long queue forms, not all of whom are prospective buyers. However, every man-jack and particularly the women want to look, not only all over your boat, but in every blasted locker - under the bunks, in the lazarette, while coming out with damnfool questions like, *'where's the toilet, Mr Howells?'*

With my boat placed in the capable hands of a broker, who I was sure would do his best to sort the wheat from the chaff - at Jean's invitation, I took the train to New York.

What a city!

What a skyline!

Those steep-sided canyons!

Dripping, without the neon-cast shadow of a doubt, when you're strolling down Wall Street at night, with the glittering and endlessly repeated news that this is not only a city that never sleeps, but keeps continually counting its money.

Jean's pad turns out to be a walk-up, three flights to the top of the building, cold-water apartment, located in what's known as a 'brownstone'.

We trudge up the stairs, Jean fiddles with the lock, eventually gets the door open – in we go.

The furniture is covered with dust sheets. The place seems not far removed from a morgue, yet the temperature, out on the asphalt-melting street, must be nudging ninety. In the apartment, the atmosphere is unbearable - not a breath of useable air.

Jean walks over to the air conditioner - one of those bolt-on jobs that are placed, half-in, and half-out of the lower part of a window.

The gadget isn't working.

We enter the bedroom, which offers a double bed, under a dust sheet, together with a bedside radio, some nice pictures, a double-fronted wardrobe, an adjacent shower and toilet.

Then we move to a well laid out kitchen - and why shouldn't it be. Jean works in the hotel industry as a call-order chef; there are plenty of purposeful, razor-sharp knives about.

Jean tries a tap (the 'hot' one, as it happens) nothing comes out of it. *'Mon Dieu'*, says my host, and then the French equivalent of *'the boiler's probably buggered'*.

The lights don't work. The telephone's dead.

The fridge is silent, not the slightest trace of any sort of mechanical buzz - the list of debacles seems endless.

And it is still, as hot and airless as ever.

What a dismal place: who could possibly live here?

But while I'm taking all this in, I'm beginning to realize that Jean is looking at me in a somewhat quizzical manner.

There's a trace of a smile on his lips.

His eyes are twinkling.

He seems (but how can it be?) as if he's been *'testing me out'*.

My new-found shipmate is *testing me out* ?

To what end, is my new-found shipmate *testing me out* (if, in fact, he's doing so).

But Jean Lacombe is not testing me out - he's *having me on*.

(if you don't follow me), it means, he's *pulling my leg*.

However, this stage play is coming to an end.

The dust sheets are being removed, revealing very nice furniture.

Jean strolls to the kitchen, reaches up to the fuse box, flips the switch, and the lights come on.

The fridge is buzzing, likewise the air conditioner.

The bedside radio bursts into life, confidently announcing to what it assumes is the listening world, what's going on in The Village tonight.

Times Square is within strolling distance, which makes it possible to enjoy the amazing kaleidoscope of people - all window-shopping along.

What about the 'phone?

Still dead as the dodo (*Raphus cucullatus,* just in case you have any doubt about it).

Jean strolls down the passage, makes a call from the public box gracing the corridor wall, and by the time we've decided it's too hot for coffee, Jean's telephone is active again (the wonders of AT & T).

My host is moving about the apartment (the 'phone's got a wander-about lead).

He's calling friends, bringing them up to date.

Addressing many of them as ... *'Cherreee* this,' ... *'Cherreee* that,' (there's a hell of a lot of *Cherreee's*).

While he's doing so, he's making sure I'm involved by providing a 'mimed' running commentary. A lift of the eyebrows here. A screwed-up grimace with his mouth there.

Then a hand, tracing out the obvious beautifully curved bottom of the gal he's currently talking to.

Then comes a tale of disaster: *'Non; Mon Dieu; can that be so?'*

'What's the matter?' (from me).

A dismissive wave from Jean (please be quiet) then an almost inaudible whisper, conveying the scale of the grief, *'she's not available!'* - *'she's, good gracious me - she's, pregnant!'*

It's as if he's auditioning for Radio City Music Hall, and he's sorting out the chorus line.

Eventually, it comes to a halt, with Jean smiling, what has to be, I'm sorry to say, a rather self-satisfied smile.

'Dinner for the four of us, at a very nice place, not far from here.'

'But, Jean, I told you, I'm just about flat bust. I've got less than fifteen bucks in my pocket.'

'Don't worry, mon ami: it will all take care of itself.'

And it did. We walked to the restaurant, were welcomed aboard by the owner (a sailing companion of Jean's).

Profuse greetings, embracing all the people present, friends and strangers alike; then the bold news that we just *must* sample a shipment, newly arrived from Bordeaux.

The girls arrive, show stopping ambassadors of Liberty, Equality, and absolutely stunning Fraternity.

Brilliant examples of French 'chic' - right here, not much more than a stone's throw from the hustle and bustle of Broadway.

We enjoy the meal - Escoffier couldn't have bettered it.

Some time later (quite a lot later) when New York was far astern, some idiot asked me *'what happened then?'*

'What happened then?'

But wasn't Ella Fitzgerald way ahead of the game?

How does it go?

The title, and the significant part of the lyric.

'she didn't say yes
'she didn't say no
'she didn't say stay
'she didn't say go

'so what did she do ?
'I leave it to you
'she did just what you'd do too

With an acknowledgement, not only to the sublime artist who sang the song, but an apology to Otto Harbach and Jerome Kern for the maybe unnecessary gender bending of the words.

About ten days later, I managed to sell my boat; was forced to reduce the price, but beggars can't be choosers and I just had to have the cash - there were debts to settle.

Jean took me to the airport, and when I got to the top of the aircraft boarding steps, I looked back, and I could see him amongst lots of other well wishers.

He was quite distinctive, stood out from the crowd, waving his friend goodbye.

Then a thought struck me.

How damned lucky some people are.

But of course, I wasn't considering him.

I was

thinking of me.

CHRISTOPHER WILLIAM BRASHER CBE

(1928 – 2003)

Born in Georgetown, Guyana, Brasher was a student of the Duke of York's Royal Military School and later a graduate of St John's College, Cambridge.

He was always interested in running, and became a protagonist of track and field events; in 1954 acted as pacemaker for Roger Bannister when he (Bannister) ran the first sub-four-minute mile, at the Iffley Road Stadium in Oxford.

Brasher paced Bannister for the first two laps, while his friend Chris Chataway paced the third.

Two years later, at the 1956 Summer Olympics in Melbourne, Brasher finished first in the 3,000 metres steeplechase with a time of 8 minutes and 41.2 seconds. An astonishing performance, which he pulled out of his hat, because his previous training times indicated that he would be very lucky indeed if he could even manage third place.

In the event, Brasher was disqualified for allegedly interfering with another runner, but the following day, after an investigation, he was reinstated as the gold medallist.

After this establishing performance, he pursued a progressive journalistic career, becoming sports editor for The Observer newspaper, and then joined the BBC as a reporter for the Tonight programme; later rose to become Head of General Features.

He became a successful businessman.

In 1971 he established 'Chris Brasher's Sporting Emporium', that a little later, he sensibly changed to the rather more manageable '*Sweatshop*', which was quite an improvement for an outfit retailing sports clothing.

In 1978 he designed and marketed the innovative 'Brasher Boot', sold as '*a walking boot with the comfort of a running shoe*'.

Three years later he founded, with his friend John Disley, the London Marathon.

In 1983 he became the second president of the Association of International Marathons and Distance Races, an office which he held until 1987.

He was married to tennis champion Shirley Brasher, née Bloomer.

As his business enterprises prospered, Brasher and his wife spent time and money on another of their joint passions - bloodstock and horse racing.

By the mid-1990s they had a string of eight horses in training.

Christopher Brasher was awarded the CBE in 1996.

He died in 2003, at his home in Chaddleworth, Berkshire, after an illness lasting several months.

photo: **Press Association**

Chris Brasher

not only talented, but clever

not only focused, but absolutely ruthless

but then again

just look at the magnificent result

Chris Brasher

(appreciation)

I met Chris when we were both at Plymouth for the start of the 1960 single-handed race.

This event was supported by The Observer.

At the time he was the paper's sports correspondent, covering just about everything, including 'messing about in boats' which was the euphemism used to describe those enthusiasts who spent their spare time pottering from headland to headland, along the coast of Britain – and there's surely nothing wrong in that.

Chris' limited experience didn't prevent him from enthusiastically supporting the concept of transatlantic racing, and he penned lots of column inches describing the participants, their boats, and what he saw as a significant broadening of a particular type of sporting endeavour.

He was present throughout the preparatory period, and not only went out of his way to help where he could, but took considerable trouble over the organization of the pre-race dinner, which was held at Pedro's (previously commented on here) the fashionable bistro, located not far from the dock where the competitors were berthed.

The menu and wine list for this meal (which I carefully saved) have been reproduced in this volume as an addendum to Chapter 3 of this text. And it is still, all these years later, amusing to note the way in which Chris incorporated the names of the yachts, with most of the names of the skippers, together with the choice of food on offer.

I gave my original menu to The Royal Western Yacht Club for inclusion in their archives, while keeping a photocopy for my own family record.

Over the years, when friends expressed an interest, I showed the menu, and got as much amusement observing their reactions as they seemed to get when taking note of the document itself.

The critical mention here is *over the years*, because the timescale being talked about is fifty years, and during that period, *very* few of those quite well-sighted people ever made mention of the one thing on the menu that really was extraordinary.

(you missed it yourself?) have another look at what was on offer at Pedro's where the bottom line reads - cigares, cigarettes, piquires de mescalin.

Piquires of what?

Mescalin, Dear Boy, *mescalin*, which, although it was incorrectly spelt (missing a final 'e') was hardly the stuff you would expect to be available, *as an injection*, at a dinner party, with those present being the sort of citizens who could be assumed to be rather more interested in matters nautical, than mainlining the stuff that Aldous Huxley reportedly experimented with.

There was also dubious 'previous' in the sinister shape of Aleister Crowley, and the sex psychologist Ellis.

All this was, of course, the sort of elaborate joke that Chris sometimes indulged in.

I thoroughly enjoyed (as did Jean Lacombe) that type of backhanded humour, particularly because, at the time, there was just the slight undercurrent that the occasion might be about to record the day when single-handed ocean racing was about to bite the dust.

Mescaline: also known as peyote, has been in use for over 3,000 years, starting with, apparently, the Native Americans in Mexico.

It is a mind bending substance, similar in some ways to LSD, with the added attraction that it provides 'geometricization' (?) of three-dimensional objects.

Just the thing for an apprehensive seaman?

About to depart on a single-handed passage that would hopefully end within sight of

the skyline of New York.

19

demolishing the myth

the half-crown bet
what half-crown bet ?

The first single-handed transatlantic race, held in 1960, turned out to be a seminal event. Perhaps not much to begin with – only five entries; nevertheless the idea caught on, as people realized that the train about to leave the platform was not headed for a weed-encumbered siding, where they parked the third-class carriages, but what was available had the hallmark of an inter-city express that, properly managed, would provide first-class transport to fame and ultimate fortune.

From that first race, the event evolved into a competition which now has a recognized place in the international yachting calendar.

The Royal Western Yacht Club carried on with the task of providing the venue, plus the essential infrastructure, and it was agreed that a four-yearly interval was about the right amount of time between the dates when they primed the pistol and fired the gun.

Thus: there was a race in 1960, 1964, 1968, 1972, 1976, and so on, but after the year 2000 the RWYC took the decision to split the race into two events, one catering for smaller boats - intended for amateurs and young sailors - the other for professionals.

The amateur event raced as the OSTAR; meaning, the Original Single Handed Transatlantic Race, while the professional version (involving huge sums of money and highly-paid skippers) was raced as The Transat from 2004.

However, there was a caveat. The Royal Western decided that yachts below 30 feet in length would have to be excluded, which was rather an odd decision, because, in the first race, all the entries but one were under that stipulated limit - so, if the rule had applied then, there wouldn't have been an event.

But that's as maybe.

The OSTAR, from the early days, went from strength to strength.

The second race was won by Lt Eric Tabarly, a serving French naval officer, sailing a purpose-built vessel; but I think most knowledgeable people would agree that Eric should have won if he'd been sailing a leaky plastic bathtub.

He was a superb seaman, both in crewed and single-handed vessels. Fearless.

A knowledgeable boat-handler, possessing gifts of endurance not given to many people. And not only that, he carried on deploying them when most of us would have given up and called an end to that particularly catastrophic day.

At the time of the second single-handed race Charles de Gaulle was the President of France, intent on what he saw as the restoration of that country's prestige. With this no doubt well in the forefront of his mind, he arranged (after Eric had won the event) for his protegé to be flown home immediately, where he was greeted with a tickertape welcome down the cheering length of the Champs Élysées, and the immediate award of the Légion d 'honneur.

So hadn't things moved on?

(You may recall) that it took nine months, from the ending of the first race, to the presentation of the prizes.

And it was at about this time, that high-powered and well-connected organizations became involved - these were businesses which were legitimately concerned with promoting their clients interests.

And it was also about this time, that all sorts of intriguing ideas were being floated, amongst them that Francis Chichester had been involved in the conception of the race.

Francis, in at the beginning?

The people who were there at the beginning, knew it wasn't true.

What to do?

It all seemed rather trivial - so it was allowed to pass.

That proved to be a mistake, and all sorts of things happened, most of which could have been avoided, if the advantageous dream had been successfully nipped in the realistic bud.

There were other, but this time favourable happenings.

In 1984 - twenty-four years, it should be noted, since the inaugural event - three gents met in a Cornish pub; and where better place to meet?

They were, Lloyd Hircock, Tim Hubbard, and Alan Wynne Thomas, and it must have been a convivial evening because they came up with a cracker-jack idea.

They thought, quite correctly (and I'm very glad they did so) that there shouldn't just be prestigious prizes for the first three boats/and skippers home - that was well taken care of.

But what about all those people who had put such an enormous effort into getting themselves, and their boats, into a position where they could just take part?

It may sound a relatively easy thing to accomplish, but there are all sorts of hurdles to overcome.

In the first instance, it takes not only a substantial amount of money (you have to own suitable yacht) there's also the little matter of the whole of one summer away from your business, or whatever the commitments people accumulate which make it difficult to up-sticks and set sail, single-handed from Plymouth to New York.

There's also emotional involvement.

Single-handed transatlantic racing is not a risk-free business.

There have been fatalities. In one event, there were two before the race, and two during the event, so for those people left waving on the quayside, it may not be just the matter of strolling home and taking the dog for a walk.

And when this is taken on board, perhaps even the most self-engrossed competitor, fulfilling a boyhood dream, should at least take note of the fact that 'worry', *for the other person*, is sometimes not the sort of commodity which is easily put aside.

So, to have a nicely crafted object which could be presented to people, not for winning (that's a singular position) and not just for turning up.

But actually *making* the passage - *getting, safely, to the other side.*

That seemed worth recording.

So far so good.

But there was a nagging little problem, which was the claim being made that Francis Chichester was not only alongside Blondie Hasler, but had actually, according to some reports, been the person who set the wheels in motion.

Over the years I had been getting letters from David Lewis, complaining he was seeing stuff in various yachting journals to that effect - and would I do something about it.

With the best will in the world - what could I do about it?

When it seemed appropriate to do so, I would write to the editors of various yachting journals, pointing out the mistake that was being made: not all of them got a reply.

On several occasions, I found myself in the invidious position of being presented with the *'half-crown club'* trophy, when, standing in the wings, were one or two people who were displaying - not a smile of appreciation, but the smirk of a successful conspiracy spread broad across their features.

No names - no pack drill.

But they were there.

Now, I was a very small pebble on that particular beach, but there were other people about who, to say the very least, loomed sufficiently large in the international sailing firmament to command respect. And not only respect, when they spoke, it was time to listen.

And the time to speak had, at last, arrived.

First up to the plate was **Lt Commander Michael W. Richey MBE.**

He was the Executive Secretary of the Institute of Navigation when it was formed in 1947.

He then became director of the renamed Royal Institute of Navigation, until he retired in 1982.

He was also the founder of the Journal of Navigation and served as its editor from 1948 to 1986.

He played a prominent role in the international working groups that introduced 'traffic separation at sea', first in the Dover Strait, and then worldwide.

From this grew the International Association of Institutes of Navigation, with Richey as its first Secretary General and later President.

This work was recognized by the award of the Superior Achievement Medal by the U.S. Institute in 1966. The Medaille d'honneur of the French Institute in 1969, and the Gold Medal of the Royal Institute in 1979.

As a small-boat seaman he completed many single-handed voyages in the yacht *Jester*, in a succession of OSTAR races.

This is, by any standard a substantial CV, so we can be sure that Mike, when he gave an opinion, did so when he was certain of his ground.

Here is an extract of a letter he wrote to me, on the subject being discussed.

*   *   *   *

14 : 12 : 2007

Dear Val

Thanks for your letter and its enclosures. I am somewhat in two minds about what, if any action should be taken to alter the title of the Half-Crown Club, so I'll leave it 'till last (private matters followed, but he returned to the subject).

I have had the odd award from the Half-Crown Club from time to time and have always enjoyed its name, founded though it is on a myth. I have also over the years spent a lot of time telling different Commodores, Secretaries and so on of the Royal Western that the wager was a myth – clearly to no avail.

Myths are hard to expunge (Joan of Arc, Shakespeare's Henry V, Che Guevara) and so on.

I am not quite sure what's at issue now. But if you simply want to know how I see the matter (bearing mind that I was not a competitor) I would say that the title of the body (Club, isn't it?) should remain.

Then, at some convenient juncture, the Royal Western might see fit to acknowledge the fact that the wager was mythical.

With all good wishes, Val: and I hope to see you (literally, as I have just had a cataract operation) at the Master Gunner in January.

Yours ever, and all the best of The Season's offerings … Mike

*   *   *   *

Nice letter, from a nice man, who knew exactly when to express an opinion, having judged that the time had arrived to do so.

Then there was another missive, from a similarly well-qualified person, who had also got fed up with being ignored.

Lt Colonel Ewen Southby-Tailyour OBE - was educated at The Nautical College, Pangbourne, and Grenoble University, before being commissioned into the Royal Marines in 1960.

For thirteen winters he served with landing craft in Norwegian waters, where Blondie Hasler first saw action.

He was seconded to the French Commando Marine in the Mediterranean, and the Sultan of Muscat's armed forces during the Dhofar war, where he was awarded the Sultan's bravery medal.

He served in the Falkland's campaign as the navigational and amphibious advisor to the commanders, for which he was appointed OBE. More recently he served with the Foreign Office in Serbia and on the Dalmatian coast.

He is a member of the Royal Yacht Squadron. The Royal Naval Sailing Association and is the second Life Honorary Flag Officer of the Royal Marines Sailing Club (his father was the first).

In 1982 he was elected Yachtsman of the Year and awarded the Royal Cruising Club's Goldsmith Exploration Award for sailing in the Falkland Islands and, later, the Ocean Cruising Club's Award of Merit for sailing single-handed in the Norwegian Arctic - in winter.

Ewen's father joined the Royal Marines with Blondie, and his godfather, Patrick Phibbs (Blondie's early sailing mentor) was responsible for much of his (seafaring) upbringing on the Bristol Channel pilot cutter, *Olga*, and the Polperro hooker *Elizabeth Mary*.

As a child Ewen sailed with Blondie in *Petula* and entered for all Blondie's two-handed round Britain and Ireland races.

He is married and lives in South Devon. He owns a twelve-ton gaff-cutter, *Black Velvet*, a vessel which is used for environmental research.

There is also a consultancy specializing in amphibious matters.

His son holds an 'offshore' yachts skipper's ticket, and his daughter is a master diver.

Ewen writes extensively for the yachting press.

So this was the gent who sent me a copy of a letter he had posted to the RWYC of E on 28th September 2008.

* * * *

From: S.E. Southby-Tailyour
To: The Commodore
The Royal Western Yacht Club of England

ORIGINS OF THE OBSERVER SINGLE-HANDED TRANSATLANTIC RACE

I really do hate to be a dampener, but I must put the record straight (as I try to do every four years, but without much success), nevertheless I will try again.

As it was the RWYC that organised the 1960 OSTAR I believe it is wrong for the Royal Western to perpetuate an untruth. If our Club can't get the historical facts right, then it is hardly surprising that the media doesn't either.

On the OSTAR website, the myth is perpetuated that the Observer single-handed trans-Atlantic race was ... 'founded by world circumnavigator Francis Chichester and cockleshell hero Blondie Hasler'.

But this is, emphatically, not true.

Although in his books he encouraged the idea that he was one of the instigators, Chichester was, in practice, the fourth entrant of five to declare for the original race (after Blondie, David Lewis, Val Howells, and before Jean Lacombe) and he did so a full two years after Blondie had first mooted the idea to David Astor of The Observer on 11th of January 1957.

Chichester waited that time after seeing Blondie's idea pinned to the RORC (Royal Ocean Racing Club) noticeboard before writing to Hugh Somerville of The Yachtsman in 1959, objecting to the 'unreasonable requirements' that demanded the removal of all engines and a qualifying cruise as a condition of entry.

When asked for his comments, Blondie replied ... 'publish Chichester's letter if you like, but it sounds half-witted to me. If he had read the rules when they were published in 1957 … … '

By the time Chichester entered the arena, Blondie had spent two years in correspondence with, amongst other organizations and individuals, The Slocum Society of America, seeking sponsorship and a starting line.

It is true that Chichester, in the closing months before the race, took on much of the administration, but that is a very different matter. He took no part in the conception, the drafting of the rules, nor, as an individual, with the 'half-crown bet'.

That the wager existed was disputed by David Lewis and still is by Val Howells; and, if it had existed, then it was not Chichester's idea (although, in two of his own books, he implied that it was).

Although lost in the mists of time, it is feasible that at some point, all four of them together (Lacombe had yet to officially enter) declared that if no sponsor could be found, they would each put in a half-crown, with the winner taking all. But even this is not verified by Val Howells, the sole remaining participant.

The thoroughly researched and complete truth will be found in my book 'Blondie' (Pen & Sword 1998 – a copy of which is held in the Club library).

I really do think it is incumbent on the Royal Western Yacht Club to perpetuate the truth, and not a myth, and would ask that your records, both private and public, be amended.

Yours sincerely … … Ewen Southby-Tailyour.

* * * *

Even that isn't the end of the matter:

Over the years, when BBC Radio Wales had an obscure spot to fill, they were apt to 'phone me, offer a few bob, and then (as I never could afford to refuse) turn up at my door, announcing themselves as coming from the Beeb in order to get the programme in the can – off the top of my head, without a script - just nicely modulated waffle. I had done it scores of times before.

On this occasion the producer was Louise Booker, and she had taken the trouble to enquire what was available in the BBC Archive.

There was something there – a long-playing vinyl disc, with this item carrying a programme recorded in London, on 3rd of November 1960.

Louise thought it was interesting stuff, so she used the introductory music for my own small programme *(Turning the Page)* which was duly recorded and transmitted.

Another year went by, and it seemed there was another slot to fill, so I was wheeled out again, with the producer being John Gower, and the interviewer Sian Pari Huws.

By this time I had realized that the programme recorded in 1960 held quite significant material – you could actually hear the OSTAR 1960 competitors talking to each other in a civilized manner.

We were also honest enough to describe how close we had come to disaster, demonstrating, yet again, that the line between success and failure is sometimes finely drawn.

There was something else about that November 1960 programme which made it quite significant.

Supposing there had been a *'half-crown' bet* ?

Each person putting up the brass, with the winner 'taking all'.

Wouldn't the occasion - the recording of the programme - have been just the place to mention the wager, and award the prize money, right there and then? It would have been convenient, because it was the first time since the race that the people concerned had actually got together.

Of course, nothing of the sort occurred.

And now we all know why (*there never was a half-crown bet*).

The advice now is - pay attention to what the people who took part in the first single-handed transatlantic race had to say.

It makes interesting reading - offered as a careful transcript of that particular radio programme.

photo: **author**

left to right

Mike Richey, Ewen Southby-Tailyour, his wife Patricia

distinguished

dependable

very good company, with an appreciation that

Defence of the Realm

is so much more than just another phrase

Photo: **Celtic Vision, Narberth, SA67 7DB**

the

Half-Crown Club

memento

this particular trophy presented to the author in the year

2000

when the race was sponsored by

Europe One
(the largest radio station in Europe)

TRANSATLANTIC TRAVELLERS

Reference: 26613 (1)   Date: 03/11/1960

This item is held in

SOUND – ARCHIVE/BH – RESEARCH – CENTRE

View Holdings - View Credits - Abbreviations Guide

Category: RADPROG.   Catalogue Number: 903272

Item Title: Trans-Atlantic Travellers.   Format: MONO

Station: PROG.   Duration: 0 : 28 : 46

Time in: 0 : 00 : 00   Reference Number: 26613 (1)

SBH: the British competitors in the single-handed yacht race across the Atlantic discuss their voyages with Commander George Villiers.

Producer: John Blunden.

PRE: Side 1. In June 1960 five yachtsmen set out from Plymouth for New York in the first single-handed transatlantic race.

The four British competitors talk about their experiences with Villiers, who introduces the programme with a montage of the men consecutively, explaining their reasons for taking part in the race.

Villiers intersperses brief biographical information: the remainder of the programme is a discussion.

The men talk about Gr.125: their choice of routes; 165: the performances and handling of their craft (Hasler's was an experimental yacht)); 195: their self-steering devices; 210: their feelings of loneliness; 245: their physical and mental fatigue.

Side 2; Gr.110: food, provisions and attempts at fishing; 160: moments of fear and despair; morale; 210: religious, spiritual and superstitious aspects of the voyages; 230: whether they would like to take part in such a race again (they all would !).

NTS: for further biographical information about the speakers see copy of Radio Times billing in the script file; DTF: script (Radio Times Billing). OTN: CTLO 34646 TXN/TDT:WEHS 03-Jan-1961. ANT: none CON. Taking Part: Francis Chichester (the winner); Colonel H.G.Hasler; Valentine Howells; Dr David Lewis; George Villiers.

BBC

(TRANSATLANTIC TRAVELLERS)

WEHS 03 : 01 : 1961   Rec 03 : 11 : 1960

George Villiers, interviews 1960 OSTAR competitors

Francis Chichester, Blondie Hasler, David Lewis & Val Howells

Villiers: you don't have to be a sailor to realise this race was a hazardous undertaking. In fact, many experienced yachtsmen openly voiced the opinion that it shouldn't take place at all, so the organisers took the precaution of limiting the entry to those who'd already given proof of their ability to sail and navigate alone. The four British entrants left Plymouth together on the 10th of June 1960, and it would be difficult to imagine four men of more varying personality. The winner in 40 days, 12 hours and 30 minutes was Francis Chichester; photographer, mountaineer, expert in aerial navigation and pioneer airman.

Chichester: I love sailing, I like navigating, I like racing, and I like voyaging. So this race was the perfect answer for my requirements.

Villiers: second was Colonel Blondie Hasler, ex-marine commando, now a designer of small craft, who took 48 days in his experimental boat 'Jester'.

Hasler: I came in more from a love of experimenting, and trying to develop a new kind of sailing boat, which will be both seaworthy and easy to handle. The type of vessel that will enable people to cross open water, with less effort than they have in the past.

Villiers: next, Dr David Lewis; another mountaineer and all-round athlete, making a medical study of the problems of fatigue and loneliness.

Lewis: I'm very interested in people's reactions to stress: one has the same thing in mountaineering, which I'm also interested in, together with similar pursuits. So this race was a good opportunity to find out if something out of the ordinary was happening.

Villiers: and the last to arrive, Valentine Howells, in whom the spirit of adventure and perhaps of buccaneering, still seems to survive.

Howells: I entered for the sport of it, just for a bit of fun. And I had a lot of fun. These people went hell-for-leather, bound for New York, but I dillied and dallied in a tropical island and had a nice time.

Villiers: it's well-known that there are many ways to cross the Atlantic, under sail, so I wonder which route was chosen, and why: Chichester ?

Chichester: I sailed the conventional Great Circle route, which is the shortest distance between two points; and I need to have a very good reason to diverge from that. At the same time, before I started, I did work out on paper what we call in the Air Force 'the dry swim'. For every possible route, I worked out how fast I could expect to sail on each track, and concluded that the Great Circle was the best, taking into consideration the winds and currents likely to be encountered.

Villiers: and Hasler, which one did you chose ?

Hasler: I chose to sail considerably north of the Great Circle, chiefly because of the knowledge I'd gained by reading accounts of the routes they used to favour in the great days of sail. It seemed to me the consensus of opinion was, that it was better to be north of the Great Circle, rather than on the Great Circle, or south of it.

Villiers: before you started, there was a suggestion that you took the northern route, because you like ice in your whisky ? Is there any truth in that ?

Hasler: That's the most dreadful slander. In this respect, I'm more English than the English. I like my whisky warm, very warm.

Note: *this is a good example of the type of often sardonic humour Blondie liked to employ. When he said ... 'that's the most dreadful slander' he was smiling broadly, and everyone thoroughly enjoyed the joke.*

Villiers: and Dr Lewis, which route did you take ?

Lewis: I took the Great Circle route. And I would like to add two things:

one, I think I'm right in saying that Francis is the first man to sail the Great Circle from England to New York, alone. And the other thing is, that he kept this very, very secret.We only knew he was going to take that route when he went with Val to buy some fishing net, to put around his boat ... 'to catch flying fish'. That proved, to the rest of us, that he *was* going to sail the appropriate Great Circle, where, of course, there are no flying fish at all.

Note: *an example of the type of 'joshing' humour that suited David's depreciatory style of delivery. He was often 'off-hand' in his comments, which could be misinterpreted: but, of course, not on this occasion, we all knew it was a joke.*

Villiers: Howells ? We all know you took the southern way, and that you arrived at delectable islands. But of course you didn't finish there; you reached them, and then sailed on.

Note: *when Villiers used the phrase ... 'southern way,' it was a slip of the tongue. As an experienced navigator, he would have known that 'southern way' implied the Trade Wind route, which was not the track sailed by Howells (poor little me) who took what is known as the 'intermediate', or low-powered steamer route.*

Howells: yes, thanks for that. Actually, I sailed a route that took me not far south of the Great Circle; only a couple of hundred miles below that track. But then, as you get further to the west'ard, the Gulf Stream becomes something to reckon with: you have to decide whether you're going to go north of the Stream, or south. As it's on the warmer side, I decided to go south, and didn't wear a lot of clothes for a month. And this is what Blondie didn't achieve. He went within 250 miles of Iceland and froze to death. That's true, isn't it? *(with a broad smile).*

Hasler: I went within two hundred and eighty miles of Iceland.

Howells: and the water temperature was 33 degrees ?

Hasler: I didn't measure it.

Howells: Ah ! *(laughter).*

Note: *... the expression 'ah !' should be interpreted as ... 'what an opportunity lost,' and that's what amused those present.*

Villiers: Chichester, how did you find conditions ? Was your route what you expected it to be ?

Chichester: no, it wasn't. I would say the conditions were, I don't know, 'stinking', is the word that occurs to me, on the spur of the moment. I got wet when I left Plymouth, and didn't dry out until I got to American waters 37 days later. That was the first dry day I had. Everything got covered in mildew. I was beating into a North Atlantic swell, encountering headwinds, for 37 days out of 40.

Villiers: so, for anyone else starting on this journey; is there any particular advice, or do you just make your choice and abide by it ?

Howells: my advice would be: take plenty of beer ! (*appreciative laughter*).

Villiers: now, the actual behaviour of your craft. Chichester: a lot of people thought you were over-canvassed; that you had taken on more than you could handle by yourself. How did that come out ?

Chichester: I think that's true. My mainsail is about 400 sq ft., and my genoa nearly as large. When you're asleep, with these sails set, you still have something to think about, because you have got to 'use' this amount of canvas, if you want your boat to sail at near its maximum speed in moderate winds. Then, when you've turned-in, and are fast asleep, the breeze freshens, and you have to get out and reduce canvas, it seems nearly always in the dark. It's certainly a handful, no doubt about it. Then when the wind-speed drops, you have to reset everything again. Later, you have to reduce canvas, even if it's only a squall. Two hours later, you have to change back again to more canvas. So much work to do, and it's very wearing.

Villiers: Colonel Hasler, with your experimental rig, you overcame a lot of that trouble didn't you ?

Hasler: I certainly overcame the difficulty involved in reefing and un-reefing; generally handling sail. But I may have done so at the expense of having a boat that was slower than she would have been under a conventional rig, on certain points of sailing.

Villiers: could you explain what your rig actually was ?

Hasler: well, my sail plan is set on one of the oldest rigs in the world. It's almost pure Chinese, as used on Chinese junks. Practically every time I've tried to depart from that design, it hasn't worked, and I've had to go back to the original.

Villiers: Dr Lewis, are you thinking of changing your rig ?

Lewis: I would be tempted, if it wasn't for the fact that I'd bought a new mainsail and a new foresail before this race. I was very impressed with Hasler's rig, especially after I'd broken my mast. He came up to me, and circled round, reefing and un-reefing, just by pulling a single line, which was the most impressive show I've ever seen.

Howells: just showing-off ?

Hasler: (*with a broad smile*) yes.

Lewis: I think he *was* showing-off; and that impressed me worse than anything.

Villiers: Howells; financial considerations apart, would you change rig ?

Howells: financial considerations are never apart, as far as I'm concerned. But I don't think Blondie is being strictly honest when he says his rig is slower; for making ocean passages, it may not be slower.

Hasler: yes, but you passed me, you may remember; you passed me very easily at the start.

Howells: (*as a joke*) that's the only thing I remember about the race with any pride.

Villiers: you were all fitted with self-steering devices. I want to know how they worked out: Chichester ?

Chichester: I think we will probably all agree, that this race would have been almost impossible without self-steering gears. We had differences in design; but I was forced to improvise mine, almost in the last month or two, as the self-steering apparatus that I had previously settled on didn't work out, so I was thrown back on building a conventional one. It was certainly more unwieldy that I would have liked.

Howells: very successful though.

Hasler: very successful.

Chichester: yes, it worked well.

Villiers: did yours work well, Doctor ?

Lewis: I was happy with it, but I can think of some improvements. My big fear, on the homeward passage, when encountering rough weather, was that the gadget might break, and I would have to sit out in a cold cockpit and actually steer.

Howells: surely everybody agrees, that in about ten years' time, there will be few small cruisers without self-steering gears; and this is something we've done a little towards, if nothing else.

Villiers: you agree with that Hasler ?.

Hasler: very much so, yes.

Villiers: the fact that you had to have self-steering devices, is only because you were alone. An ordinary ocean racer has sufficient crew to have somebody at the helm, in watches. I want to know more about this: how alone you felt on the journey - Howells ?

Howells: you do feel very much alone, after you've been at sea for a month, and have only seen four ships, or something like that. I don't like being alone. I know some of the others have subjugated themselves to this experience, just to find out how it would feel. But I would have avoided it - would have taken a stowaway - if I thought I could have got away with it *(with a smile)*.

Villiers: Doctor, you were 'one of the others', who supposedly did it to find out about loneliness. What have you found out ?

Lewis: I think that at the start of a single-handed passage, it's difficult to come to terms with loneliness. To adjust to being alone was, for me, a major undertaking. But after a time you get into it. You begin to feel 'at one' with the sea and the wind. You feel (mistakenly) that you have things under control. But then, when things go wrong, you realize that you have no one to blame but yourself, which is quite a big thing for me, because I *always* blame someone else. But I wouldn't sail alone for preference.

Villiers: did you consciously combat the feeling of loneliness ?

Lewis: no, I don't think so.

Villiers: you just took it as it came ?

Lewis: I think it automatically fades away, after a few days at sea, when you get into the routine .

Howells: you mean to say, you didn't feel lonely during the last week at sea ?

Lewis: not nearly as much as I did during the first few days: I was miserable.

Howells: but this is something different, isn't it. Nervousness at the beginning, but a sense of achievement at the end - yet your sense of loneliness is the same. You are still ... on your own !

Villiers: Col Hasler, I can see you're shaking your head. Are you in agreement with that ?

Hasler: no, I don't think I'm quite in agreement with what Val and David have said, possibly because I live more alone in my ordinary life. In fact, I would rather *be* alone when there's a difficult job to do, providing it's within my power to do it. For me, solitude removes one of the biggest problems of taking a small boat across an ocean (the possibility of personal conflict occurring between members of the crew). This gives rise to the anxiety experienced by the skipper of the boat, with that person feeling responsible for the safety of the other people aboard. This, to me, is an added burden. I would rather be alone - provided I can do it.

Villiers: do you hold with that, Chichester ?

Chichester: yes, I agree with Blondie. Though I rather cheated the loneliness, in a way, because I wrote 50,000 words on the trip. I used to settle down in the morning, when the terrors of the night had departed, and 'write away', imagining that I was talking to my wife or to some friend. It seemed to alleviate the loneliness to a great extent. I only felt seriously lonely when there was calm, and I had time on my hands.

Villiers: in addition to the feeling of loneliness, there is of course the effects of extreme fatigue. On occasions, I believe, Col Hasler, you have suffered hallucinations associated with fatigue. Did it happen during this voyage ?

Hasler: no, it didn't. Nevertheless, you're quite right - I have suffered hallucinations when I've been desperately tired. But in the course of this race I was never desperately tired, because I was always able to lie down and sleep before that stage was reached.

Villiers: but with your great rig, Chichester, surely you must have endured a lot of physical fatigue ?

Chichester: I did get fagged out, especially in the storm. The trouble is, in a storm, you can't sleep properly. You're thrown about so much that you can't rest; even if you do manage to drop off to sleep, you are not properly asleep. You're feeling the movement all the time. You don't get rested. All previous single-handed seamen, when writing about their experiences, have stressed this problem. It's always been the major difficulty posed by single-handed passage making.

Howells: but surely we've got past that now. The fact that we've developed self-steering devices, means that a step forward has been taken relating to the problem of fatigue. I didn't have any difficulty at all. I spent about 80% of the time on my back, either writing or reading, or planning work aboard the boat. I just didn't have a problem.

Chichester: Valentine, could you rest during a storm? When you were being thrown about in your boat ?

Howells: yes, I was certainly thrown about. But after two months at sea, you get used to this sort of thing, don't you ?

Chichester: perhaps you had a more comfortable bed than I.

Howells: mine was fairly hard boards.

Villiers: well, it seems that none of you really suffered from mental fatigue during the passage. What about physical fatigue? Did you manage to keep fit ?

Lewis: I did personally. But I also found this rather surprising fact; that I had no hallucinations, whereas I have had them in the past, due to stress. And I'm quite sure the reason for this is, that you require not only being alone, and stressed, but you require monotonous occupation, coupled with intense fatigue to experience hallucinations. When you're doing something active, they (hallucinations) tend to go away. They always have for me, in the past. When I sailed to Norway, and when I did a long canoe trip on one occasion. I'm sure that the self-steering gears have accounted for the fact that none of us have encountered these difficult phenomena. All of us, to a certain extent, had periods of rest and recuperation. I know I did.

Howells: everyone looked very fit when they got to New York; that's a significant point, isn't it ?

Villiers: it might be due to the type of food you carried. How did your provisions work out ?

Hasler: mine worked out very well. I had fresh vegetables most of the way, for 4 weeks or so. I also had the traditional salt beef in brine, which lasted all the way there and all the way back, which I like very much as a preserved meat.

Villiers: but you Howells, you had a patent egg mixture didn't you ?

Howells: it wasn't patent, sir: *potent* is the word *(laughter).*You get a bucket, a galvanised one, and you get 48 fresh eggs. You throw the eggs in the bucket. Then you get 12 lemons, and squeeze the lemons over the eggs. After three days you have the most horrible looking mess you have ever seen in your life. Then you throw in 3 or 4 lbs of demerara sugar, carefully tip in a gallon and a half of rum, and mix it all up. You decant this stuff into stone jars (if you put it into a tin receptacle, it may rust through the metal). Whenever you feel low, or dispirited, you go below and have a nice big tot of 'Live Long'.

Villiers: I think it's one of the best recipes for fatigue, loneliness, and everything else I've ever heard of.

Howells: I only lost 6 lbs in the 50 odd days of the passage; and I was cooking for myself. If I had been cooking for myself ashore, for the same length of time, I would probably have lost more than that.

Villiers: so, Chichester; how did your rations work out ?

Chichester: I lived like a fighting cock. But I know these characters around the table, and when I say that I only lost 10 lbs., they are going to retaliate by saying I hadn't got any more to lose *(with a broad smile)*. But I lived extremely well. I cooked myself a good dinner every day, even in storm conditions. The only thing I ran short of was the traditional stuff, which is whisky.

Villiers: how many times did you dress for dinner?

Note: *this question, to Francis, had been 'cooked-up' by the others, and was delivered with a smile.*

Chichester: ah ! Now you're on another sore point. I was much busier than I expected to be. It was not until I got into American waters that the weather was calm enough to encourage me to dress for dinner, then I got my smoking jacket out. But the continuous movement of the boat had chafed through the sleeve. And apart from that, it was covered in mildew and completely unusable, so I was excused.

Villiers: Dr Lewis; from strictly a medical angle, did you learn anything about 'provisions' from this journey ?

Lewis: from a strictly practical angle, next time around, I would bring enough food. I left Plymouth somewhat short of stores. Everything was such a rush that I didn't work out the varied amount of food I was going to need, so I was short of a number of items, especially water. I had a lot of dehydrated food, but didn't have enough water to reconstitute it. So I lost about 20 lbs on the passage. Looking back through my notes, on what I ate each day, they indicate that I was not eating as much as I should have. I didn't run out of food, but got very tired of stews three times a day !

Villiers: what about natural food: did you get any fish? Chichester ?

Chichester: no, I'm sorry to say, I never caught a single fish. I tried very hard when approaching the Great Banks. This being a traditional fishing area, I assumed I would be able to catch something, so I got the tackle out and fished away. I was down below, suddenly I heard a noise, and climbed into the cockpit. There were three of the largest whales in the world, just alongside. I looked around, and there were about one hundred more surrounding the boat. I don't know whether it was my fishing which annoyed them, or the fact that someone was playing a record of 'Burl Ives' on the radio which brought them up. But I came to the conclusion that they didn't want me to fish in their waters, so I took my tackle in.

Villiers: what I haven't asked you, Howells; during this journey, did you have moments when you thought … this isn't good enough, I wish I hadn't started?

Howells: I thought I shouldn't have started - the day we started, if you see what I mean *(laughter)*.Nothing struck me with greater force than the fact that I had made a mistake by starting; and from what I've been told, there might have been one other who thought the same thing, at about the same time. I was worried that I'd left my wife with a new baby (my son Christopher, was born just a few days before the race started) and with that in mind, I thought I shouldn't have started. Then, after a reasonable distance had been made good, I was worried that I wouldn't be able to keep on, and would have to go back with my tail between my legs. It seems your views alter relative to your geographical position.

Villiers: so you had no particular situation that will always remain in your memory. But what about you Hasler: did you have a bad moment?

Hasler: I certainly had a moment of fright; at least one, but one in particular. When I was trying to get past the southwest corner of Ireland, in order to go up on my northern route, by a piece of remarkably lousy navigation, I thought I was about 20 miles further to seaward than I was. I had just written in my log how wonderful it was to be out in the open Atlantic. It was foggy at the time, and I was in my bunk. My boat Jester was close-hauled, but she put herself about, on to the other tack, which she hadn't done before. So I went up on deck to see why she'd put herself about, and there was a large chunk of Ireland, showing through the fog, right in line with the direction she'd previously been pointing.

Villiers: what about you Doctor ?

Lewis: well, that last story rings a bell with me, because I thought I was about 40 miles off the coast of Nova Scotia. This also was in fog, after 3 days of heavy weather. I'd been a little shaken the day before, by being damaged by a warship, which came up on the wrong side (the weather side) and drifted down on me and damaged my mast. So I hadn't slept much the night before. Something of the same thing happened to me (that had happened to Blondie). I heard a dull, rhythmical roar, coming through the fog. I wondered what it was, then suddenly realised I must alter course. As I came about, I saw, through the fog, the breakers and surf on the rocks of Nova Scotia, not much more than 100 yards away. I must admit I sat at the tiller, trembling, for an hour after that. All my bad moments came together, because the next day the spinnaker boom came detached from the sail, hit me on the bridge of my nose, and broke the base of my skull, which healed in the course of a couple of weeks, but was dreadfully painful at the time.

Villiers: so you accomplished a significant part of your journey with a broken skull ?

Lewis: yes.

Howells: *(obviously in jest)* … this guy's got a pretty thick skull you know.

Francis: has it healed now David ?

Lewis: *(with his trademark wry smile, and not being in any way put-out)* I think there's an unkind innuendo in those remarks.

Note: *David Lewis was man of extraordinary fortitude, as any examination of his subsequent sailing career will bear out (read 'Ice Bird' if anyone doubts the veracity of this remark).*

Villiers: I sense an atmosphere here. Do they *really* think it doesn't make much difference, whether your skull was broken or not ?

Lewis: they probably attribute my safe arrival to the fact that it did get broken.

Note: *broad smiles all round, as an appreciation of the way he'd delivered the shaft.*

Howells: well, Providence has been looking after both Blondie and David, but I don't think it did much for you, Francis.

Chichester: yes: I don't know whether a boat develops a personality or what - I don't understand these things. But I do know that this same Nova Scotia coast served up something for me. I work out my navigation very carefully, particularly when heading towards a coast which the Admiralty Pilot describes as being rugged and rocky, but which I never actually saw, because of the continuing fog. I reckoned I had 20 miles clear ahead to me, so I turned in. But when I tried to sleep, the sails began slatting-about. The seas hit the boat hard every time I was dropping off. Then the self-steering gear began playing up. Finally, I couldn't stand it any longer and went up on deck and tacked the boat. Immediately, everything went to sleep. The sails went to sleep. The seas seemed to die down; everything was quiet, and I slept soundly until dawn. But when I looked at my plot, I found that the edge of the chart I was working on had been turned-in, to get it to 'fit' on the chart table, and I had read the scale on the lower (incorrect) chart. This meant that I was only 3 miles off the coast when I tacked. Had I gone to sleep, it might have been rather unpleasant.

Villiers: of course, this may be an example of 'sailors fortune'. But it also brings us to the subject of superstition at sea. Howells: I think you carried an American dime with you.

Howells: yes; but I didn't need it. I didn't 'nearly ' run aground, like these chaps, by making a major navigational error. What's interesting, is the sometimes marginal difference between success and failure. If they had all run aground, I would have finished first, instead of next to last (but delivered with a disarming smile). On the point of superstition: I think that religion may be tied up in this to a certain extent. I'm certainly more God-fearing now than I was when I started; and not quite so cocky. I may appear, or sound, cocky; but when I was in the middle of the Western Ocean, I didn't feel cocky. When you look back on it, you may wish to reappraise the power of prayer, because I certainly did 'consult the Almighty', when I got into difficulties, which I did, many times.

Villiers: do you feel any of this Doctor?

Lewis: I didn't have exactly the same feeling. I didn't feel the need for prayer particularly (delivered with a smile: see note below) but I did feel that being alone, especially in storms, when the sea was particularly impressive, was a great spiritual experience which I can only describe in those words: that is, being alone, but involved with powerful forces, over which you have only limited control. I felt that I was in the presence of very powerful forces indeed..

Note: *David was quite open about the fact that he was a non-believer. He had been scandalised by the claim (made by Sheila Chichester) before the race, that Francis had been healed of lung cancer through 'the power of prayer'. So when he was asked, by Villiers, if he had appealed to the Almighty to intervene on his behalf (or words to that effect) he turned the question aside by introducing a 'spiritual experience' which he probably felt was also something of a mirage. He was smiling his 'butter wouldn't melt in my mouth' smile, throughout this part of the conversation.*

Villiers: Colonel Hasler: I think it's true to say that you four gentlemen have pitted yourselves against elements; become involved with risks, and hazards, as a matter of choice. When you started this race, I think everybody thought you were off on a hare-brained scheme, and that you had initiated it. Are you going to do this sort of thing again? Or have you worked it out of your system ?

Hasler: I would certainly like to sail again in another single-handed transatlantic race.

Villiers: are you with him in that hope doctor ?

Lewis: definitely.

Villiers: what about you, Howells ?

Howells: I would like to go again; but if my wife overhears me, she will probably cut my throat. It took me two years to persuade her to let me go this time. But there is one point I would like to make, that so far hasn't been made. In some sports, in some fields of endeavour (say the Grand National) you get 38 starters and just 4 finishers, with possibly one or two shot along the way. And then, in ten-day bicycle races, some people drop dead over the pedals. Well, we had 5 starters, and we had 5 finishers; so this is something we can be proud of. This is the good thing. I don't think that everyone thought it was going to turn out this way. There were doubters who assumed that somebody would end up in Ireland - that it would be unlikely if everyone arrived in New York. So can't we can look on this as is some sort of minor achievement?

Villiers: and finally Francis Chichester; you have not only won the inaugural single-handed transatlantic race. You were a great pioneer airman - flew alone across the Tasman Sea, many years ago. Have you worked off the feeling? Or are you going to indulge in another of these grand adventures?

Chichester well, I must say that I've had the most happy, exciting few weeks in my life. These last six months have been tremendous fun really. I have also learned an awful lot about sailing, so one naturally has the feeling, that you would like to see if one couldn't do a lot better. Naturally, these young chaps are already beginning to feel their weight and planning another challenge. I think it would be great sport, to turn out and see if it couldn't be done in a much faster time.

Howells: it doesn't matter how many races we have, I think it's going to be a jolly good man who beats your time, Francis: 41 days, it's going to take some beating.

Note: *this was a mutually agreed 'wrap-up' to the programme, delivered by a fellow competitor, and meant as a gesture to Francis, who was not only delighted to receive the accolade, but did so with a degree of genuine emotion.*

As an end-piece: the next single-handed transatlantic race was held in 1964. The race was won by Eric Tabarly, followed by Chichester, and Howells. They were all able to significantly reduce the time that had been set by Chichester in 1960. A trend that has continued throughout the years, with the winner of the Faraday Mill OSTAR 2005 making the passage from Plymouth to New York in 17 days, 21 hours, and 41 seconds.

In June 2000, Francis Joyon, sailing *'Eure et Loir'*, made the passage from Plymouth, England, to Newport, Rhode Island in the almost unbelievable time of ...9 days, 23 hours, and 55 minutes.

20

Eira Margaret

&

Christopher David

photo: **author**

Eira Margaret & Christopher David

couldn't make it to Plymouth
for the start of OSTAR 1960

**but they were aboard the vessel every mile of the way
on the passage to
New York**

ACKNOWLEDGEMENT

Mr Simon Trice

D & D
Computers
Narberth
SA67 7AA

not only for the
software and hardware
but the essential technical support
that old buffers need
when they are trying hard to just
keep up
with this galloping digital age

V.N.H

10 : 05 : 11